THE POLITICS OF HONG KONG'S REVERSION TO CHINA

Also by David Wen-wei Chang

CHINA UNDER DENG XIAOPING: Political and Economic Reform

CHINESE COMMUNITIES AND POLITICAL DEVELOPMENT IN SOUTHEAST ASIA COUNTRIES

ZHOU ENLAI AND DENG XIAOPING IN THE CHINESE LEADERSHIP SUCCESSION CRISIS

Also by Richard Y. Chuang

THE INTERNATIONAL AIR TRANSPORT ASSOCIATION: A Case-Study of a Quasi-Governmental Organization

The Politics of Hong Kong's Reversion to China

David Wen-wei Chang
University Rosebush Professor of Political Science
University of Wisconsin, Oshkosh
Fulbright Scholar to China, 1992–93

and

Richard Y. Chuang
Professor of Political Science
Northern State University, Aberdeen, South Dakota
Fulbright Scholar to China, 1996–97

Foreword by Hungdah Chiu
Professor of Law
University of Maryland, Baltimore

First published in Great Britain 1998 by
MACMILLAN PRESS LTD
Houndmills, Basingstoke, Hampshire RG21 6XS and London
Companies and representatives throughout the world

A catalogue record for this book is available from the British Library.

ISBN 0–333–68462–1

First published in the United States of America 1998 by
ST. MARTIN'S PRESS, INC.,
Scholarly and Reference Division,
175 Fifth Avenue, New York, N.Y. 10010

ISBN 0–312–17367–9

Library of Congress Cataloging-in-Publication Data
Chang, David W., 1929–
The politics of Hong Kong's reversion to China / David Wen-wei
Chang, Richard Y. Chuang.
p.   cm.
Includes bibliographical references and index.
ISBN 0–312–17367–9 (cloth)
1. Hong Kong—Politics and government.   2. Hong Kong—Relations–
–China.   3. China—Relations—Hong Kong.   4. China—Politics and
government—1976–   I. Chuang, Richard Y.   II. Title.
DS796.H757C44 1997
951.2505—dc21   96–52814
                                                               CIP

This book is printed on paper suitable for recycling and made from fully managed and
sustained forest sources.

10   9   8   7   6   5   4   3   2   1
07   06   05   04   03   02   01   00   99   98

Printed in Great Britain by
The Ipswich Book Company Ltd
Ipswich, Suffolk

Contents

Foreword
Hungdah Chiu

THE SINO-BRITISH DECLARATION OF 1984

On 26 September 1984, after almost two years of negotiations, the United Kingdom (UK) and the People's Republic of China (PRC) initialed a Joint Declaration on the reversion of Hong Kong to China.[1] The agreement was formally signed on 19 December 1994, and instruments of ratification were exchanged on 27 May 1985.[2]

The Joint Declaration contains eight parts, three annexes, and two memoranda. Since Part 8 of the Declaration provides that '[t]his joint declaration and its annexes shall be equally binding', there should be no doubt on the legal validity of the entire document. Moreover, this declaration, as provided in Part 8, 'is subject to ratification and shall enter into force on the date of the exchange of instruments of ratification', just like any other formal treaty concluded between states. Therefore, though this document takes the form of a 'declaration', it is a formal international agreement similar to a treaty under international law. The validity of an international agreement is not dependent on the name given to the document, be it called 'treaty', 'agreement', 'declaration' or any other name. All international lawyers, including those in the United Kingdom and the PRC,[3] support this view. In view of this, if the PRC reneges on its assurance on Hong Kong after 1997, the UK could invoke the Joint Declaration to make a diplomatic presentation to the PRC even if Hong Kong was by then Chinese territory. However, this appears to be an unlikely event. More probably the two sides might interpret the application or implementation of provisions of the Joint Declaration differently. For this situation, the Joint Declaration provides no procedure to resolve the dispute.

In case of negotiating a settlement on a dispute relating to the application or interpretation of the Joint Declaration, the UK is in an unfavorable position. This is because, despite the lengthy content of the documents, the Declaration contains certain subtle grey areas, vague in nature, which would allow the PRC to maneuver its application without literally violating the Declaration.

The Joint Declaration contains more than 8000 words and is, perhaps, the second longest international agreement ever concluded by the PRC.[4] It spells out in detail the PRC's policy toward Hong Kong, the post-1997 Hong Kong regime, and its international relations. The highlights of the declaration are as follows:

1. After 1997, Hong Kong will become a Special Administrative Region of the PRC under Article 31 of the PRC Constitution.[5] It will enjoy a 'high degree of autonomy' except in foreign and defense affairs.

2. Hong Kong will be vested with executive, legislative and independent judicial power, including that of final adjudication.

3. Hong Kong's chief executive will be appointed by the PRC after elections or consultation in Hong Kong. The government of Hong Kong will be composed of local people.

4. Hong Kong shall maintain the capitalist economic and trade systems for 50 years after 1997.

5. The existing social and economic system will remain unchanged. Freedom of speech, movement, the press, assembly, strike, and religion and other freedom will be protected by law. Similarly, private property rights will be protected.

6. Apart from displaying the national flag and national emblem of the PRC, Hong Kong may use a regional flag and emblem of its own.

7. Hong Kong may participate in relevant international organizations and international trade agreements. It may establish official and semi-official economic and trade missions in foreign countries, using the name 'Hong Kong, China' to maintain and develop relations and conclude and implement agreements with states, regions and relevant international organizations in appropriate fields.

8. The PRC defense force stationed in Hong Kong shall not interfere in the internal affairs in Hong Kong and the expenditures for these military forces shall be borne by the PRC's Central People's Government.

ANALYSIS OF THE JOINT DECLARATION

Under the above arrangements, Hong Kong, on the surface, will enjoy a 'high degree of autonomy', but a closer analysis of the Declaration and the PRC's 1982 Constitution casts serious doubt on the durability and credibility of such autonomy. First, under Article 1 of Annex 1 of the Declaration, the PRC's National People's Congress (NPC) shall enact a basic law of the Hong Kong Special Administrative Region to guarantee the continuation of Hong Kong's capitalist system and lifestyle for 50 years and other matters as provided in the Joint Declaration. While under the PRC's law, Hong Kong may elect roughly 40 delegates to the NPC,[6] but the practical use and strength of 40 Hong Kong delegates among the 3400 delegates[7] in the NPC's decision-making process would be insignificant. Moreover, Article 67, paragraph 4, of the Constitution, provides that the Standing Committee of the NPC shall have the power 'to interpret statutes'; thus both the legislative and interpretative powers of the Basic Law for Hong Kong are in the hands of the NPC. Under such circumstances, the so-called 'high degree of autonomy' is at the mercy of the NPC and thus without credible guarantee.

Second, under Article 2, paragraph 1, of Annex 1 of the Declaration, 'after the establishment of the Hong Kong Special Administrative Region, the laws previously in force in Hong Kong . . . shall be maintained, save for any that contravene the Basic Law.' As stated above, the Standing Committee of the NPC has the right to 'interpret statutes'; therefore, the Standing Committee could annul those local Hong Kong laws which it dislikes on the ground that they contravene the Basic Law.

Third, while Article 2, paragraph 2 of Annex 1 of the Declaration provides that the Hong Kong 'Legislature may on its own authority enact laws in accordance with the provisions of the Basic Law and legal procedure', Article 67, paragraph 8 of the PRC Constitution provides that the Standing Committee of the NPC has the power 'to annul those local regulations or decisions of the organs of state power of ... autonomous regions ... that contravene the Constitution, the statutes or the administrative rules and regulations', thus effectively placing a severe restraint on the power of the Hong Kong legislature.

Fourth, under Article 89, paragraph 14, of the PRC Constitution, the State Council (Cabinet) has the power 'to alter or annul inappropriate decisions and orders issued by local organs of state administration at different levels'; therefore the PRC's State Council can interfere, based on a legal foundation, with the Hong Kong government's administrative function at any time if it chooses to do so.

Fifth, Article 1, paragraph 3 of Annex 1 of the Declaration provides that the 'chief executive of the Hong Kong Special Administrative Region shall be selected by election or through consultation held locally and be appointed by the Central People's Government.' Since the PRC has the final say on the appointment of the chief executive, to what extent the Hong Kong people have the free will to choose their chief executive is open to serious doubt. In a genuine federal country, the election of the chief executive of a member state is the sole decision of the people of that state without any participation of the central government. For instance, in the United States a governor of a state is elected by the people of that state and there is no way for the president or federal government to block that selection.

Internationally, the agreement was well received by the United States, Japan, southeast Asian countries and Western European countries,[8] all of whom have a stake in the continuation of the stability and prosperity of Hong Kong – the third largest financial center of the world – in the post-1997 period.

After the announcement of the Joint Declaration, the financial and real estate markets in Hong Kong gradually recovered and, at least on the surface, the city began to thrive again.

The Declaration was greeted with relief by the Hong Kong people, though not with enthusiasm, because they realized that the alternative, a unilateral 'solution' proclaimed by the PRC, would be even worse. Moreover, the Chinese promise of a high degree of autonomy for Hong Kong and the preservation of its existing socioeconomic system and lifestyle seems, at least on paper, reasonable.

THE ENACTMENT OF THE BASIC LAW

The Joint Declaration is to be implemented by a Basic Law of the Hong Kong Special Administrative Region ('SAR') which will be enacted by the PRC's National People's Congress; therefore, the Basic Law is of vital importance in maintaining Hong Kong's prosperity in the post-1997 period. According to the PRC, the constitutional basis of the Hong Kong Special Administrative Region is Article 31 of the 1982 PRC Constitution which states:

> The state may establish special administrative regions when necessary. The systems to be instituted in special administrative regions shall be prescribed by law enacted by the National People's Congress in the light of specific conditions.[9]

However, some Hong Kong groups pointed out that the capitalist system to be continued in Hong Kong for fifty years after 1997 would be contrary to at least two articles of the PRC Constitution, namely:

> ARTICLE 5. The state upholds the uniformity and dignity of the socialist legal system. No law or administrative or local rules and regulations shall contravene the Constitution.[10]
> ARTICLE 6. The basis of the socialist economic system of the People's Republic of China is socialist public ownership of the means of production, namely, ownership by the whole people and collective ownership by the working people.[11]

These groups would like the PRC to revise Article 31 of the Constitution to provide a more specific guarantee for the Hong Kong capitalist system in the post-1997 period. However, the PRC has been reluctant to even discuss the issue.

On 4 April 1990 the president of the PRC promulgated the Basic Law of the Hong Kong Special Administrative Region (SAR) adopted by the National People's Congress on the same day.[12]

On the surface, the 159 articles of the Basic Law appear to ensure the 'high degree' of autonomy for Hong Kong in the post-1997 period. However, an analysis of several key provisions indicates that the PRC wants to retain final control, especially in matters relating to the autonomy of the Hong Kong SAR's political system.

First, the residual powers, i.e. those powers not delegated to the Hong Kong SAR by the Basic Law, are to be reserved for the PRC Central People's Government (Article 20),[13] and both the interpretation and amendment of the Basic Law are to be entrusted to the PRC's National People's Congress (NPC) and its Standing Committee (Articles 158 and 159).[14]

Second, laws enacted by the legislature of the Hong Kong SAR must be submitted to the NPC's Standing Committee for the record and, if the latter considers that an SAR law is not in conformity with the provisions of the Basic Law regarding affairs within the responsibility of the Central Authorities or regarding the relationship between the Central Authorities and the Region, the Standing Committee may return the law in question which shall immediately be invalidated (Article 17, paragraph 3).[15]

Third, PRC law applicable to the SAR shall be confined to those laws relating to defense and foreign affairs as well as to other matters outside the limits of the autonomy of the Region as specified by the Basic Law (Article 18, paragraph 3).[16]

However, in the event that the Standing Committee of the NPC decides to declare a state of war or, by reason of turmoil within the Hong Kong SAR which endangers national unity or security and is beyond the control of the SAR government, decides that the Region is in a state of emergency, the Central People's Government may issue an order applying the relevant national laws in the Region (Article 18, paragraph 4).[17] Under such circumstances, the PRC may in fact cancel the 'high degree of autonomy' for the Hong Kong SAR.

Fourth, the Hong Kong SAR shall enact laws on its own to prohibit any act of treason, secession, sedition, subversion against the Central People's Government, or theft of state secrets, to prohibit foreign political organizations or bodies from conducting political activities in the Region, and to prohibit political organizations or bodies of the Region from establishing ties with foreign political organizations or bodies (Article 23).[18] It should be noted that the PRC has considered the spread of democratic ideas as subversive; therefore, this article is intended to deter Chinese or foreign groups from using Hong Kong to spread democratic ideas to China.

With respect to the appointment of the Chief Executive of the Hong Kong SAR, the Basic Law rejects direct election by the Hong Kong people. The PRC shall select an Election Committee of 800 members to elect the Chief Executive (Appendix I of the Basic Law).[19] The election is therefore under the control of the PRC. Although the Basic Law provides that 'the ultimate aim is the selection of the Chief Executive by universal suffrage', the candidate shall be nominated 'by a broadly representative nominating committee in accordance with democratic procedures' (Article 45 paragraph 2).[20] Through the nominating committee, the PRC shall assure that only politicians approved by it can be put on the candidate list.

On the composition of the Legislative Council of the Hong Kong SAR, the Basic Law provides that the Council shall be constituted by election 'in accordance with principles of graduate and orderly progress' and the 'ultimate aim is the election of all members of the Legislative Council by universal suffrage' (Article 68).[21] In a decision adopted by the NPC on 4 April 1990 on the formation of the first Hong Kong SAR government and the first Legislative Council, only 20 members of the 60-member Council shall be directly elected. Ten members are selected by an election committee and 30 members are selected by functional constituencies. Their terms of office shall be two years, but starting with the second term of the Council, the term of office for members shall be four years. In the second term, the directly elected members shall increase to 24 and, from the third term on, that number will be 30 (Annex II of the

Basic Law). Under this arrangement, the PRC can assure
that at least half of the Legislative Council will be under its
control.[22]

When the draft of the Basic Law was released in January
1990, Martin Lee, a prominent Hong Kong lawyer and democracy advocate who serves on the Hong Kong Legislative
Council, commented that 'instead of a high degree of autonomy, what we are getting from the Basic Law is a high
degree of control'.[23]

THE ISSUE OF ELECTION OF THE LEGISLATIVE COUNCIL

In order to appease the Hong Kong people's dissatisfaction
with the Basic Law, which allows only one-third of the Legislative Council to be directly elected by the people when
Hong Kong is returned to the PRC, the Hong Kong government decided to increase the number of directly elected
seats in the 60-seat Legislative Council in 1991 from 10 to
18. The British government hoped that the 1991 election
would be a success, and if so, it would ask the PRC to allow
Hong Kong to have more than 20 directly elected seats in
the Legislative Council.[24]

The election was held on 15 September 1991. Liberal pro-
democracy United Democrats of Hong Kong (UDHK) candidates and their allies won 16 of the 18 seats. Not one
pro-Chinese communist candidate was a winner. The two
seats that did not go to the United Democrats and their
allies were taken by a conservative pro-business candidate
and an independent. Despite such an impressive result for
the democracy candidates, the turnout was only 39.2 per
cent of the 1.9 million registered voters.[25] It appears that
most Hong Kong people are either uninterested in politics
or considered the election a futile exercise that will not change
the way Hong Kong is governed now or in the future.

On 7 October 1992, the newly appointed British Governor of Hong Kong, Christopher Patten, announced a plan
to increase voters in future legislative elections.[26] For the
1995 election, the purpose of which was to choose members of the Legislative Council through to 1997, the Basic

Law calls for 20 directly elected seats, 30 functional constituency seats, and 10 seats elected by an Election Committee.

Governor Patten's plan, taking advantage of the lack of a provision prohibiting the reform of the election process of the functional groups and the election committee, is to increase the electorate from about 110 000 people to most registered voters for electing the 30 members in the functional constituency election, where interested groups such as lawyers, trade unionists and businessmen vote for members of the Legislative Council.[27] His plan also calls for direct elections for the lower level district boards and municipal council members who are now largely appointed. Those elected to serve in lower level boards or councils will make up the Election Committee, who will elect the remaining 10 members of the Legislative Council. In other words, under Governor Patten's plan, all members of the Legislative Council in the 1995 election will directly or indirectly be elected by the people of Hong Kong.

The PRC, however, immediately denounced the plan as a violation of the Basic Law.[28] The reason is simple; a Legislative Council so composed bears the mandate of all the people of Hong Kong and would have the ability to stand up for the Hong Kong people and resist the PRC's interference in Hong Kong affairs. The PRC has publicly announced that it will dissolve this Council and conduct another election after its takeover of Hong Kong on 1 July 1997.

FUTURE PROSPECTS

Will the PRC's 'one country, two systems' work to maintain the prosperity and stability in Hong Kong after its reversion to the PRC in the post-1997 period? This depends a great deal on political developments in the PRC. Until recently, Hong Kong's capitalist system and the PRC's communist system have coexisted side by side and resulted in mutual benefit. But the systems are essentially incompatible and the British presence in Hong Kong has served as a buffer to make the coexistence between the two possible and insulate Hong Kong from the political turmoil in China. The PRC, by insisting on removing that buffer and insulation without providing a credible substitute, attempts to mix the two essentially incompatible systems together in a great experiment. Only the future will tell whether such an experiment will succeed.

While the PRC has moved toward a more liberal economic system, it is unlikely to change further in the foreseeable future, and its political system remains a dictatorial one. To continue its economic liberalism without corresponding political reform appears to be difficult if not impossible. The PRC's recent sentencing of the famous human rights activist Wang Dan to long-term imprisonment points to an era of hard rule.[29] If this is the trend, then the PRC will encounter more difficulty and resistance in its rule in Hong Kong, where the people have long enjoyed generous freedoms of free speech, press,[30] publication, demonstration and others. On the other hand, to allow people in Hong Kong to have genuine freedoms under PRC rule could have a demonstrative effect on the people in mainland China, who would most likely demand similar freedoms. The crucial question is how long can the Chinese communist authorities resist the worldwide trend toward democracy? The ruthless suppression of the 4 June 1989 Tiananmen democratic movement[31] has not silenced that movement: it has continued to flourish in China in one form or another.[32] The reversion of Hong Kong to China, while gratifying to all Chinese because of their inherent nationalism, may also mark the beginning of the process of the demise of Chinese communist rule.

Preface and Acknowledgments

Great Britain takes pride in maintaining Hong Kong's prosperity and stability. She would like to stay on beyond 1997. London knows well that Hong Kong would always need China as its hinterland for survival. Thus the British government had to take the initiative to approach China. Murray C. MacLehose, as governor of Hong Kong, attempted to negotiate a new lease for the New Territories. The British believed that such a suggestion might appeal to the Chinese government because it would insure that Hong Kong's prosperity and stability would remain undisturbed beyond 1997 and thus would help China achieve economic reform and international trade expansion. Britain believed this would also be welcomed by the 6 million people in Hong Kong who might even participate in the British negotiation with China, provided, of course, that the Beijing regime would accept a Hong Kong delegate during negotiations.

To Britain's surprise, the Beijing government informed Governor MacLehose during his first visit to China that China had no interest in discussing a new lease. She insisted on recovering all lost territories of Hong Kong, Kowloon and the New Territories in 1997 and insisted that the restoration of sovereignty and administration would not be negotiable. The Beijing regime argued that the cession or lease of the above-mentioned territories were the result of unequal treaties unilaterally imposed on China by 'gunboat diplomacy without China's freely given consent. The treaties themselves were, therefore, invalid according to international law. Nevertheless, mutual goodwill and respect still prevailed in Sino-British initial contact.

However, during the later negotiations, the convergence of basic Sino-British mutual interests beyond 1997 focused on the preservation of economic prosperity and political stability in Hong Kong. Few or no definitive commitments were made to guarantee the continuity of the existing quality of life for the people of Hong Kong except for obscure generalizations such as 'high degree of autonomy' and preservation of 'life-style'. How these obscure generalizations would translate into political realities was left to the future Basic Law (mini-constitution) to be enacted by the Beijing government. This mini-constitution will govern the Hong Kong Special Administrative Region (HKSAR). Many Hong Kong people disapproved of the undemocratic document but, although their future has been officially sealed, millions of residents refused to remain totally silent.

The actual negotiation of Hong Kong's reversion to China began formally when Margaret Thatcher first visited Beijing in 1982. This meeting was the beginning of a process which finally resulted in two major documents: the Sino-British Joint Declaration and the Basic Law. Both continue to guide London and Beijing in their joint policy behavior, but neither side has fully complied. Two unexpected major events interfered with the smooth transition originally anticipated by the British, who continue to have commercial interests in Hong Kong and China, by the Chinese, who wish to achieve an orderly and conflict-free regaining of sovereignty in Hong Kong, and by the people of Hong Kong, who are deeply concerned about the continuation of their relative autonomy. One painful event was the pro-democracy movement in China in 1989, which shocked and moved the people in Hong Kong. The other was Governor Chris Patten's unilateral proposal in 1992 for political reforms in 1994–5, which shocked and angered the Chinese government. The residents in Hong Kong sadly had little control over their own destiny in 1993 when both London and Beijing were again waging a frustrating diplomatic war in clear violation of both the Joint Declaration and the Basic Law.

The story of Hong Kong's reversion claims attention globally, especially among its trading partners. People in many walks of life in many countries wish to see Hong Kong remain prosperous and stable. We have thus decided to write this book.

We have learned much from our case-study on Hong Kong's reversion. We believe that a rapid economic integration in the southeastern region of China, including Hong Kong and Taiwan, will emerge in the early decades of the next century. We base our conviction on a number of factors, some of which are discussed in Chapter 1. First, inside China economic development and social changes will inevitably lead to greater systemic restructuring of the political system in favor of popular participation and greater constitutional freedom. Such a result of changes and reforms will come peacefully. The momentum of reform will distinguish China as an innovator of a unique new model of one-party democracy similar to that in the Republic of Singapore. Second, we are convinced that civil war in the Taiwan Straits is unlikely in view of recent internal antagonism in Taiwan against the independence movement, regardless of potential foreign influences pulling the island away from mainland China. Third, we believe, as do many in Hong Kong, that the British legacy of government and legal system may not survive long after 1997. The professional and business elite in Hong Kong will have little difficulty adapting to the style of leadership imposed by China. Hong Kong, China and Taiwan may soon cooperate economically and emerge into one single global force of national, social and economic modernization. We anticipate that cultural and economic influences from mainland China will soon persuade the leaders of Taiwan to seek an earlier reunification with a 'progressive' China which, by then, may be far removed from today's 'Socialism with Chinese characteristics'. It may look more like 'capitalism with Chinese innovations'.

Dr Chuang wishes to express his deep appreciation to the chairperson of the Political Science Departments of University of Wisconsin-Oshkosh for grants in research time and funding; the Pacific Cultural Foundation in Taiwan and the Association of Chinese Social Scientists in North America for partial funding; the Fulbright Scholarship Board for the appointment to teach and do research in Beijing; the Robert Black College Dean and staff of the University of Hong Kong for assisting in his residency and in granting him access to the university library.

Dr Chuang wishes to express his appreciation to President John Hutchinson and Vice President Sam Gingrich, Northern State University (NSU), and the Association of Chinese Social Scientists in North America for partial funding;

the Hong Kong Economic & Trade Office in San Francisco, the Hong Kong and Macao Office of Mainland Affairs Commission in Taiwan, and the Institute of Current China Studies in Taiwan for providing news digests, publications and original documents; and colleagues at Hong Kong Chinese University for providing survey research materials.

Mr Vilas Genke of UW-Oshkosh Political Science Department has been most helpful for many years in many ways as Program Assistant to Chang, and so has Ms Karen Elliot of the department of Social Sciences and History of NSU to Chuang.

We also wish to thank many other friends in Hong Kong, Taiwan and the United States, and those in the Social Science Academies in mainland China. They invited us to attend conferences or give lectures on Hong Kong.

Both of us would like to express our sincere thanks to Professor Tom Hansen of the English Department at NSU for the initial editing of the manuscript and Professor Ming Ming Pu of the same department for indexing the book. Dr Chuang would particularly like to express his special thanks to *Revue de Droit International* (Geneva, Switzerland) and *Asian Affairs: An American View* (Washington, DC) for permitting him to use some of the published materials, albeit with revisions and updating, for this book.

Intellectually, we are also indebted to Professor Robert A. Scalapino, former Director of the Institute of East Asian Studies, the University of California–Berkeley, and Professor Joyce Kallgren, University of California–Davies, and former Associate Director of the Institute for East Asian Studies. Their encouragement and advice are also appreciated.

Finally, we would like to express our sincere thanks to Professor Hungdah Chiu of the University of Maryland for writing the Foreword.

University of Wisconsin–Oshkosh   David Wen-Wei Chang
Northern State University, Aberdeen, SD   Richard Y. Chuang

List of Abbreviations

ACE	Association of Chinese Enterprises
ADPL	Alliance for Democracy and People's Livelihood
APSS	Association of Post-Secondary Students
ASPDMC	Alliance in Support of the Patriotic Democratic Movement in China
BC	British Citizenship
BDTC	British Dependent Territories Citizens
BLCC	Basic Law Consultative Committee
BLDC	(Hong Kong) Basic Law Drafting Committee
BN(O)	British National (Overseas)
BOC	British Overseas Citizenship
CCBL	Consultative Committee for the Basic Law
CCP	Chinese Communist Party
CFA	Court of Final Appeal
CI	Certificate of Identity
CPPCC	Chinese People's Political Consultative Conference
CRC	Cooperative Resource Center
DABHK or DAB	Democratic Alliance for the Betterment of Hong Kong
DP	Democratic Party (formerly United Democrats of Hong Kong)
EEC	European Economic Community
EXCO	Executive Council
FSHK	Federation for the Stability of Hong Kong
FTU	(Hong Kong) Federation of Trade Unions
HKFW	Hong Kong Federation of Women
HKMAO	Hong Kong and Macao Affairs Office of the State Council
HKPSPPM	Hong Kong People in Support of Patriotic Pro-Democracy Movement in China

HKSAR or SAR	Hong Kong Special Administrative Region
ICAC	Independent Commission Against Corruption
ICJ	International Commission of Jurists
JLG	(Sino-British) Joint Liaison Group
KMT	Kuomingtang (the Nationalist Party in Taiwan)
LDFHK	Liberal Democratic Federation of Hong Kong
LEGCO	(Hong Kong's) Legislative Council
LP	Liberal Party
MP	Meeting Point
MSAR	Macao Special Administrative Region
NCNA	New China News Agency (Xinhua)
NPC	National People's Congress
PC	Preparatory Committee
PL	Provisional Legislature
PLA	People's Liberation Army
PRC	People's Republic of China
PWC	Preparatory Working Committee
SCMP	*South China Morning Post* (Hong Kong)
SSRC	Social Science Research Center (University of Hong Kong)
UDHK	United Democrats of Hong Kong
UNCCPR	United Nations Covenant of Civil and Political Rights
UNCESCR	United Nations Covenant of Economic, Social and Cultural Rights
UNHRC	United Nations Human Rights Commission

1 Introduction

THE HIGHLIGHTS IN TRANSITION DEVELOPMENT

On 17 September 1995, the first and also the last general election for all the 60 members of Hong Kong's Legislative Council (LEGCO) took place, under Governor Patten's reform and leadership. Nearly half of the population were eligible to vote. However, only approximately one-third of those eligible actually participated, an indication of political apathy reflecting the majority perception of the bleak political future of Hong Kong after 1 July 1997, when China resumes its sovereignty.

Surprisingly the democratic forces won a smashing victory at the poll, even though the pro-China parties and independent candidates, with Beijing's all-out backing for the first time, were expected to do much better. When the pro-democracy 'Jubilant Democratic Party (DP) celebrated their sweeping legislative victory on Sunday, Beijing renewed its promise that the legislature would be disbanded on 1 July 1997'.[1] The New China News Agency (NCNA) in Hong Kong, which represents the Hong Kong and Macao Affairs Office of the State Council in Beijing, vehemently declared, in spite of the election result, that 'the attitude of the Chinese government on this issue [disbanding of the new legislature] is consistent and will not be influenced by the result of the election'.[2] Furthermore, Beijing often considers the Democratic Party (formerly United Democrats of Hong Kong) as a foreign 'subversive organization' against China. The DP's future after 1997 is difficult to be certain of now. Later chapters will reflect in detail the meaning and impact of this major watershed election[3] and the future potential policy reaction from China.

On the other hand, Britain is supposed to remain in complete charge until 1997. Yet time and again it has been demonstrated that Beijing, through the NCNA as its shadow government, has been gathering a momentum of influence ever since the Sino-British Joint Declaration in 1984. The

1

declaration and its annexes have set in motion events which have been watched closely everywhere in the world, because Hong Kong, in culture and in life-style, is a successful merger of the East and the West, a demonstration of Britain's innovative achievement of balance inside Hong Kong itself and in harmony with powerful China until 1982. Prime Minister Margaret Thatcher on her trip to Beijing in 1982 learned at first hand how adamantly the Chinese leadership insisted on Hong Kong's return to China in 1997. Between 1984 and 1997 many of us – scholars, diplomats, businessmen and, especially, the six million residents of Hong Kong – witnessed, and will continue to see, frustrating Sino-British diplomatic attempts to achieve a smooth transfer of sovereignty back to China. And the Chinese legislature has the authority to create a Hong Kong Special Administrative Region (SAR).

Much of the literature about Hong Kong's transition seeks to decipher the precise definition of 'one country, two systems', the Chinese intention to govern Hong Kong, Macao and, eventually, Taiwan.[4] Each of these three unrecovered territories of China has its uniqueness in history and politics. However, Hong Kong is the first of Beijing's experiment to achieve, in fifty years' time, greater integration and harmony with the motherland. The people of Hong Kong are proud of their Chinese heritage and identity. However, they prefer not to be governed at the present time by the communist-dominated central government in Beijing.[5] The crisis of transition for the Chinese population in Hong Kong began in 1982 when Sino-British negotiations disallowed them a direct voice on their own future destiny. The reasons for such denial were obviously in the interests of both Britain and China. It is our task in this book to describe and analyze the motives and dynamics that lie behind the ways in which the people, through emigration and elections, have registered their feelings of betrayal and uncertainty. These popular reactions, in stages from 1984 to the present, have become sources of embarrassment to both Britain and China.[6]

The Beijing regime's policy position seems to have been deeply influenced by its intention to prevent the spillover of democratic sentiment on the mainland itself and by its insistence on eventually applying 'one country, two systems' to Macao and Taiwan. Beijing was deeply shocked in 1989 when it learned how much democratic self-government the people of Hong Kong had expected from the British before the 4 June pro-democracy movement in China. The Chinese leaders were stunned by the enormous support for democracy in China. People demonstrated in the streets of Hong Kong during the time of the student occupation of Tiananmen Square. Thus, fear and prudence forced China to tighten its constitutional control against a 'high degree of autonomy and the life-style' in Hong Kong later, during the final drafting of the Basic Law.[7]

The British government was under pressure from the people of Hong Kong to quickly implement the promise of 'representative government before 1997'. It was under pressure from China not to do so and not to unilaterally interpret the Joint Declaration of 1984. Through a series of policy papers and the White Paper in the late 1980s, the colonial government in Hong Kong skillfully manipulated the poll interpretation of popular opinion in order to postpone the scheduled partial direct election from 1988 to 1991. Gradually, the concerned residents and the small percentage of qualified voters in Hong Kong lost confidence and even trust in the British government. Citizenship, the right to reside in Britain and to own British passports, was another issue aggravating the relations between London and some people in Hong Kong. In short, residents of Hong Kong, except a few thousand families who are permitted by Britain to emigrate to the UK, have had to emigrate to other countries or to remain totally silent so as not to antagonize their future rulers. Fundamental conflicts of such a nature continued among three often mutually exclusive interests: those of the expatriate British, those of the authoritarian Chinese, and those of the Hong Kong residents.

Britain was not strong enough to negotiate. The Chinese nullified past treaties with Britain, effectively depriving London of its basis for any valid claim to continue governing Hong Kong. On the other hand, Britain will never be in a position to physically oppose China in the way she defended the Falkland Islands against Argentina. Since the people of Hong Kong did not actively oppose China's claim to regain sovereignty, Britain had insufficient popular support to negotiate vigorously with China. Thus, London could only rely on less effective resources in its bargaining to secure Beijing's concessions. For example, by preserving good relations with China, Britain can remain in Hong Kong as consultant to the future government there. This would best help Britain to protect her enormous property ownership on the island and to enjoy commercial and investment concessions in both Hong Kong and China. From the Chinese point of view, Britain, before and after 1997, would continue to be in the best position to help maintain and improve prosperity and stability in Hong Kong. In addition, mainland China itself needs foreign investment and trade. Britain could play a major role in China's economic reform and modernization, especially in view of Hong Kong's potential as China's largest investor and trade partner in the coming decades. Furthermore, China depends heavily on Hong Kong as a transit export–import city. Hong Kong's own prosperity and stability is, therefore, critically important to China for many years yet.

This mutual dependence was clearly the calculated source of bargaining strength the British relied upon during the negotiation for the Joint Declaration in 1982. Britain still had 15 years to govern Hong Kong legally without interference from China, at least theoretically. Thus she expected to be legally free to introduce reform for representative government in Hong Kong before 1997. To retain Chinese goodwill up to and beyond 1997, however, Britain agreed in 1984 to set up a Sino-British Joint Liaison Group for the purpose of transition and mutual consultation. In practice, however, many different interpretations of the Joint Declaration, the Basic Law, and seven letters detailing additional Sino-British official understandings have, unfortunately, emerged to make the 1997 'smooth transition' impossible. And yet, neither side can afford to ignore the other. After the unexpected 1989 pro-democracy movement, however, relations were greatly strained.

The Basic Law drafting convention was still in progress in 1989–90. The delegates from Hong Kong crafted every possible device in order to maintain stability and obtain a greater guarantee for the promised high degree of autonomy and the protection of their life-style for individual freedom.[8]

However, their effort failed. Martin Lee and Szeto Hua, as delegates, were unable to influence their opposite numbers from China, who were directed to follow the instructions of the government in Beijing. The final pro-China Basic Law was eventually approved by the National People's Congress in December 1990. Together with the Joint Declaration, the Basic Law would help in achieving a smooth transition. After July 1997, the Basic Law will become Hong Kong's Constitution. We will describe and analyze the Basic Law in some detail in succeeding chapters to illustrate potential future problems between China and Hong Kong.

In 1990, democratic forces, which were yet to be formally organized as political parties, fought each other for success in the 1991 Legislative Council election. Their overwhelming victory against pro-China candidates apparently convinced the British government under John Major of its moral responsibility to carry out electoral reform with or without Beijing's cooperation. The arrival of Governor Christopher Patten in early 1992 suddenly changed the political climate in favor of rapid institutionalization of election reform. On 7 October, Patten unilaterally announced a reform proposal in his annual public report to the Legislative Council. Thus a new crisis emerged with China. Patten's personal trip to Beijing did not succeed in securing Chinese cooperation. Rather, Patten's sweeping democratic proposal caused China to accuse the British of violating the Joint Declaration, the Basic Law, and the Sino-British understandings which were reached through the exchanges of the seven letters at the ministerial level. Together, they were labeled as the 'Three Violations'.[9]

The new crisis led to 17 rounds of secret diplomatic talks in Beijing in 1993 between the British Ambassador and Chinese Vice-Minister for Foreign Affairs. Details of the talks will be analyzed in later chapters. The breakdown of the talks has naturally led to separate unilateral implementation of the transition since late 1993. Verbal war and mutual blame, through the media, have become a daily routine. The people of Hong Kong have remained victimized, with no respect for or trust in either Britain or China. Meanwhile, Governor Patten pushed his reform legislation through the Legislative Council. The British irreversibly changed from conciliation to confrontation with China, whose goodwill had been once considered fundamental to Britain's long-term future commercial investment opportunity in China. We believe that the 4 June incident in Tiananmen Square and the victory of pro-democracy forces in the 1991 election were responsible for the courage of the British in implementing a popular reform for more democracy before 1997.

With strong demand in Hong Kong for participation in democratic development and with the strong backing of Whitehall for Patten's 1994–5 election reform, the Chinese government, too, began to pursue its own separate path of transition. More determined than before because of the 'British violation', the Hong Kong and Macao Office of the State Council in Beijing prepared for the deadline of 1 July 1997 by appointing dozens of pro-China residents as Hong Kong Affairs Advisors and hundreds of local District Affairs Advisors. In addition, a Preparatory Working Committee was organized in 1993 to study transition problems and implementation strategies. The PWC was, in fact, merely the 'advanced subgroup' to the Preparatory Committee which, according to the Basic Law, could not be organized legally until January 1996. Meanwhile, China suddenly encouraged and supported pro-China candidates to participate in the 1995 LEGCO 'illegal election'.

The Beijing government has begun to search for candidates for the future Chief Executive to be nominated to the National People's Congress for appointment in 1996. Such future candidates will not go through popular election but will be appointed by China after informal consultation with a Hong Kong group. In addition, how the future 'provisional legislative council', which is to replace the recently elected Legislative Council, will be created is not yet known in detail. Beijing must first of all analyze the critical impact of the repeated election victories of the United Democrats in 1991 and of the new Democratic Party victory in 1995. Perhaps the most stunning shock to Beijing has been the humiliating defeat of candidates from the pro-China Democratic Alliance for the Betterment of Hong Kong (DAB). The defeated prominent leaders of the DAB themselves have suddenly moved closer to the position of anti-China voters and, especially, have begun to support Governor Patten's post-victory appeal to London to grant British citizenship to some three million residents. In the wake of election defeat, Beijing needs to recalculate the number of the patriotic pro-China residents and their desire to preserve prosperity and stability.

THE PRESSURE OF TIME FOR CONFLICT RESOLUTION

Responsibility for this state of affairs cannot be neatly assigned to either the British government or the Chinese regime. Neither side deliberately undermined Hong Kong's popular interests. They seem to have miscalculated the people's hidden passion for a guaranteed 'autonomy and life-style', while putting their own interests first during the secret diplomatic negotiations. New events and circumstances after the Tiananmen Square Incident of 1989 have forced both Britain and China to reevaluate the power of the silent majority among the population in Hong Kong. Britain, for example, was encouraged to adopt a confrontational attitude for reform to satisfy the people's support for democratic representation and participation. Voters welcomed the lowering of the voting age, the creation of nine new functional constituencies, the popular election of District Board members and the new massive extensions of enfranchisement in both 1994 and 1995 elections. The Beijing government, contrary to its denunciation of the election, encouraged the DAB candidates and other pro-China independent candidates to participate in the election process. China turned out its full mobilizing forces in support of its preferred candidates,[10] although remaining unwavering in its commitment to abolish the newly elected Legislative Council after 1 July 1997. It becomes clear that China will modify its position in recognition of popular majority sentiment in order to assure a smooth transition. Finally, the people of Hong Kong, although deprived of an effective voice during Sino-British negotiations from 1982 to 1993, seem to have been quietly listened to by both China and Britain. The transition deadline pressured them to seek conflict resolution. The end result of conflict resolution is a partial fulfillment of what

the silent majority voters have wanted. Their new voting power
has emerged from Patten's reform implementation. Beijing
is now put under severe scrutiny to show how it will deliver
its promise of a 'high degree of autonomy' and a continuation of the current 'life-style of the people'. We believe
the communist government will yield realistically to the
majority of the people after 1997 if there is no evidence of
foreign influence in Hong Kong plotting against Hong Kong's
genuine unification with the motherland under the Basic
Law. China will have a strong incentive to make the Hong
Kong experiment a convincing success in order to accomplish its reunification with Taiwan under the same 'one
country, two systems' formula.[11]

On the whole, Beijing's emphasis in negotiations since
1982 has convinced us that China's approaches and methods, as followed flexibly in some circumstances and stub-
bornly in others, have proven its determination to carry out
its territorial nationalism and sovereign independence against
foreign interference in its internal affairs. For example, Beijing
rejected Britain's attempt to re-lease the New Territories and
Britain's request for 'continuous administration' of Hong
Kong after sovereign transfer in 1997. Beyond these two
fundamental principles, all matters can be negotiated and
reconciled. This policy position on territory and sovereignty
is clearly the same as has been offered to Taiwan. In the
case of Hong Kong, in particular, it has been a matter of
national pride against past humiliating Western imperialism. In the case of Taiwan, it has been Beijing's fear of
potential American and Japanese interference in China's
internal dispute in a civil war unfinished since 1945. Territorial nationalism to reclaim all lost lands has been the
unifying ideology under both Sun Yat-sen's Kuomintang and
Mao Zedong's communist party, whether against Russia, India,
Japan or the British in Hong Kong.[12]

Although the Chinese government has not perceptibly
softened its position regarding Taiwan, in spite of Washington's upgrading of so-called 'unofficial relations' with Taiwan, the most recent London visit of Foreign Minister Qian
Qichen, 1–4 October 1995, unexpectedly created an even
greater spirit of cooperation relative to Hong Kong's transfer.[13] This was Qian's first trip after three and a half years

of confrontation. London and Beijing have again agreed on high-level mutual visits and periodic smoother consultation between the Patten government and Beijing, and the New China News Agency in Hong Kong has formally accepted the liaison functions between the two governments. It also seems likely that the Joint Liaison Group, as established by the Joint Declaration in 1984, will soon operate more efficiently on matters of consultation and transition.

As 1 July 1997 approaches, Beijing needs to maintain this new atmosphere of confidence for the people in Hong Kong. To do this will require continued cooperation from the British government in Hong Kong. Foreign Minister Qian Qichen agreed that all issues of contention can be resolved except the 'dissolution issue' of the newly elected Legislative Council. The HKSAR government, under provisions of the Basic Law, will come into existence before 1 July 1997. Beijing's schedule for this is as follows:[14]

1. December 1995: termination of the Preparatory Working Committee.
2. January 1996: creation of the Preparatory Committee, according to the Basic Law, to formally establish China's Special Administrative Region in Hong Kong (SAR).
3. April 1996: creation of a Nomination Committee by the Preparatory Committee.
4. July–September 1996: recommendation of the SAR Chief Executive to China's National People's Congress for his or her approval or rejection and the final announcement, in December 1996, of all major administrative officials.
5. Early 1997: the establishment of Hong Kong's Provisional Legislative Council.
6. 1 July 1997: official sovereign transfer acceptance by China.

The Patten cabinet in Hong Kong was happy with China's spirit of cooperation. Governor Patten himself was elated over the change of atmosphere because the people of Hong Kong had been partially heard in London and Beijing since the 1989 pro-democracy movement in the streets of British Hong Kong. However, there were many issues to be settled in the months ahead. These included matters of the construction of the new airport and Container Pier No. 9, and the organization of the Court of Final Appeal. It appeared certain that the British, the Chinese people in Hong Kong and the communist government would cooperate, creating prosperity and stability by recognizing the common purposes of all three sides.

CHINA'S GUIDING PRINCIPLES IN THE HONG KONG EXPERIMENT

It is not difficult to analyze the Chinese government position in terms of unyieldable principles on the issue of national sovereignty, on the one hand, and flexible spirit of negotiation at the working level, on the other. It appears that the overall communist position can be summarized in terms of non-interference in domestic affairs and territorial recovery. Given the past 150 years of Western and Japanese encroachments on China's borderlands – whether involving Hong Kong, Macao or Taiwan or the British-Indian presence in Tibet or the Russian interference in Xingjiang or the Japanese creation of Manchukuo in the 1930s – the communist government after the 1949 revolution has so far refused, in principle, to make any territorial concession. It made war on India in 1962, had border disputes with the Soviet Union, and concluded peaceful border settlements with Pakistan and Burma. Chinese actions in military and diplomatic behavior since 1949 lead us to make the following observations about deeply entrenched attitudes which appear to be guiding the policy debates in Beijing:[15]

National sovereignty and administrative independence

Beijing has been determined to regain full Chinese sovereignty over Hong Kong since the very beginning of unofficial negotiations between 1979 and 1982.[16] Mao Zedong regretted his concession of sovereignty over Port Arthur to Stalin in 1950. He quickly reclaimed it in 1956 after Stalin's death. The Chinese did not tolerate India's claim to inherit the British right to station military guards in the Tibetan capital. On the other hand, Zhou Enlai made peaceful and generous border settlements with Premier U Nu of Burma and Ayub Khan of Pakistan. In short, on sovereignty and territory China has not yielded since 1949 to bullish and aggressive foreign claims.

One country, two systems

In the interest of domestic peaceful settlement, the use of military force is unnecessary, counter-productive and morally indefensible. Beijing also learned this humiliating lesson in 1969 during the military skirmish with the Soviet Union over Damaski Island. In the case of Hong Kong, military force has been totally unnecessary for the recovery of sovereignty. Taiwan, on the other hand, has a strong defence capability. However, the use of armed forces in such a civil war context may precipitate American intervention on Taiwan's behalf. Thus, the Beijing government has proposed a 'one country, two systems' general formula for both Taiwan and Hong Kong for reunification. Under this proposal, use of military power is conceivable only if Taiwan declares independence or if 'foreign influences' enter Taiwan. This formula should serve to stabilize the relations of two systems in 'one China', while all other peaceful activities and exchanges work to improve mutual relations. The application of this formula to Hong Kong is shrewd because China can benefit economically from Hong Kong. The critical factor was China's need to borrow Hong Kong's economic experience in Deng Xiaoping's economic reform since 1978. The Communist regime was fully aware that Chinese residents love China but prefer to live under the British because they also resent communism.[17] Thus, everything considered, wealthy Hong Kong can still enjoy its benefits under the British legal system while becoming a part of China. If this experiment succeeds well with the people of Hong Kong, it can be used to convince their Chinese brethren in Taiwan.

The preservation of 'prosperity and stability'

If Hong Kong's profit-making opportunities diminish or if any other serious destabilization should occur, the livelihood of some six million people and their future destiny will be in serious jeopardy. The Chinese leadership realizes that China, too, will benefit from Hong Kong's prosperity and stability, which will greatly contribute to China's modernization. The British, too, even at the moment of losing Hong Kong, depend on her well-protected artificial prosperity and stability as they bargain for China to grant them the opportunity, in both Hong Kong and China, for commercial profits beyond 1997. For the interests of all three parties, prosperity and stability in Hong Kong must not disappear because of the coming transfer of sovereignty.[18] Every year since 1984, however, some 40 000 to 50 000 well-educated Hong Kong Chinese have chosen to emigrate to other English-speaking countries for a life of security and liberty. They resent political oppression and potential instability within China itself, before or after 1997, that can affect prosperity and stability in Hong Kong.

The British lack of bargaining power

British diplomats possess greater skills in negotiation than diplomats from most other countries. In both technique and strategy either for advance or for retreat at the diplomatic table, British negotiators have been the most effective bargainers in most circumstances. However, in 1982–4, the Chinese diplomats confidently understood that opportunity and time for the British to bargain were severely limited, and that the people of Hong Kong would never organize to encourage the British to stay on, although they did believe the British were under a moral obligation to make the best possible bargain on their behalf. The Chinese people in Hong Kong have always had emotional and cultural ties with China. Obviously Chinese negotiators knew well that Britain could not continue on the island of Hong Kong itself without releasing from China the huge area of the New Territories. Chinese negotiators expected Britain to make concessions in an attempt to keep Hong Kong undisturbed.

Hong Kong people governing Hong Kong

Self-government was one of the attractive promises implicit in the concept of 'one country, two systems'. Written into the Basic Law, self-government is defined as a 'high degree of autonomy' and preservation of 'life-style'. The Basic Law specifies that most of Hong Kong's agreements with other countries will be honored and that the British legal system will continue to operate until after 2047. In short, self-government is complete except in defence and foreign policy areas, which are to be handled from Beijing. On the surface, Hong Kong will make its own laws, conduct its own trade, regulate its own currency, and so on. However, uncertainties lie in the daily task of actual implementation. The Beijing government may restrict autonomy to prevent Western influences from reaching China itself. Nevertheless, China is committed to a general concept of autonomy, which will also be applied to Taiwan to allow Taiwan people to govern Taiwan. Macao has made the same arrangement as another Chinese Special Administrative Region for transfer in 1999. Until the Tiananmen Square Incident of 1989, the people of Hong Kong had relied heavily on this unilateral promise of self-government.

The crisis of the pro-democracy movement

The interpretation – in terms of its actual implementation – of 'one country, two systems' has been much affected by the 1989 killing in Beijing. Overnight, the people of Hong Kong came to the assistance of the Chinese student demonstrators there. The crisis brought to Hong Kong streets one million demonstrators protesting against the communist regime. Money and medical supplies were collected and shipped to Beijing to help the students in the city. The people of Hong Kong realized that their own future after 1997 would be affected by this same corrupt government, which would be implementing the Basic Law and the Joint Declaration of 1984. They wanted political reform to take place in China to better assure their own future 'high degree of autonomy' and the 'preservation of life-style'. The 1989 crisis encouraged the British but frightened the Beijing government. It provoked the younger generation of students in Hong Kong to demand change, before the transfer, in favor of autonomy and liberty. Since the crisis, anti-Chinese political forces in Hong Kong have been on the rise and the British have felt morally compelled to introduce parliamentary representation while there was still time to do so. The end result of all this was diplomatic breakdown eventually between London and Beijing before Governor Patten's reform proposal was made public on 7 October 1992.[19]

The irony of benign neglect

Both China and Britain committed a monumental mistake in ignoring the Hong Kong people by keeping them out of the negotiations. The unexpected subsequent crisis of 1989 provoked Britain to reverse its benign neglect before Hong Kong's transfer to China. Had Hong Kong been allowed to participate in an open negotiation to protect its viable community, both London and Beijing would have had less liberty for secret bargaining with each other, and the chance of a 'betrayal' would not have been possible. Britain and China, indeed, were severely criticized by Hong Kong people for their deliberate neglect of Hong Kong interests. Following the 1991 election victory in Hong Kong, John Major's government, unable to ignore strong anti-China sentiment in Hong Kong, reversed the previous British policy of willing compliance to one of confrontational political reform under a new and dynamic governor installed in 1992. This was a courageous step to further democratic political developments in Hong Kong. The Beijing government, too, discovered this strong anti-communist sentiment but was not able to overcome it and achieve any kind of reconciliation with the majority of the voters in the 1991 election.[20] It is our view that China will soon have to carefully cultivate the goodwill of the people and allow democratic participation in election politics. Beijing's animosity toward autonomy and lifestyle in Hong Kong may not be obvious after 1997. After all, policy mistakes will adversely affect Taiwan and cause instability in China itself.

The meaning of 'territorial nationalism'

China has persisted in maintaining that if a territory was ever a part of China and if Chinese people have continued to live there, such 'undisputed' land must be returned to China. As a concept this 'territorial nationalism' conveys the belief that the overwhelming majority of the people on mainland China strongly insist on the 'unity of land' and 'the unity of nation'. Thus, an undivided Chinese nationhood requires reclamation of all lost territories. Perhaps the Chinese cultural tradition of the 'extended family' is responsible for such a unique psychology of identity. There is a widely shared common sentiment in Hong Kong today: 'We love China but we hate communists.' Taiwan's majority population is also in favor of eventual, but not immediate, reunification with the mainland. They, too, dislike communism. A minority of less than 30 per cent of the population entertain the concept of an independent Taiwan.[21] We thus believe that there is indeed a commonly shared 'territorial nationalism' among the Chinese. The innovation of 'one country, two systems' for a period of 50 years appears to be a communist plan for transition before full unity.

China's suspicion of foreign plots

Through the last 150 years of modern China's humiliating history, Chinese leaders have learned that foreign imperialists seek special extraterritoriality and treaty rights in China in order to chip away China's territories on the peripheral borders. China lost Hong Kong to the British in 1842. The Japanese took Taiwan by war in 1895. Imperial Russia marched into Northern Manchuria and Outer Mongolia. After 1945 at the end of World War II, the Chinese people were elated that the Western powers agreed upon Taiwan's return to China after the Japanese surrender. Currently, Western interests in human rights in China and foreign support for Taiwan and Tibet often infuriate the Chinese government and people. These are construed as foreign plots to interfere in China's domestic affairs. A very recent example was the 1995 American congressional suggestion for the president to appoint a negotiator to deal with China on behalf of Tibet.[22] We believe, for other reasons, that the Chinese people are indeed united in support of their central government against foreign plots to instigate separatist movements in the peripheral territories of China. The political crisis in Taiwan currently is a case in point. The bitter reaction from Beijing against a 'private visit' of President Li Teng-hui of Taiwan to the United States is an indication of much greater future conflict between Beijing and Washington. When the British, before 1982, suggested a continuation of leasing the New Territories, China abruptly rejected this idea. When the British offered to return Hong Kong's sovereignty to China in return for China's consent to grant 'administrative authority' to Britain, China rejected it also. Beijing insisted on recovering both sovereignty and direct administration of Hong Kong.

China genuinely fears foreign interference in its own internal affairs. This psychological predisposition may merely be modern China's groundless paranoia. It is, however, a significant factor in China's diplomatic encounter with any foreign countries perceived as scheming against China. This factor was, of course, present during the Sino-British negotiation in 1982 and again in 1993 when Governor Patten's election reform instituted a representative government in Hong Kong. Thus, the 17 rounds of negotiation ended in complete deadlock and mutual acrimony.

The impact of the Hong Kong experiment on China

The Beijing regime wants to recover a prosperous Hong Kong without any undesirable impact which could disturb communist domination in China. We believe this goal to be somewhat unrealistic after 1997. The last 20 years in China, since Deng's economic reform, teaches us that the regime is deliriously aware and fearful of the impact of foreign democracies on China. In the 1980s, it failed to stem the so-called 'cultural pollution' from Hong Kong. Coastal China today is changing toward liberalization. Provincial governments and private economic entities from the interior have also found numerous outlets for direct trade and international investment through facilities existing only in Hong Kong. As an inevitable result of this, the central government in Beijing is losing control over certain economic developments. Income gaps now separate different regions in China. We believe that economic decentralization will in time lead to political reform and greater democratization. Deng Xiaoping's vision of 'one country, two systems' is failing to insulate the healthy influence of Hong Kong.

'One country, two systems' is a two-way street. There are areas of daily life experience that cannot be insulated or regulated by the autocratic government. Direct and indirect trade and investment, cultural activities, business travel, tourism and the free media from Hong Kong will affect every part of China in the years to come. However, for the survival of Marxist government, the Beijing regime will no doubt institute damage control to minimize the influence of freedom and democracy from Hong Kong. In short, China dictated the terms of the Joint Declaration and drafted the Basic Law for the purpose of the socialist self-defense. Such self-defensiveness certainly will not be conducive to achieving genuine reunification with Hong Kong or Taiwan.

STRUCTURE OF THE BOOK

Chapter 2 is a comparative study of the Sino-British Joint Declaration on Hong Kong and the Sino-Portuguese Joint Declaration on Macao. These two joint declarations embody China's grand design of 'one country, two systems' and constitute the foundation upon which the two Basic Laws are to be based. China gives more autonomy to Hong Kong than to Macao. It is expected that, in its possible future deal with Taiwan, China will give Taiwan greater autonomy than Hong Kong.

The Tiananmen Incident of 1989 made the Hong Kong people more acutely aware of the potential role of the Chinese military. Chapter 3 deals with the question of stationing Chinese forces in Hong Kong. The Tiananmen Incident also reminded the Hong Kong people that they may need to secure a safe haven elsewhere should the situation in Hong Kong become unbearable after 1997. Chapter 4 deals with this question.

After the Democrats won the 1991 election convincingly in the wake of the Tiananmen Incident, Governor Patten seized this opportunity to push unilaterally for major political reforms. China resisted strongly. The Sino-British confrontations are elaborated in Chapters 5 and 6.

Chapter 7 provides a detailed account of Hong Kong's politicians and the development of political parties, both of which may have an important impact on Hong Kong before and after 1997. Chapter 8 discusses the politics underlying the organization of the Court of Final Appeal in Hong Kong and contrasts the differing ways in which China and the Western countries understand the concept of human rights.

The brief concluding chapter explores the impact of the Hong Kong experiment on Taiwan – when and if Taiwan is likely to unify with China.

2 Joint Declarations on Hong Kong and Macao

Under the terms of the Sino-British Joint Declaration[1] and Sino-Portuguese Joint Declaration,[2] Hong Kong and Macao are to be returned to China at the end of this century, respectively by the United Kingdom on 1 July 1997[3] and by Portugal on 20 December 1999.[4] After their transfer, they are each to be governed by a Basic Law, which China is to enact and promulgate long before the actual transfer.

HISTORICAL BACKGROUND

Prior to the adoption of China's open door policy in 1979, Hong Kong was virtually the only place through which China maintained contact with the outside world. Through Hong Kong, China has annually earned a large amount of foreign exchanges, a function which Hong Kong continues to perform today. Hong Kong, which includes Kowloon and the New Territories, has an area of 404 square miles and a population of six million. About 98 per cent of its population are Chinese. In a sense, Hong Kong is a Chinese community. Macao, about 40 nautical miles west of Hong Kong, is a small peninsula. It has an area of only six square miles and a population of about 400 000. Here too about 98 per cent of the people are ethnic Chinese. Its major industries are tourism and casinos and its economy is dependent on Hong Kong. Compared with Hong Kong, Macao is much less economically important to China. Politically, however, Macao is just as important.

The questions of Hong Kong and Macao are a product of history, as the government of China has always said. They are the result of unequal treaties, although the case of Macao is slightly different.

Following the Opium War in 1840, China ceded Hong Kong to Britain under the terms of the Treaty of Nanking.[5]

19

After another war between the two, China ceded the southern tip of the Kowloon Peninsula in 1860.[6] In 1898, China was forced to lease the rest of the peninsula (the New Territories) to Britain for 99 years.[7] As the lease of the New Territories approached expiration in 1997, the British took the initiative to negotiate with China. Without the leased New Territories, which comprise about 92 per cent of all the area and contain all major fresh water reservoirs and industrial plants, Hong Kong island and Kowloon alone cannot survive. After two years of painstaking negotiation,[8] the two countries initialed the Joint Declaration on 26 September 1984. It came into force on 27 May 1985.

The Macao situation is somewhat different. The Portuguese merchants first came to Macao in 1553. By bribing local Chinese officials, the Portuguese managed to get permission for permanent residency beginning in 1557. Later, due to the commission or omission of certain acts on the part of local Chinese officials, the Portuguese acquired the de facto rights to govern Macao, beginning in 1573.[9] Perceiving China's obvious weakness after the Opium War, Portugal pressured China to conclude a treaty[10] in 1887 giving Portugal the right to perpetual jurisdiction there.[11] Under the treaty, however, Portugal cannot transfer this right to a third party without China's consent.[12] In other words, China still has residual sovereignty. This is similar to the 1903 Panama Canal Treaty in accordance with which Panama retained residual sovereignty.[13] In June 1986, China and Portugal started negotiations. The Joint Declaration was initialed on 26 March 1987 and came into force on 15 January 1988.

An explanation of the Chinese policy toward unequal treaties concluded by previous governments and of its plans for dealing with Hong Kong, Macao and Taiwan is necessary before we discuss the Joint Declarations themselves.

CHINESE VIEW ON UNEQUAL TREATIES

Communist regimes recognize, in principle, only those treaties which are concluded by themselves, but not necessarily those which were concluded by the previous non-communist regimes.

China is no exception. An editorial in the Chinese Communist Party's official newspaper, *People's Daily*, illustrates this point. It states:

> At the time the People's Republic of China was inaugurated, our government declared that it would examine the treaties concluded by previous Chinese governments . . ., treaties that had been left over by history, and would recognize, abrogate, revise, or renegotiate them according to their respective contents . . .[14]

China has repeatedly stated that it does not recognize the validity of these unequal treaties regarding Hong Kong, Kowloon and Macao and has claimed that they are Chinese territories over which China has sovereignty. At same time, China has also declared:

> With regard to the outstanding issues, which are a legacy from the past, we have always held that, when conditions are ripe, they should be settled *peacefully through negotiations* and that, *pending a settlement, the status quo should be maintained.*[15] (Emphases added)

Although the unification of China is a longstanding 'national desire'[16] China, for various reasons, did not take any action toward Hong Kong or Macao. Not until quite recently was it ready to negotiate with Britain and Portugal. In fact, in both 1967 and 1974 Portugal voluntarily offered to return Macao to China, but China declined.

To unify Hong Kong, Macao, and particularly Taiwan, with China, the Communist Chinese government has conceived the previously mentioned strategy of 'one country, two [or several] systems'. This idea had been in the making several years before the Third Plenary Session of the Communist Party's 11th Central Committee of 1973, and it took shape shortly afterwards. Deng Xiaoping said:

> There are two ways to settle the issues: peacefully and non-peacefully. The non-peaceful way, or the way to settle the issues by force, was deemed inappropriate. How could these issues be settled peacefully? It requires taking into full consideration the history and present conditions of Hong Kong and Taiwan. . . . All work should be based on

reality. So, it is indispensable for us to respect the history and reality of Hong Kong and Taiwan when we consider the questions. Our proposal for reunifying the mainland and Taiwan is reasonable. After the reunification is realized, Taiwan can still practice capitalism while the mainland maintains socialism, or 'one country, two systems'.[17]

This arrangement is essential because, Deng said:

[I]f the capitalist system in Hong Kong and Taiwan is not guaranteed, stability and prosperity there cannot be maintained and peaceful settlement will become impossible. So, on the Hong Kong questions, China must first of all guarantee that the present capitalist system and lifestyle will remain unchanged for 50 years after 1997.[18]

China entered into negotiations with Britain because of its longstanding position of Chinese sovereignty over Hong Kong, and to these negotiations it brought the principle of 'one country, two systems'. The sovereignty issue did not exist in the case of Macao because when China and Portugal established diplomatic relations in 1979, Portugal had already recognized China's sovereignty. However, the concept of 'one country, two systems' also governed the negotiations on Macao.

COMPARISON OF THE TWO JOINT DECLARATIONS

The Sino-British negotiations on Hong Kong started in September 1982 and concluded two years later. For about half a year there was no progress at all because the two sides deadlocked on the sovereignty issue. Britain, in the wake of its Falkland Islands victory, wanted to exchange recognition of Chinese sovereignty for its continued administration beyond 1997. China would not agree, and the negotiation tensed. For example, in October 1983, Beijing declared September 1984 as the deadline for an agreement to be reached, or else China would proceed with its own plans for Hong Kong.[19] Furthermore, a formal deadline of 30 June 1985 was set in the Joint Declaration for the exchange of instruments of ratification to take place.[20] This deadline implied that if the exchange of instruments of ratification did not take place by that date, the Joint Declaration would never come into force. On the other hand, it took only nine months (June 1986 to March 1987) for China and Portugal to reach agreement on Macao. The absence of the sovereignty issue accounted for the accelerated negotiations. Furthermore, the Chinese negotiating team, essentially the same team that negotiated with Britain, was experienced. The Sino-Portuguese Joint Declaration on Macao states only that it would enter into force on the date of the exchange of instruments of ratification. It did not set a deadline.[21]

Since Portugal did not have many bargaining chips, it was not certain before the negotiations whether China would apply the Hong Kong model to Macao. However, due to several Chinese internal events, such as student demonstrations and the purge of Hu Yaopang in late 1986 and early 1987, Portugal found an opportunity to strike a better bargain. Portugal threatened that unless the final agreement suited certain basic concerns, they would simply hand Macao back within a year or two. This was exactly what Beijing feared. A premature hand-over of Macao under these circumstances would damage Hong Kong's prospects for economic and political stability prior to 1997.[22] In retrospect, China essentially used the same formula to handle Hong Kong and Macao. The spirit, format and wording of the two documents are quite similar. Some provisions are virtually identical.

The Sino-British Joint Declaration on Hong Kong consists of the Joint Declaration proper and three annexes. The Joint Declaration proper sets forth China's basic policies towards Hong Kong after 1997. It provides a framework in which the people of Hong Kong can work for a 'secure and prosperous future'.[23] The basic points are as follows: Britain will return Hong Kong to China on 1 July 1997; prior to 1 July 1997, Britain will be solely responsible for the administration of Hong Kong; except for foreign and defence affairs, Hong Kong will enjoy a high degree of autonomy as a Special Administrative Region (SAR) of China;[24] the SAR will be governed by a Basic Law to be enacted by the National People's Congress of China;[25] and the current social and economic (capitalist) systems and life-style in Hong

Kong will remain unchanged for 50 years after 1997, during which time the socialist policies applied in the mainland will not be applied to the SAR.[26] Annex I is an elaboration by China on its basic policies. Annex II deals with the Sino-British Joint Liaison Group, and Annex III details the land leases. These annexes are designed for smooth transition and are as binding as the Joint Declaration. Associated therewith is a separate Exchange of Memoranda on the status of persons, nationality and related issues. The entire Declaration contains over 10 000 words. The Sino-Portuguese Joint Declaration on Macao consists of the Joint Declaration proper and two annexes. Annex II to this Joint Declaration combines Annexes II and III to the Sino-British Joint Declaration. Associated therewith is also an Exchange of Memoranda dealing with the status of persons and nationality issues. The contents of these components are generally comparable to the Sino-British Joint Declaration. Portugal will return Macao to China on 20 December 1999.[27] However, the Sino-Portuguese Declaration is much shorter. It contains less than 6000 words. There are many provisions in the Sino-British Declaration which deal with shipping, finance, aviation, and so on. These do not appear in the Sino-Portuguese Declaration since Macao is not a center for such activities.

While 'one country, two systems' is the underlying principle for the Sino-British Declaration, these four exact words are not used in that document. In contrast, they are used in the Sino-Portuguese Declaration on Macao. Apparently, China has since become more deliberate in using this phrase, perhaps in part because it may have Taiwan in mind.

Twelve years after the Sino-British Declaration came into effect on 27 May 1985, Hong Kong will, as previously mentioned, be returned to China on 1 July 1997. The Sino-Portuguese Declaration, which came into effect on 15 January 1988, also has a transitional period of about 12 years. Transitional matters in both cases are being overseen by the Joint Liaison Groups and Land Commissions. Both Land Commissions and Joint Liaison Groups came into existence when the two Declarations took effect. While both Land Commissions will cease to exist when their respective transfers of administration take place, the duration of the two Joint

Liaison Groups differs. The Sino-Portuguese one will cease to exist on 1 January 2000,[28] eleven days after the transfer of administration takes place; the Sino-British one will also continue to function until that date – a full two and a half years after the transfer of administration.[29] Presumably, the transition in the Hong Kong case is more complicated; hence, more time for liaison is needed.

As for the method by which the membership of the legislature is to be determined, Paragraph 1 of Annex I to the Sino-British Joint Declaration provides that the legislature shall be constituted by elections. Although it is debatable whether 'elections' means direct popular elections, indirect elections, or both, they are elections nevertheless – that is, legislators are not to be appointed. The counterpart in the Sino-Portuguese document states, however, that the majority of the members shall be elected.[30] In other words, up to 49 per cent of the membership could be appointed. This method of selection is definitely less democratic than that of Hong Kong.

The chief executives of the two SARs are both to be selected by elections, or through consultations held locally, and to be appointed by the Central People's Government. Due to the central government's appointment power, the Chief Executive cannot really be very independent. Principal officials of the HKSAR, equivalent to secretaries, are to be nominated by the Chief Executive, but they also are to be appointed by the central government.[31] For the Macao SAR, the process is essentially the same, but even assistant secretaries, a rank lower than secretaries, are to be appointed by the central government.[32] In this regard, the central government exercises more control over Macao.

Since foreign and defense affairs are the responsibility of the central government, the Sino-British agreement provides that the central government can station military forces in the HKSAR.[33] However, the agreement specifically states that the military forces shall not interfere in the internal affairs of the HKSAR.[34] The Sino-Portuguese agreement only states that the Central People's Government shall be responsible for the defence of the Macao SAR, and nothing else. It is not clear whether the omission of 'shall not interfere in the internal affairs of the Macao SAR'[35] is intentional. And if so, it is also not clear whether this implies that the military forces could legally interfere in Macao's internal affairs. What is clear is that the omission has caused uneasiness for some people.

Careful readers of the two Declarations have also discovered one other difference, which may or may not be important. The Sino-British agreement states that 'Hong Kong's previous capitalist system and life-style shall remain unchanged for fifty years.'[36] The Sino-Portuguese agreement states that 'the current social and economic systems and life-style shall remain unchanged for 50 years'.[37] The word 'capitalist' is not there. This could mean a greater degree of socialism is intended for Macao.

The question of nationality and passport[38] is always a sensitive one among nations. China insists that it will not accept dual nationality. Each person in Hong Kong and Macao will have to make a choice.

This does not pose much of a problem to people in Hong Kong. The vast majority of the ethnic Chinese there will have to choose Chinese nationality since the passport issued by Britain to people in the dependent territories (British Dependent Territories citizens – BDTC) does not entitle the holder to right of abode in Britain. China considers BDTC only as a travel document for traveling outside of China, not a document denoting nationality. In any event, the BDTC or its modified version, British National (Overseas) – BN(O), will cease to exist sometime after 1997.[39] The number of British born in Hong Kong is relatively small and they usually have close ties with Britain. Most, if not all, of them will choose British nationality. Whether they can also acquire Chinese nationality is no major concern to them.

The choosing of only one nationality does pose a serious problem for people in Macao. There is a larger number of Macao-born Portuguese than Hong Kong-born British. Portugal has ruled Macao more than 430 years. Many of the Macao-born Portuguese do not have close ties with Portugal any more. Macao is their home; yet they are Portuguese. During negotiations, the Portuguese government tried, without avail, to seek Chinese permission to allow these people to have dual nationality. The ethnic Chinese in Macao who hold Portuguese passports have a similar problem. The holders of the Portuguese passport, unlike those of the BDTCs, do have the right of abode in Portugal. Furthermore, the Portuguese government has announced that, unlike the BN(O)s, the Portuguese passports can be handed down to future generations.[40] Thus, those ethnic Chinese also have to make a difficult choice. The Chinese government in this case takes the same position as in the Hong Kong case. The Portuguese passport will be considered only as a travel document for people who have Chinese nationality.

PROCESS OF THE ENACTMENT OF THE HONG KONG BASIC LAW

The Joint Declarations, Annexes and Exchanges of Memoranda are all international agreements.[41] Their implementation requires domestic action by the signatories. The two Joint Declarations respectively state that China will, in accordance with the provisions of Article 31 of its constitution, establish a Hong Kong Special Administrative Region (HKSAR) and a Macao Special Administrative Region (Macao SAR) upon resuming the exercise of sovereignty thereof. They further state that the basic policies of the China regarding Hong Kong and Macao, as set forth in the Declarations, will be stipulated respectively in a Basic Law of the HKSAR and of the Macao SAR. The two Basic Laws are to be enacted by the National People's Congress (NPC) of China. What follows is a description of the process by which China is to enact the Basic Law for Hong Kong. The process for Macao, not discussed below, will be similar.

The NPC established a Basic Law Drafting Committee (BLDC) for Hong Kong in 1985. The BLDC was thus a governmental organization of China. The BLDC was composed of 59 members, of which 23 (about 40 per cent) are Hong Kong residents and the rest mainlanders. To canvass the opinions of the HK people and to facilitate the work of the BLDC, the Hong Kong members of the BLDC organized a Consultative Committee for the Basic Law (CCBL). This committee was composed of 180 members who are all Hong Kong residents, including non-Chinese. The CCBL is considered to be a private organization of Hong Kong. Due to the fact that the selection of its 19-member Executive Committee was done in an undemocratic way, the BLDC did not necessarily reflect the real views of the Hong Kong people.[42]

There were to be three drafts for the Basic Law. It took the BLDC almost three years to complete the first draft, which was published in April 1988. The document is entitled 'The Draft Basic Law of the Hong Kong Special Administrative Region of the People's Republic of China (for Solicitation of Opinions)'. According to the drafting schedules, there was a five-month period during which the Hong Kong people could express opinions and concerns to the CCBL. Following this, the CCBL was to submit a report to the BLDC in October. Then the BLDC, after considering the report of the CCBL and the opinions from all other sources, such as the British government (through diplomatic channels), was to make another draft in early 1989 for submission to the NPC. After the NPC acted on it, with possible revisions, that revised edition was again to be published for public input. And after that round of consultation and possible further revision, the NPC would promulgate the final version some time in 1990. The politics of the drafting of the Basic Law will be analyzed in Chapter 6.

3 The Stationing of Chinese Forces in Hong Kong

The possibility that the People's Liberation Army would be stationed in Hong Kong after the reversion had been a continuing concern of the Hong Kong people since the signing of the Joint Declaration. However, the Tiananmen incident in June 1989 prompted the Hong Kong people to pay immediate and serious attention to this issue. In this chapter we will analyze the role of the military in the context of Hong Kong's reversion to China in July 1997. After explaining the importance of the Chinese military in politics, we will discuss five major issues: the military's attitude toward Hong Kong, the stationing of forces in Hong Kong, the planning and training of the forces, the negotiations to determine which military bases and defence lands China will take over, and the role of the People's Liberation Army (PLA) in Hong Kong after 1997.

THE CHINESE MILITARY AND POLITICS

Chinese politics has two somewhat contradictory sayings: 'The Party controls the gun' and 'The regime comes out of the barrel of a gun'. Either statement perhaps could be true during a particular period of time. What cannot be denied, however, is that the military has always been an important player in Chinese politics.

The military is especially important in time of war or internal disorder. An obvious example was the military's role in the Tiananmen Incident in June 1989. But the military has also had an enormous impact on China's policy toward Taiwan and Hong Kong, taking a militant position on the reunification of these two areas with China.[1] It is not clear to what extent the military may have contributed to the

Chinese government's refusal to renounce the possible use of force against Taiwan, or even against Hong Kong.

THE MILITARY'S ATTITUDE TOWARD HONG KONG

The Joint Declaration reflects China's willingness to carry out the so-called 'one country, two systems' principle in Hong Kong.[2] In 1984 the political system of Hong Kong was, as it continues to be today, substantially different from the communist/socialist system that prevailed in most of China. Therefore, this Joint Declaration is not a document without significance. China at least made some important concessions or guarantees. For this reason, the Declaration produced euphoria in both China and Hong Kong at that time.

However, either during the negotiations or shortly after they concluded, the Chinese military expressed dissatisfaction with China's guarantee not to change Hong Kong's capitalistic system for 50 years after 1997. According to reports, some who attended a military seminar for high-ranking officers did not understand why Deng Xiaoping was willing to make such a guarantee. Others felt that Deng was just too soft.[3] Yang Shangkun, then vice-chairman of the Central Military Commission and a professional soldier, was also reported to have said, 'Son of a bitch, no change after 50 years! If I dispatch a big army over and ask for a change by tonight, it can't be later than tomorrow morning!'[4]

Proposals introduced in 1992 and 1993 by Hong Kong Governor Christopher Patten to democratize the enclave met with strong resistance from China.[5] The Chinese military frequently and openly criticized the Hong Kong government, expressing the view that if Britain and Hong Kong would not withdraw the reform proposals, China might as well just take over Hong Kong.[6] According to some sources, the Chinese military had contingency plans to 'take care of' Hong Kong. One plan envisioned a conflict limited to China and Britain; in a second plan the United States was also involved. A third plan added another player, Taiwan.[7] In September 1993, the *Far Eastern Economic Review* reported that the PLA had begun to assemble and train the troops that would be stationed in Hong Kong after 1997.[8] As the Sino-British negotiations on political reforms appeared to come to a dead end, Deng Xiaoping and other Chinese officials repeatedly hinted that China might consider taking over Hong Kong before 1 July 1997.[9]

After the Sino-British negotiation on political reforms broke up in November 1993, China appeared to want to demonstrate its power in an attempt to encourage Britain to withdraw its reform proposals. In the first five months of 1994, Chinese fighters invaded Hong Kong air space three times.[10] Nevertheless, Hong Kong went ahead with District Board elections on 17 September 1994.

STATIONING OF PLA FORCES

The answer to the question of whether the People's Republic of China has the right to station forces in Hong Kong after 1 July 1997 is a definite yes. The right to station troops in its own territory is an integral part of a country's sovereignty.[11] Whether the people of Hong Kong wanted PLA forces there is another question, one which was of increasing concern since the 4 June 1989 Tiananmen Incident. Since then, Hong Kong worried about whether China would actually station troops there, and if so, when, where, how many, and what kind?

Will there be troops?

Even prior to the Tiananmen Incident, some people in Hong Kong felt that the presence of the PLA would be undesirable. They suggested that after 1 July 1997 the PLA should hire the Gurkhas, from Nepal, who now man about half of the Hong Kong garrison, rather than itself dispatching troops, so that Hong Kong could avoid the stigma of 'the Red Army entering the city'.[12]

Shortly after the Tiananmen Incident, many members of the Legislative Council suggested amending the Basic Law to allow China to station troops in Hong Kong only during war.[13] A survey commissioned by *Ming Bao* (a major newspaper in Hong Kong) reported that the stationing of the PLA in Hong Kong was people's number one concern for the 1990s.[14]

Some people suggested that China could reserve the right to station forces in Hong Kong but announce that it would not actually do so. Psychologically, the benefits of this action would be immeasurable. This decision would not reduce China's military capability. China could station forces intended for Hong Kong in Shenzhen and easily dispatch them across the border.[15] However, to China the right to station forces in Hong Kong is symbolic of its sovereignty over the territory; therefore, China insists upon retaining this right.

When to station?

When Britain started to trim its garrison forces in Hong Kong, the question arose of gradually replacing those troops with the PLA. In 1987, when Sino-British relations were reasonably good, Britain had the impression from the eighth meeting of the Joint Liaison Group[16] that China would not station forces in Hong Kong before it resumed control.[17] In February 1988, when asked whether China would station forces in Hong Kong before 1 July 1997, the chief Chinese delegate of the Joint Liaison Group said that it would not, but that it might send a small number of military personnel to Hong Kong to inspect barracks and installations.[18]

After the Tiananmen Incident, China reportedly expressed a strong desire to station forces at certain military bases in Hong Kong before the takeover. The advantage of this step would be better adaptation to the new environment and a smoother transition.[19] Following the collapse of negotiations on political reforms in November 1993, reports of China's taking over Hong Kong prior to 1 July 1997 became even more frequent and vivid. Several Chinese military delegations, representing the General Staff Headquarters, navy, army, and the 42nd Army, quietly visited various bases and installations in Hong Kong in early 1994. Since then, Sino-British relations have improved somewhat.[20] However, it was reported in early 1996 that Britain would not object to China's sending an advance group of several hundred military personnel to certain military bases and facilities in Hong Kong to prepare for the transfer.[21]

Where to station?

The British garrison was stationed in various barracks throughout Hong Kong. The headquarters of the British Forces were in the Central District of Hong Kong, housed in the Prince of Wales Building, which reportedly was also the nerve-center of the British intelligence operation in the Far East. A Royal Navy dockyard was adjacent.

China wanted to station part of its forces in a barracks the British already had abandoned because of urban development projects.[22] Britain was concerned about the possible reactions of the local residents, especially after the Tiananmen Incident,[23] and was prepared to lodge a strong protest to China.[24] China, however insisted on stationing forces in downtown Hong Kong.[25]

The image of the PLA, by no means good before the Tiananmen Incident, became much worse after that. Four months after the Tiananmen suppression, 51 per cent of the respondents to a survey conducted in Hong Kong by the *South China Morning Post* stated they did not want the PLA in downtown commercial districts. However, they had no objections the troops being stationed in the newly developed cities. About 20 per cent of the respondents wished the PLA to station near the Hong Kong/Chinese border. A quarter of the respondents even specified the places the PLA should station, such as Lo Wu and Sha Tau Kok, on the Hong Kong/Chinese border.[26]

An August 1993 survey by the Social Science Research Center of Hong Kong University showed that although close to half of the respondents agreed to China's stationing forces in Hong Kong, the majority were worried that the PLA would not observe Hong Kong laws, could not get along with Hong Kong police, and would adversely affect Hong Kong's international image. If the PLA came to Hong Kong, 75 per cent of the respondents wanted the soldiers stationed in border areas. Only 20 per cent would be willing to have the PLA in urban areas.[27] China, however, would not accept any preconditions, stating repeatedly that stationing troops is a right of sovereignty.

How many troops and what kind?

The question of how many troops of the PRC would station in Hong Kong had also been a concern of the Hong Kong people – preferably, the fewer the better.

Britain maintained only a symbolic military presence in Hong Kong, primarily to patrol the border to stop the illegal entry of Chinese. The military also helped the police to maintain order, when necessary. In 1987, there were about 12 500 troops in Hong Kong.[28] Of those 3000 were civilian employees and 5000 were in support services such as medical, transport, and communication. Combat forces did not exceed 4500.[29] The total garrison in 1994 had been reduced to 9500 troops.

Britain has suggested that China did not need a large force in Hong Kong because much of the present military responsibility for patrolling the border would be transferred to the police, which would be enlarged proportionally, and because China already has troops in Shenzhen or nearby. Britain suggested a figure between 4000 and 5000 troops – the equivalent of the British combat troops then in Hong Kong.

China never mentioned any specific figure for its future forces in Hong Kong – the information might be a military secret. Reports have mentioned figures of from 3000 to 5000[30] to 14 000.[31] A Chinese official once remarked, however, that the force would not be very large because the central government would be responsible for all of the expenses. In late May of 1996, the Commander of British Forces in Hong Kong visited the future PLA unit in Shenzhen. He stated after his return that the force level could be between 9000 and 10 000[32] When asked what kind of forces China would station in Hong Kong, a Chinese member of the Joint Liaison Group stated that they should include all the types of armed forces that Britain had had in Hong Kong.[33] That would include army, navy and air force. However, a 1995 newspaper article stated that there are to be no air force troops, only army and navy.[34] A more recent account states that there will be ten helicopters but no fighters.[35]

PLANNING AND TRAINING OF THE FORCES

As early as 1990, the Central Military Commission had included the stationing of forces as an agenda item. The commission instructed the General Staff Headquarters, General Political Department, and General Logistics Department[36] to study the relevant provisions in the Basic Law dealing with the British forces in Hong Kong so that they could advise the Chinese delegation of the Joint Liaison Group.[37] Sometime before Christopher Patten came to Hong Kong as governor, the Central Military Commission established a special unit to plan for the stationing of forces in Hong Kong after 1997. By the end of 1993, the General Staff Headquarters and the General Political Department had developed a training program for the future forces.[38] In mid 1994, the Central Military Commission established the 'Office of June 30'[39] to be led by the deputy chairman of the commission, Zhang Zeng.[40] At about the same time, the Chinese Ministry of Defence began construction of a US$21 million Military Command and Training Center in Shenzhen to be used for the training of troops to be deployed in Hong Kong.

The Central Military Commission determined that the future PLA commander in Hong Kong should be a major-general or lieutenant-general; not too old; and ideally a Cantonese familiar with Guangdong and Hong Kong affairs. One possible name has already surfaced, that of Lei Mingqu. In December 1993, Lei was a lieutenant-general and a deputy political commissar of the Guangzhou Military Region who had been stationed in Guangdong for a long time and had been a member of the Party's Central Committee. Under the Basic Law, future PLA troops stationed in Hong Kong were to be under the direct command of the Central Military Commission. Therefore, Lei's membership of the Party's Central Committee could serve as a useful link to the central government. That information was not completely accurate, however. In 1994, it was Major-General Liu Zhengwu, not Lei Mingqu, who was named the future PLA commander in Hong Kong. Liu was 48 years old then and was to be promoted to lieutenant-general after 1997. He was the commander of the PLA's 42nd Army which is a major component of the Guangzhou Military Region.[41]

Most of the soldiers of the future Hong Kong force will be selected from the Guangzhou Military Region.[42] Their training will consist of (a) political education (Deng's 'socialism with special Chinese characteristics', China's constitution, and the Basic Law); (b) legal education (the military code and Hong Kong laws); (c) social and history education (social and historic developments in Hong Kong after the Opium War and Hong Kong customs and culture); (d) military training (skill in using light arms, in self-defence, and in dealing with riots); and (e) language training (learning English and Cantonese conversation skills).

Soldiers are to be high-school graduates, and officers, college graduates.[43] Presently, 57 per cent of the officers of the Guangzhou Military Region and 40 per cent of the soldiers meet that educational standard. Most of them come from the countryside of Guangdong, and therefore the Cantonese and 'custom and culture' requirements pose no problems for them.[44]

The discipline and morals of the forces to be stationed are of great concern to the residents of Hong Kong. This concern appears legitimate in view of the less than desirable image presented by some of the PLA. There have been fights between some PLA soldiers and Hong Kong truck drivers in Shenzhen.

To ease these concerns, the Guangzhou Military Region invited more than 200 people from Hong Kong to visit its barracks and bases in Guangzhou. The company they visited is famed for its excellent training and the level of the soldiers' education and civility. The deputy regional commander stated that the quality of the forces to be stationed in Hong Kong in the future would be even better than this company.[45] A leader in the visiting delegation advised that China should pay special attention to the image of the PLA when they are off duty. She suggested that adequate allowances be given to the soldiers to buy civilian clothes so that they would not have to wear uniforms when off duty.[46] However, shortly after this visit, it was reported that some model squad leaders being trained in Guangdong for deployment to Hong Kong were disciplined for illegally setting up toll gates along a highway to collect tolls from cars.[47] Incidentally, this has been a popular way for farmers, soldiers and workers to make money.

The Chinese authorities have been concerned about the soldiers' discipline. The 'Office of June 30' compiled a 'Handbook for Future PLA Forces in Hong Kong' including detailed regulations on items such as uniform, dress, holidays, conduct outside the base, contacts or relations with Hong Kong residents, visits of families or relatives, and vacationing. Those who violate these regulations will be punished.[48]

NEGOTIATION ON MILITARY BASES, FACILITIES AND LANDS

Sino-British negotiation on this issue took almost seven years, from 1987 to 1994. The PLA was concerned about the cost of the military bases, facilities, and military lands – worth billions of US dollars – that the British handed over to China. Some of the facilities were located in the downtown areas of Hong Kong, Kowloon and the New Territories, and some were far from the cities. The British did not agree with the PLA position that it would take over all military infrastructure then under the jurisdiction of the British military whether in the city or not. They planned to turn over as few facilities as possible, and as far from the city as possible.

Britain used several arguments to support its position. First, the Chinese have always said that stationing troops in Hong Kong was only to signify its sovereignty. Britain argued that China would not require a large force to achieve this objective and therefore the PLA would not need many bases or much land. China took the position that it could station up to 12 500 troops – the highest level Britain had had – and would require many bases and much land. Second, Britain argued that its long-term plan had moved its naval base/headquarters to Stonecutter Island. The new base could be the future PLA naval base, and the PLA navy would not need any facilities in Hong Kong proper. Furthermore, according to the long-range plan of the city, land was to be created at the naval base for urban and economic development. Third, Britain contended that barracks then in the city were far from the city when they were built years ago.

During the course of negotiations, China reiterated three principles relevant to this issue: first, the military facilities it would take over from the British should be adequate for defense; second, China also supported Hong Kong's economic and urban development and would not stand in its way; and third, agreement on these issues should be reached through consultation. Those were positions that Britain found it difficult to refute. China's trump card was through consultation. It would dispute any unilateral action taken by the British whether there was merit or not.

On 17 May 1993, Britain moved its naval base to Stonecutter Island over the repeated protests of China. China earlier had informed the British that it would not use the new base on Stonecutter Island, but would rather build a new one close to the former British base. Britain wished to pacify China by guaranteeing that the harbor to be built on Stonecutter Island would be comparable to the old one. China then demanded that the new harbor be able to accommodate an aircraft carrier. When Britain contended that China did not have an aircraft carrier, China retorted that it might have one later. Subsequently, a newspaper reported that China planned to construct two mid-sized (40 000 tons) aircraft carriers.[49] Britain had asked China during the course of negotiations what level and kind of forces China intended to station in Hong Kong, so that it could review the potential base land requirements. China replied that such information was a state secret. China in turn asked Britain for detailed information on all bases and military lands in Hong Kong for her future reference. Of course, Britain did not totally comply either.

Britain was willing to give only a limited number of military installations and lands to China because the British knew very well that the PLA, after obtaining them, might sell them later for profit. China's Three Headquarters, Air Force, Navy, and the Second Artillery Corps (missile) all have holding companies in Hong Kong,[50] headed by people related to the high-ranking government, party and military officials. Enormous pressure from the PLA caused Britain to soften its position and to give China more facilities, both in and outside of the city – but on the condition that when and if the PLA no longer needed these bases, they should be returned to the government of the Hong Kong SAR. The PLA could not pocket the proceeds.

After seven years of off-and-on negotiations, the two sides reached an agreement on 30 June 1994.[51] According to the agreement, the British were to hand over to China on 1 July 1997 fourteen military locations for defense purposes, with no conditions as to whether or not the PLA could sell them later. Another 25 locations currently in the possession of the British military were to be handed to the Hong Kong government when the British military no longer had any use for them. Those 25 parcels of land were large enough to build 15 000 housing units, which could generate HK$ 65 billion (roughly US$ 8.3 billion) for the Hong Kong government. The Prince of Wales Building, then headquarters of the British forces, was to be given to the PLA for its headquarters.

Britain may have made some of these concessions with an eye to gaining an agreement with China concerning financial arrangements for the construction of a new airport on the island of Chek Lap Kok. Those negotiations had been going on for three years. Both the negotiations on the military sites and the ones on airport finances had been complicated by the Sino-British disputes over political reforms, which started in October 1992 and formally broke up in November 1993. It was speculated that Britain was willing to make some concessions on the military land in order to achieve a breakthrough in the airport negotiation.[52] Indeed, an agreement on airport finance was reached on 4 November 1994, four months after the military land agreement.[53]

THE ROLE OF THE PEOPLE'S LIBERATION ARMY IN HONG KONG AFTER 1997

According to the Joint Declaration signed in September 1984, the maintenance of public order is the responsibility of the government of the Hong Kong SAR.[54] PLA forces to be stationed in Hong Kong are to be for defense and therefore should not interfere in the internal affairs of the SAR.[55] The Basic Law enacted by China pursuant to the Joint Declaration states that in time of need the SAR government could ask the Central People's Government for assistance from the garrison to maintain public order for disaster relief.[56]

Thus, even in cases of public disaster, the PLA in Hong Kong would not intervene unless the SAR government requests it.

Provisions are made for two exceptions, however. First, if the Standing Committee of the National People's Congress (NPC) declares war, national laws would prevail over the Basic Law, and the PLA in Hong Kong could then intervene without a request from the SAR government.[57] Second, if the Standing Committee of the NPC decides that turmoil in Hong Kong creates a state of emergency beyond the control of the government of the SAR that would endanger national unity or security, the central government could order the application of the relevant national laws to the Region.[58] The central government alone is empowered to determine whether the turmoil is beyond the control of the SAR or whether a state of emergency exists.

In reaction to mass demonstrations in Hong Kong supporting the pro-democracy movements in Tiananmen, Deng Xiaoping stated that the people of Hong Kong could criticize the Chinese Communist government after 1997, but they would not be allowed to subvert it. The people of Hong Kong have to ask themselves whether a Tiananmen-style tragedy could happen in Hong Kong.

The primary task of the PLA in Hong Kong after 1997 seemed not to be defense against foreign invasion in the traditional sense, but rather prevention of 'turmoil' or 'subversion' and suppression should they occur.

According to Zhang Zhen, vice-chairman of the Central Military Commission, the ten top functions and duties of the future PLA in Hong Kong were the following:

1. Defend the sacred territory of the motherland – Hong Kong and its surrounding islands, Hong Kong's airspace and waters – and prevent encroachment by foreign countries;
2. Prevent and attack activities of subversion and sabotage by foreign powers aimed at Hong Kong society;
3. Prevent and crush efforts by foreign powers to take advantage of Hong Kong's unique environment and conditions to use it as a base for carrying out subver-

sion and sabotage of inland construction of socialism and the Four Modernizations;

4. Prevent hostile forces, and pro-British and pro-United States extreme rightist forces in Hong Kong from manufacturing political unrest;
5. Prevent and attack riots planned and manufactured by hostile forces and extreme rightist pro-British and pro-United States forces in Hong Kong;
6. Prevent and attack hostile foreign forces and extreme rightist pro-British and pro-United States forces in Hong Kong from attempting such treasonous actions as independence or creating 'political entity';
7. Prevent and attack hostile forces from Taiwan, and Taiwan independence forces, from manufacturing political unrest and disorder;
8. Assist and support special zone police departments in maintaining social stability and other tasks in the Hong Kong special zone;
9. Defend and uphold the government's implementation and practice of the policy toward Hong Kong of 'one country, two systems', and carry out the Basic Law enacted by the National People's Congress, not tolerating the subversion and sabotage of hostile forces; and
10. Assist and support work efforts if and when major disasters or other times of difficulty fall upon Hong Kong.[59]

Only one item on Zhang Zhen's list (no. 1) pertains to defense in the traditional sense. One other item (no. 10) deals with natural disaster. The other eight are aimed against sabotage of the 'one country, two systems' by 'hostile forces' in or outside Hong Kong.

Since 1978, China has practiced what the popular Chinese saying accurately describes as loose control in economics and tight grip in politics. These two principles will very likely be applied to Hong Kong. China will largely give Hong Kong a free hand in the economic sphere. Economic freedom can also benefit the enterprises in which the Chinese government or the children of high-ranking officials invest. However, there will be tight control in politics. Freedom of the press, expression, assembly and demonstration will all be curtailed drastically. In most cases, knowing what China's policies are, people will exercise self-restraint, a process that has already begun in Hong Kong. Ultimately, it appears that China will be able to exercise tight political control, which can and will be backed up by the PLA to be stationed in Hong Kong.

4 Safe Haven, Visas, and Right of Abode

The Tiananmen Incident of 1989 was a real shock for the people of Hong Kong. Since then they have been concerned about the stationing of the PLA in Hong Kong which is discussed in Chapter 3. Many Hong Kong people wish to find a safe haven somewhere should the situation in Hong Kong become unbearable. Those who are 'British nationals' and hold British passports expect that their 'mother country' would grant them the right of abode in the United Kingdom should they need to leave Hong Kong. However, such is not necessarily the case. This chapter will analyze both the right-of-abode problem and Hong Kong's out-migration problem arising from its people's lack of confidence in the future HKSAR under China's rule.

BRITISH NATIONALITY LAWS AND HONG KONG

The United Kingdom has perhaps the most complex nationality laws in the world. Various kinds of citizenships or statuses have been created for different purposes.

One of the more recent nationality acts, the British Nationality Act, enacted in 1981 and implemented on 1 January 1983,[1] provides for six types of citizenships or statuses: British Citizenship (BC), British Dependent Territories Citizenship (BDTC), British Overseas Citizenship (BOC), British Subjects, Commonwealth Citizenship, and British Protected Persons. Only the first three will be discussed here.

British citizenship is acquired automatically by those born in the United Kingdom, those who have a parent who is a British citizen, or those with a parent who has settled in the United Kingdom. Thus, a child who is born in the United Kingdom neither to a British citizen nor to a resident of the United Kingdom cannot acquire BC automatically.

43

The latter two kinds of citizenship include persons connected with certain Commonwealth countries other than the United Kingdom. In dependent territories (including Hong Kong, Gibraltar and the Falkland Islands, among others), the rules for acquiring citizenship are similar to those for acquiring BC except that the connection is with the dependent territory rather than the United Kingdom. Any United Kingdom and colonies citizen who had not acquired either BC or BDTC as of 1 January 1983 became a BOC. The BOC is mainly intended for those born in former colonies or dependencies who opted to remain British when their native countries became independent. The BOC status was initiated when the 1981 Nationality Act came into force and, with a few exceptions, could not be acquired thereafter. There are only about two hundred thousand BOCs in the world. Of the three types of citizenships mentioned, only BCs have an automatic right of entry and abode in the United Kingdom.

Some 3.25 million of Hong Kong's 6 million people are BDTCs, 3.19 million by birth and 53 000 by naturalization. It is noteworthy that the Hong Kong BDTCs constitute well over 90 per cent of all BDTCs worldwide. It would be safe to speculate that Britain created the BDTC mainly for Hong Kong.

Obviously the title BDTC will cease to be appropriate after 1997 because Hong Kong will no longer be a British dependent territory. Accordingly, the Declaration states that all Hong Kong BDTCs will lose their BDTC status as of 1 July 1997 but will be able to acquire another suitable status known as *British National (Overseas)* – BN(O).[2] The BN(O), like the BDTC and BOC, does not have the right of abode in Britain.

PROBLEMS OF THE VARIOUS KINDS OF BRITISH CITIZENSHIP

With the exception of 'British Citizenship', the British nationality proper, all types of British citizenship have disadvantages. First, BDTCs, BOCs and BN(O)s do not, as previously mentioned, have the right of abode in Britain. Second, they may be denied entry to non-commonwealth countries. Third, they may also be denied entry to Commonwealth countries. Fourth, they may be denied entry to the United Kingdom itself. For example, Canada refused to issue visas to those BOCs whose passports did not include the stamped endorsement: 'The holder has the right of readmission to Britain.'[3] Canadian officials said that BOC passports were meaningless, not passports at all. France recently denied Hong Kong BDTC holders entry although it did not require visas for BDTC holders.[4] In May 1988, a number of Hong Kong BDTCs – members of a tourist group that planned to stay two days in Britain – were denied entry.[5] Similar cases occurred in June.[6] Those denied entry were sent back to the preceding stop on their itinerary. British Foreign Secretary Sir Geoffrey Howe ordered an investigation of these cases. It appeared that the reason that British immigration officers denied the travelers entry, was that they suspected their intention was to work and settle in Britain. Some Hong Kong BDTC holders were allowed entry to Britain, but immigration officers stamped their passports with the mysterious mark '+' and entry was limited to two days.[7]

The Hong Kong government began to issue the BN(O) on 1 July 1987. It promoted the new passport worldwide, insisting that it would have the same efficacy as the BDTC. Whereas many countries announced that they would recognize the passport, it seemed that the vast majority of Hong Kong's residents did not have full confidence in it. From July to November 1987, there were only about 15 700 applications for BN(O)s, whereas 55 000 applied for BDTCs during the same period.[8] Similarly, in June 1989, there were only 3335 applications for BN(O)s but 26 067 for BDTCs.[9] Many BN(O) holders had encountered travel problems; some even applied for the revocation of their passports and reverted to the status of BDTC.[10]

It was announced in January 1988 that BN(O)s would be permitted only a non-renewable six-month stay in Britain, reduced from one year. Members of the Hong Kong legislature considered this another example of the British abandonment of Hong Kong.[11] A member of the Basic Law Drafting Committee doubted that Britain would protect BN(O)s traveling abroad after 1997; he believed that Britain would merely inform China and let it take care of the matter.

THE BRITISH GOVERNMENT'S RESPONSE TO THE HONG KONG BDTCS

Ninety-eight percent of Hong Kong's six million people are of Chinese origin. The overwhelming majority are either children of Chinese refugees or are themselves refugees from China. Besides the British, Americans and Japanese, those who have migrated from the Indian subcontinent make up a significant ethnic minority. Many of the latter have severed the connection with their native countries. The approximately 3.25 million BDTCs have the right of abode in Hong Kong and cannot be deported. The rest – with the exception of resident BCs, who have rights similar to those of the BDTCs – are either residents or non-residents. They have lesser rights and can be deported. This chapter deals with the concerns of the 3.25 million BDTCs to whom Britain has a moral obligation.

The BDTC's 'wish list' – in an approximate order of preference – can be simplified as follows:

First, to give the right of abode in the United Kingdom to

1. all Hong Kong BDTCs;
2. non-Chinese BDTCs (mainly people of Indian descent);
3. Hong Kong veterans (those who fought for the British against the Japanese during World War II);
4. widows of the aforementioned veterans;
5. civil servants who occupy 'sensitive' positions;
6. civil servants (approximately 150 000).

Second, if no right of abode is granted to BDTCs, to give an endorsement on BDTC or BN(O) passports permitting the holder to:

1. enter the United Kingdom without a visa;
2. make multiple entries into the United Kingdom.

Third, to give the said right of abode to students from Hong Kong who are now at school in the United Kingdom. No one who knows British legislative history on nationality and immigration could have high hopes that the British government would respond substantially to this wish list. Prior to 1962, British nationals in Hong Kong qualified for full British citizenship, which entitled them to live and work in the United

Kingdom. In 1962, however, Britain instituted the Commonwealth Immigration Act, designed to reduce 'coloured immigration'.[12] The British Nationality Act of 1981 was directed specifically at Hong Kong. During parliamentary debate on that bill, the opposition (Labour) charged that it was 'an immigration control bill dressed up to look like a nationality bill'.[13] M.D.A. Freeman, the official annotator of this act, commented, 'The Act is permeated by racism and sexism.'[14]

The racist aspect of the British Nationality Act of 1981 is further evidenced in Section 5, which resulted from an amendment. Although Section 5 does not specifically mention Gibraltar, it provides access to British citizenship for the people of Gibraltar. Additionally, the British Parliament passed an act in March 1983 that provides for the acquisition of British citizenship by the people of the Falkland Islands. Thus, the majority of the world's white BDTCs are eligible for British citizenship.

Section 4 of the British Nationality Act of 1981 provides a mechanism by which some BDTCs can acquire British citizenship. Section 4 is, however, applicable only to those BDTCs who have served in the government of a dependent territory. The approval or rejection of an application is entirely up to the home secretary's discretion. Although the act requires that discretionary decisions be made without regard to race, color or religion, the home secretary is not required to explain the acceptance or rejection of an application. Furthermore, such decisions cannot be appealed or reviewed in any court. During the period from 1980 to 1988, only 46 veterans and eight civil servants from Hong Kong were granted British citizenship.[15]

Admittedly, the number of BDTCs in Hong Kong is exceedingly large compared with that in Gibraltar and the Falkland Islands. The United Kingdom does indeed have practical difficulties in admitting 3.25 million BDTCs. However, the British government's response to virtually all Hong Kong's requests was a flat no. The government has showed very little flexibility and has taken no concrete action. Britain's Foreign Secretary Sir Geoffrey Howe consistently asserted that 'Nothing would undermine confidence in Hong Kong more' than Britain's acceptance of applications for British passports, for the right of abode, or even for guaranteed readmission to Britain.[16] Sir Geoffrey implied that denying BDTCs the right of abode in the United Kingdom would cause their confidence to remain intact or even to increase. No one could understand this kind of logic. Hong Kong's people made one simple request: 'Guarantee us a "home of last resort" so that we don't have to worry. This will increase our confidence in Hong Kong.' *The Times* of London observed that if Hong Kong's 3.25 million BDTCs were granted the right of abode in the United Kingdom, not all of them would immigrate there; most would find more suitable places to immigrate.[17] According to a survey conducted in Hong Kong on 22 June 1989, if Hong Kong BDTCs were granted the right of abode in the United Kingdom, only 6 per cent would be willing to immigrate there.[18] From 1981 to 1988, 197 000 people emigrated from Hong Kong. Only 9000 (4.6 per cent) immigrated to the United Kingdom.[19] In addition, it would be physically impossible for all Hong Kong's 3.25 million BDTCs to travel to Britain within a short time period. If three Boeing 747s were chartered every day, it would take eight years to transport 3.25 million people to Britain.[20]

OTHER COUNTRIES MORE GENEROUS

For many years, Canada, Australia and the United States had admitted more immigrants from Hong Kong than the United Kingdom had. From 1984 to 1988, Australia and Canada accepted tens of thousands of Hong Kong residents each year. In the aftermath of the Tiananmen massacre, the United States was considering revising its immigration laws to accommodate more immigrants from Hong Kong.

As mentioned in Chapter 2, Portugal will return Macao to China in 1999. Ninety-eight per cent of Macao's 400 000 population is of Chinese origin. About one-third of the population hold Portuguese passports. Unlike the United Kingdom, Portugal has only one type of citizenship, and all Portuguese passport holders have the right of abode in Portugal.[21] It is noteworthy that Portugal is a much smaller country than Britain in terms of both population and area. It is ironic that Portuguese passport holders in Macao were able to live in the United Kingdom after 1992 when the European Economic Community became further integrated.

The French government recently granted citizenship to more than a hundred high-ranking Chinese executives of French companies in Hong Kong.[22] These individuals never even had to set foot on French soil to apply for citizenship. The purpose of this action was to alleviate concern by guaranteeing the executives an 'escape route', thus enabling them to work wholeheartedly without anxiety about their future. The French government's actions implicitly rejected Britain's argument against granting the right of abode to the BDTCs.

BRITAIN'S 'MORAL COWARDICE'[23]

In April 1989, a select committee of the British House of Commons held hearings in Hong Kong for the purpose of listening to the desires of Hong Kong residents. One British newspaper reported that Conservative and Labour members of Parliament alike were unsympathetic – and the government in London even more so – in regard to the hearings.[24] Some Hong Kong residents believed the hearings were a mere formality and not grounds for optimism.

After the Tiananmen Incident, however, Hong Kong residents began hoping that the British government might become more flexible. Numerous groups and individuals – including Allen Lee, the senior member of the Hong Kong Legislative Council, and Lydia Dunn, the senior member of the Hong Kong Executive Council – went to London to do some lobbying. Lee and Dunn were received, among others, by Foreign Secretary Howe and Prime Minister Margaret Thatcher. In the meantime, Hong Kong residents anxiously awaited the verdict, a report by the House of Commons Foreign Affairs Committee on British Policy regarding Hong Kong.

The report was released on 30 June 1989.[25] While it recognized the Tiananmen Incident's enormously adverse impact on Hong Kong, the committee maintained that not all Hong Kong's 3.25 million BDTCs should be given the right of abode in Britain. Hong Kong's people and government expressed disappointment. The committee, however, petitioned other countries to assist Hong Kong residents in case their situation worsens after 1997. It was ironic that Britain itself would not assist the Hong Kong residents. Many people viewed this as a case of simply passing the buck.

The committee, however, advocated a speed-up in the pace of Hong Kong's democratization, ensuring a full-fledged democracy by 1997. Accordingly, the committee recommended that 50 per cent of the legislators be directly elected in 1991; the chief executive be selected by a grand electoral college six months before the transfer of sovereignty; and the second chief executive be directly elected by universal suffrage. These recommendations were much more progressive than the policies contained in the White Paper of February 1988.[26] To illustrate, the White Paper recommended that ten of the 57 legislative seats – only 18 per cent – be directly elected in 1991. Hong Kong's government originally planned the direct election of a small number of legislative seats in 1988. Due to China's objections, the direct election was postponed to 1991. Then the committee recommended that 50 per cent of the legislators be directly elected, declaring that it did not believe China would object. The inconsistency of Britain's stance makes one wonder whether it truly had Hong Kong's interests in mind.

Although the committee denied Hong Kong's BDTCs the right of abode in the United Kingdom in general, it recommended that certain categories – including persons in 'important' positions, high-ranking civil servants, police officers, some thirty veterans' widows, and BDTCs of non-Chinese origin – be protected, that is, given the right of abode in the United Kingdom. However, no specific number was given for any category other than the veterans' widows. The committee's rationale for granting certain categories of BDTCs the right of abode in the United Kingdom was that if they were secure in the knowledge that they had a potential refuge in the event of an emergency, these people would stay in Hong Kong. This is an obvious contradiction of Foreign Secretary Howe's long-standing illogical statement.

'WHOLE' INSURANCE VS. 'HOME' INSURANCE

Emigration increased sharply after 4 June 1989: it was estimated that 42 000 people emigrated from Hong Kong in
1989.[27] In an October 1989 meeting, China held Britain solely
responsible for the current lack of confidence in Hong Kong.[28]
This was obviously absurd.

Regardless of the immigration policies of various countries, only a small portion of Hong Kong's six million residents can emigrate. The majority, for financial, psychological,
or other reasons, are simply incapable of leaving. It is in
their interest to maintain a successful and stable Hong Kong.
Furthermore, only a prosperous Hong Kong can ensure better
treatment from China after 1997. Needless to say, China
wants to take back a golden goose rather than a sick one.
For these reasons, Britain and China have, despite problems, worked hard to keep Hong Kong thriving. After the
Tiananmen Incident, however, extraordinary efforts were
required to restore Hong Kong's confidence. In the wake
of the Tiananmen panic, the Hong Kong government announced in October 1989 that it was planning one of the
world's largest civil engineering projects. The $16.3 billion
(in US dollars) project would comprise a new airport, a five-
fold expansion of Hong Kong's container port – already
the world's busiest – and extensive transport links to con-
nect the new port and airport with urban and industrial
areas.[29] From 1980 to 1990, China made substantial investments in Hong Kong estimated at US$10 billion.[30] Despite
an exodus of capital and corporate headquarters from Hong
Kong, many businesses, especially American and Japanese,
continued making investments there. While visiting the United
States in October 1989, Hong Kong's Governor Wilson
reemphasized to Secretary of State James Baker and Secretary of Commerce Robert Mosbacher that he welcomed
American investment. On separate occasions, Congressmen
Solarz and Porter endorsed the concept of a 'group immi-
gration insurance policy' to restore Hong Kong's confidence,
underwritten by countries such as Australia, New Zealand,
Canada, the United States, and Britain. Japanese Foreign
Minister Nakayama visited Hong Kong in November 1989.
His trip was designed to boost business confidence in the

colony in the aftermath of the Tiananmen Incident and to pressure China to observe the spirit and the letter of the Declaration.[31] Japanese investments in Hong Kong gained momentum during the last months of 1989. Trade with China after the Tiananmen Incident was not affected to any significant degree, according to Hong Kong's government.[32] Hong Kong's economy has, as a whole, continued to grow, albeit at a slower rate. Optimists suggested that Hong Kong's economy was resilient. On 17 December 1989, the Hang Seng (stock exchange) index reached 2900, compared with 2675 at the last session of the pre-4 June index.[33]

It appears that foreign investors are less worried than Hong Kong residents about the colony's uncertain future, perhaps because they know they can rely on their governments if problems occur after 1997. The Hong Kong Chinese, however, do not have this kind of security. Thus, Chinese businesses that remain in Hong Kong tend to lease rather than purchase real properties; borrow money from banks, rather than make substantial equity investments (if difficulties arise the business can be abandoned); invest for a quick return rather than long-term benefits; and keep their assets as liquid as possible. Pessimists have maintained that Hong Kong's average economic growth rate from 1970 to 1990 was 9 per cent annually and that it would be about 6 per cent annually from then on.[34] *Business International* predicted that growth from 1990 to 1995 would average only 4.3 per cent annually.[35] According to the Hong Kong government, the actual average growth rate from 1990 to 1995 was about 5.1 per cent.[36]

BRITAIN TAKING A GIANT STEP FORWARD

Following the release of the British House of Commons Committee report in late June 1989, Hong Kong's government and people continued working diligently to obtain the right of abode for all BDTCs. In late July, Foreign Secretary Howe was replaced by John Major, a substitution which perhaps indicated that Mrs Thatcher had determined a new set of foreign policies, including those concerning Hong Kong. On 20 December 1989, Douglas Hurd – who succeeded

Major as foreign secretary in another round of cabinet re-shuffling in late October – announced Britain's new policy on Hong Kong in the British House of Commons.

Britain would grant full British passports to 50 000 key individuals in Hong Kong – including their dependants; the total was an estimated 225 000 – 'who are important to the efficient working of the territory, and who currently are most vulnerable to emigration'.[37] A spokesperson for the Hong Kong government's special Working Group on Nationality stated, among other things, that Britain had decided as the most effective way to encourage people to remain in Hong Kong, to provide them with full British passports. Britain's new policy once again requested aid from the international community. Perhaps to some extent for the benefit of British domestic consumption, Foreign Secretary Hurd concluded his statement by noting that this policy was 'designed not to encourage immigration into this country but to persuade to remain in Hong Kong those whom we need to retain there if our last substantial colony is to pass successfully through the final eight years of British rule'.[38] The implementation of this policy would require legislative action by the British Parliament. Its passage was, however, no certain matter.

Details of the British Nationality (Hong Kong) Bill 1990 were announced by Britain on 5 April. Passports would be provided to 50 000 key people and their spouses and children under 18. The bulk of the passports were allocated through a points system favoring those occupations which had the highest emigration between 1987 and 1990. Passports were divided among four major categories: general allocation, 36 200; disciplined service, 7000; sensitive service, 6300; and key enterpreurs, 500. The Hong Kong Immigration Department oversaw the operation of this plan, and recommendations on individual applications were passed to the governor before being submitted to the British home secretary. A steering group, chaired by the chief secretary of Hong Kong with members comprising independent representatives of the community and the commissioner of the Independent Commission Against Corruption, assisted the governor in implementing and supervising the operation of the schemes.[39]

The British Nationality Bill of 1990 completed the legislative procedures and became law on 26 July 1990. Passports were allocated in two phases: the bulk immediately, with the remainder of about 13 per cent reserved for later. By the end of the first phase on 1 January 1994, a total of 36 840 heads of households had been registered, leaving 13 160 places to be distributed in the final phase. Application deadline for this final phase was 31 March 1994.[40] As of that date, a total of about 40 000 applications had been received. The probability of success, therefore, would be about 33 per cent.[41] The total number of people who have been granted British passports (full citizenship with the right of abode in the United Kingdom) under this Act is about 200 000.[42] British action on this matter has quelled much of the criticism by Hong Kong people and others.

BRITISH DEPENDENT TERRITORIES CITIZENS, BRITISH NATIONALS (OVERSEAS) AND HONG KONG SPECIAL ADMINISTRATIVE REGION PASSPORTS

As mentioned above, because the status of British Dependent Territories Citizens (BDTCs) will cease to exist on 1 July 1997, these citizens were advised to apply for the new form of British nationality, the British Nationals (Overseas) (BN(O)), if they wish to retain British nationality. The BN(O)s, as also mentioned before, are not entitled to the right of abode in the United Kingdom. Initially many BDTC holders or those who were eligible to apply for the BN(O)s in Hong Kong did not wish to switch to or apply for the BN(O)s, mainly because the BN(O) was not, for the purpose of securing visas, a document widely accepted by governments. However, through the efforts of the British government and with the cooperation of many other countries, the holders of the BN(O) are being admitted entry without visa by more than a hundred countries now. Thus the number of people switching to or applying for the BN(O)s has dramatically increased in recent years. For example, 30 March 1996 was the application deadline for those BDTCs who were born between 1977 and 1981, and some 52 845 people lined up in a mile-long procession. This was 20 000 people more than applied in all of 1995.[43] The total number of the BN(O)s is estimated at three million.[44]

The issuance of the future HKSAR passport has been a concern of both the United Kingdom and China. On 10 January 1996, the two countries reached an agreement. All BN(O) and Certificate of Identity (CI – issued to the permanent residents who were not born in Hong Kong) holders, who number more than five million, are eligible to apply. The passport will be issued by Hong Kong's Immigration Department after 1 July 1997. No sooner was the agreement signed than two important questions arose. Hong Kong people are concerned that the Immigration Department might not be the only authority who can issue HKSAR passports after 1 July 1997. They pointed out that the above-mentioned agreement contains a provision to the effect that Chinese embassies or consulates abroad may issue HKSAR passports to those qualified applicants overseas. While Hong Kong officials have rejected this interpretation or possibility, many Hong Kong people remain doubtful. Their fear is that China might abuse this provision by issuing HKSAR passports very loosely. Another question was whether the holders of the HKSAR passport could enter the United Kingdom without a visa. The LEGCO as well as China tried to persuade Britain to waive the visa requirement. After two months' deliberation and debate, Britain announced its policy of visa-free access to the United Kingdom for Hong Kong people. It is hoped that other European Union members will follow. At present, besides Britain only Singapore and one other small country have indicated that they will admit HKSAR passport holders without a visa. China, and perhaps Britain as well, is trying to persuade those countries which are accepting BN(O) passport holders without a visa to accept HKSAR passport holders without a visa.

FOREIGN PASSPORTS AND RIGHT OF ABODE IN HONG KONG

While many Hong Kong people have already acquired foreign passports (nationality) or permanent residency, they will have to make a difficult choice when 1 July 1997 comes, because

China does not recognize dual nationality. They have to choose either permanent residency in Hong Kong or the right to foreign consular protection, but not both. If they do not declare on their own initiative that they possess foreign nationality or permanent residency, then all those who have Chinese blood and were born in Chinese territories (including Hong Kong) will be automatically considered as Chinese citizens. The foreign passports they possess will be deemed as travel documents, which shall not entitle them to foreign consular protection within Hong Kong. Those who possess foreign nationality but also wish to retain the right to foreign consular protection must declare this to the Chinese authorities in Hong Kong. Still, these people have to live in Hong Kong for seven consecutive years before they can acquire permanent residency.[45] Legal experts in Hong Kong have a different interpretation on consular protection, however. They suggest that one country cannot, under normal circumstances, deny another country's right to protect its nationals unless there is an agreement between the two.[46]

The problems for those who emigrated to other countries but may wish to return to Hong Kong after 1 July 1997 are also complicated. If they return to Hong Kong as Hong Kong permanent residents, they will be deemed Chinese citizens; and if they enter Hong Kong with a foreign passport, then they will be deemed foreign nationals. It is expected that there will be many confrontations on this nationality[47] and permanent residency issue both before and after 1 July 1997. China wants to stress its sovereignty over Hong Kong by forcing Hong Kong people to make a choice. Hong Kong people would like to have some extra insurance by having the best of the two worlds.

ETHNIC MINORITIES AND OTHER PROBLEMS

As mentioned in 4.3 above, the non-Chinese BDTCs, who are mostly of Indian descent and may have severed their connections with their motherland, have been anxious to acquire the right of abode in the United Kingdom. But as late as April 1996 there was no major progress. One official of an *ad hoc* committee under the Executive Council which has been studying the problem pointed out that it is extremely important to know the total number of this group of people. He implied that if that number is not very large, the Hong Kong government might be able to persuade the British government to grant them the right of abode. It is estimated that there are 3000–7000 people belonging to this category. One is not sure, however, whether this number is large or small. Lu Ping, the director of the Hong Kong and Macao Office under the State Council, has indicated that he will assist the non-Chinese BDTCs (now most likely BN(O)s) in getting HKSAR passports. However, the official of the above *ad hoc* committee felt that the non-Chinese BDTCs are more interested in getting British than Chinese passports.[48]

Another group of people, which is much smaller than the non-Chinese BDTCs, has nevertheless had a similar fate. These are the widows of Hong Kong veterans who fought for the British in the Second World War. The total number was 30. While visiting Hong Kong in March 1996, John Major promised that he would help them get British citizenship by introducing a private bill in parliament. Unfortunately, the private bill was killed in the House of Commons due to the objection of certain Labour Party members. John Major expressed regret. What is more regrettable is that while the British House of Commons was debating the bill, one of those widows died. The total now became 29,[49] much smaller than in 1989. As students of government all know, a private bill has no chance of being passed if there is even a small number of legislators objecting. The chances for these widows to get the right of abode in the United Kingdom appears very slim in the near future.

One English language newspaper in Hong Kong recently reported that, according to Lu Ping, non-Chinese permanent residents of the HKSAR might be deported. That has certainly caused alarm in many quarters. To allay the fear, Lu Ping clarified through his office that none of the permanent residents of Hong Kong will be deported whether they are Chinese citizens or not.[50]

THE BOTTOM LINE: CONFIDENCE

Since the signing of the Joint Declaration in 1984, there have been, on average, between 50 000 and 60 000 people emigrating from Hong Kong annually. It is estimated that by 1 July 1997, the total will reach about 600 000. Between 1981 and 1988, the years prior to the Tiananmen Incident, emigration averaged less than 30 000 a year. Many Hong Kong people, especially the middle class and intellectuals, lack confidence in the future HKSAR. A recent survey conducted by Hong Kong Baptist University indicated that about 20 per cent of the Hong Kong people are able to leave at any time, and close to one-third of the entire population will manage to leave Hong Kong. The survey further indicated that should life be miserable after 1997, it is probable that a large number of Hong Kong people will escape. Such a situation could be comparable to that of the Vietnamese boat people in the 1980s.

5 British Implementation of the Joint Declaration and the Basic Law

In this chapter our focus is on the British path of implementation, especially after the arrival of Governor Christopher Patten in July 1992. Shortly following that, all of his reform policy actions were subject to Chinese government attack through the New China News Agency and via the pro-China media.[1] The next chapter will describe the Chinese path of the implementation (or the second stove approach) that also generated a large amount of pro-Hong Kong media reaction and critical responses from the Hong Kong government.[2]

Britain had been frustrated at its inability to discharge its responsibility eight years after the 1984 Joint Declaration. Then in July 1992 Governor Chris Patten arrived on the scene. Three months after arrival he quickly earned the support of the people in Hong Kong by initiating a new path to compel cooperation from Beijing. During the previous eight years the Joint Liaison Group (JIG) had not worked well at all. The people of Hong Kong have long felt disappointed and betrayed by the Basic Law which denied them much future opportunity to participate politically through election or referendum. The future Chief Executive, for example, would certainly be appointed by the National People's Congress rather than elected by universal balloting.[3] The Legislative Council would still not have an elected majority. Little was clearly guaranteed by the Basic Law in spite of the promised 'high autonomy' in the Joint Declaration. The Hong Kong government published a Green Paper in 1985 and a White Paper in 1988 to explain its planning for a representative government. Yet no major effective steps had been taken till Patten's arrival, although the 1991 LEGCO election clearly demonstrated the voters' preference for greater democracy in direct participation.[4]

THE NECESSITY FOR DEVIATION

The Beijing regime had been stonewalling all major steps to implement policies for democratic representation before 1 July 1997. Because of its interpretation of the Joint Declaration, the Chinese government prefers that nothing at all be changed. By the time Patten arrived in 1992 the Joint Liaison Group had met 25 times and accomplished little. The foreign ministers of both countries had met twice annually and failed to achieve agreements. Meanwhile, professional people were emigrating out of Hong Kong by tens of thousands annually. This brain drain and capital exodus was clearly threatening 'property and stability'. Under these circumstances, Britain felt compelled to act unilaterally.

The British moral and political dilemma

British colonial practice everywhere in Asia and Africa was known for its system of effective and efficient government. Its civil service system was one of the enduring legacies left behind in every former colony. British Hong Kong, in particular, has been well governed in terms of economic prosperity, efficient rule of law, individual liberty and private wealth and property under the British authoritarian, but not dictatorial, governor, who represents the Queen and executes London's policies. The British government in Hong Kong since 1842 was never confronted with popular demands for democratic reform. Since the Joint Declaration in 1984, the people were fully aware that the promised 'high autonomy' and free life-style would not be possible without democratic institutional reform. They were largely satisfied so long as the British remained in charge. Given these popular sentiments and the need to preserve the British legacy, Britain had to discharge its moral obligation before leaving. However, politically it had failed repeatedly to secure Beijing's cooperation. British Foreign Secretary Douglas Hurd had earlier worked diligently to influence the Chinese drafting of the Basic Law to include a larger number of popularly elected members in the Legislative Council prior to 1997. He further worked to have the Basic Law specify that the elected Legislative Council in 1995 would serve its full term to September 1999. By early 1992 Sino-British cooperation reached an all-time low. British ability to carry out popular demand for reform was nil. 'Smooth transition' was not likely. Thus, the London government's change of approach was not totally unexpected.

In 1989 the Chinese leadership suffered a serious blow in prestige in the Tiananmen Incident. Internal political power struggles and the declaration of martial law in China worried the people and the British government in Hong Kong. On the other hand, the Tiananmen Incident stirred the people of Hong Kong to a high pitch of political patriotism in protest and street demonstration against the Beijing government. This new and unexpected politicization also put pressure on the Hong Kong government for rapid reform. Popular confidence in China's faithful implementation of the Joint Declaration was seriously eroded after 1989. Britain was caught in a dilemma between 'smooth transition' and the need for reform to ensure Hong Kong's continuing stability and prosperity.[5]

The new Chinese attitude toward Patten after the Tiananmen Incident

As stated previously, the new Chinese attitude included, in essence, restriction against Hong Kong's political democratization through the Basic Law; the removal of Xu Jiatun for being too liberal and pro-democratic as Beijing's top representative in Hong Kong;[6] the barring of all anti-government books and media publications from Hong Kong and elsewhere from entering China; and increased border control against underground efforts to smuggle out those anti-government student leaders and intellectuals of the Tiananmen Incident. Zhou Nan, a former vice foreign minister and one-time chief negotiator of the Joint Declaration came to Hong Kong in charge of the New China News Agency. It was clear that China was determined to prevent reform and to influence changes in Hong Kong before 1997 at any cost. Its major focus was placed on the drafting of the Basic Law and its revision during the following ten months. In particular, its attention was focused against the drafting committee's liberal members from the Hong Kong side, especially against Martin C.M. Lee and Szeto Hua, who were struggling in favor of an independent judiciary and an elected future government capable of resisting pressure from Beijing.[7] The drafting members from the Beijing side, for example, would not allow more than one-third of the future LEGCO members to be popularly elected by 1997 and only half to be elected by AD 2003.

As always, all the drafting meetings were kept secret. The central government, according to the Basic Law, will remain strong through the National People's Congress. More on China's new attitude will be traced in the next chapter, which considers how Beijing has relied on the Joint Declaration, the Basic Law, and the seven additional letters of agreement between the two foreign ministers. These major documents were very closely adhered to and tightly interpreted by the Chinese government to solidify its position in repudiating the sudden violation and deviation by Britain under Governor Patten.[8] The Basic Law itself is China's instrument of implementing the Joint Declaration, and Beijing's consultation with Britain had been maintained all along before the arrival of Governor Patten to keep the London government well informed. This was done through the Joint Liaison Group (JLG) which was designated in the Joint Declaration to function for the purpose of 'smooth transition'. The JLG is required to continue several years after July 1997. In short, at Hong Kong's expense, China had been in better command of the entire process of transition from 1984 until Patten's arrival. Beijing did not believe that Britain had any right to make any political reforms before 1997.[9] Nor did China intend to give in on any reform demands by their Chinese brethren in Hong Kong. Beijing, in addition, did not want Britain to interfere with its sovereign right to determine or implement its policy of 'Hong Kong people governing Hong Kong'. The 1989 Tiananmen Incident compelled the Beijing leadership to institute tighter methods to restrict the politically awakening groups and leaders among the six million people in Hong Kong. Thus China's opposition to Patten's leadership personally was no surprise at all.

Politics in the drafting of the Basic Law

Without violating the terms of the Joint Declaration between Britain and China, the Chinese leadership had clear ideas as to how to create the future Hong Kong Special Administrative Region (HKSAR, or simply SAR). Article 31 of China's constitution empowers the Standing Committee of the National People's Congress to dictate the politico-legal relations between the central government and the local SAR.[10] Beyond being bound by certain provisions relative to national defence and the conduct of foreign policy and of those officials in Hong Kong representing the central government, the HKSAR government is completely independent and accountable only to the people in Hong Kong according to the stipulations in the Basic Law. When the Basic Law was being proposed and debated before being formalized between 1985 and 1990, the British government was allowed, indeed, to suggest and to argue for changes to the Chinese foreign ministry on its own views. However, the making of the Basic Law was perceived purely as a Chinese internal exercise of sovereign power. The drafting convention consisted of 23 delegates representing all major sectors from Hong Kong, including leaders of religion, education, labor, the legal profession and business in particular. The other 36 delegates, chosen from mainland China, mainly adhered either to the views of the central government or, especially, to the views of the paramount leader Deng Xiaoping, who actually came more than once to address the plenary sessions of the drafting convention. Deng publicly declared what Hong Kong could or could not have. He did not believe Western democracy was good for Hong Kong. He did not want to see Hong Kong destroyed by internal discord among social groups and untested political factions. There were no political parties at that time in the 1980s in Hong Kong. Nor had there ever been a British-guided universal popular election. There could not be, therefore, any valid reason to rush to political reform under Britain when she had not seen fit to hold elections of any substance during the 150 colonial years. The paramount leader spoke specifically:

Each country must find a system that best suits its needs. Also, do not expect Hong Kong to be controlled by Hong Kong people alone. The central government will not interfere with its daily management. But when the interests of the state are being endangered the central government will not stand aside. We can stand people scolding the communist party or China, but we cannot accept people who want to use democracy to turn Hong Kong into an anti-communist base.[11]

There were fewer than half a dozen delegates from Hong Kong's 23-member drafting delegation who actually fought for greater democratic elections before and after 1997. In fact, there were only two delegates who often confronted the majority delegates from the Communist side during many crucial debates. Attorney Martin Lee and educator Szeto Hua were the two most resented Hong Kong delegates, even by other delegates of conservative business background from Hong Kong. Britain, barred from the drafting convention, was watching with frustration, attempting to influence the proceedings by exchanging diplomatic letters with the Chinese foreign minister. Because of Xu Jiatun's careful choosing of delegates, the Hong Kong business circle had the greatest influence among the Hong Kong delegates and they were often in greater agreement with the views of the Beijing government on how the Basic Law should be. S.Y. Chung, Vincent Lo, T.K. Ann, and Judge Simon Li were powerful Hong Kong delegates during the drafting of the Basic Law. These businessmen themselves did not favor democratic reform at all. As trusted friends of Beijing, they easily saw debates and recommendations in similar ways as the 36 Chinese delegates did. The Mainland delegates were not of one single background. They came actually from three major backgrounds: nearly one-third (11) from a well-renowned legal circle, 15 from government circles, and ten representing minor political parties. As a delegation, however, they were dominated by Li Hou and Lu Ping, who were deputy directors of the Hong Kong and Macao Affairs Office and deputy secretaries general of the drafting convention. The first plenary meeting was held in July 1985 in Beijing under Ji Pengfei, former foreign minister and then director of the Hong Kong-Macao Affairs Office.

China considered the making of the Basic Law the most critical means through which to translate the Joint Declaration into future practice after 1997. This mini-constitution had to be at least nominally acceptable to the Chinese residents in Hong Kong. Their indirect participation, through large-scale controlled sessions of consultation, but not referendum, would be given utmost attention for revision. Whether this gesture was appreciated by the majority of Hong Kong residents requires further study. Ji Pengfei, however, was serious and sternly laid out the procedure and timetable for drafting completion:[12] (a) The 'discussion draft' had to be ready by early 1988 for the Hong Kong residents to comment upon; (b) the first revision would incorporate the result of this popular consultation; (c) the 'corrected draft' would go to the central legislature (NPC) as the first draft; (d) after the National People's Congress had reviewed it, the republished draft would again go to the people in Hong Kong in 1989 for their second-stage consultation, which would be followed by a plenary session of the drafting convention for final revision, after which it would be submitted to the National People's Congress, which would finally approve it in early 1990. Thus, in April of 1990 the people in Hong Kong received their mini-constitution under which the SAR government would be organized in 'smooth transition' and also in accordance with the Sino-British Joint Declaration of 1984.[13]

Xu Jiatun played a dominating role in Hong Kong delegate selections. The 'heavyweight' Hong Kong drafters were highly regarded as delegates representing the business tycoons who were entrusted by the British but had been won over by Xu Jiatun. Other intellectuals of influence and leaders of high repute, such as Judge Simon Li, publisher Louis Cha, educator Szeto Hua and liberal attorney Martin E.M. Lee, were chosen also. Their views differed from Beijing's plan for Hong Kong. However, their legal knowledge and democratic convictions for Hong Kong earned them recognition and respect from Xu Jiatun and tolerance from the Chinese government,[14] and their inclusion in the delegation from Hong Kong appeared to demonstrate China's open-mindedness. Indeed, the people in Hong Kong did, at first, register a genuine confidence in getting a good democratic

Basic Law. They did not appreciate, however, the secretiveness of the convention during those five long years of secret debates in small groups, and they came to believe that they were betrayed when universal popular referendum was denied. Twice popular consultations were held but participation was small each time.

At the very start, Director Ji Pengfei insisted that the Hong Kong delegation must organize a large-scale committee to conduct consultation on the draft law. He promised that 'a full play' would be given to solving problems through democratic consultation.[15] But in forming such a Basic Law Consultative Committee (BLCC), several business tycoons and T.S. Lo at first simply did not think of the consultation as necessary. Bowing to the insistence and careful arrangement by convention secretariat, T.K. Ann from Hong Kong was made the chairman and convener of such future consultative committee. This body of 180 members in Hong Kong did not have the official blessing of the National People's Congress, unlike the Draft delegates, who were formally empowered by the NPC. The upshot of the irony was that these pro-Beijing tycoons and others, such as attorney Dorothy Liu and Judge Simon Li, were all persuaded to cooperate fully with Xu Jiatun in the grand display. Pro-democratic leaders and their followers in Hong Kong resented such domination to misinterpret the 'public views'. However, it appeared that the promise of 'Hong Kong people governing Hong Kong' was, at least, a brave experiment or not an intentional betrayal. This was how delegate Szeto Hua felt. The pro-democracy voice in Hong Kong did not die because Martin Lee was elected in the partial LEGCO election in September, 1985. He continued to champion the 1988 partial direct election under the British. To his disappointment Britain was easily persuaded by China not to directly elect any LEGCO members in 1988, or at least not until after the Basic Law's approval by Beijing. In short, Beijing was able to maintain complete control over both the Basic Law drafting convention and the 180 member Consultative Committee.

The Basic Law itself consists of a preamble and nine chapters. Article 12 declares HKSAR to 'be a local administrative region, which shall enjoy a high degree of autonomy'.

Articles 13 and 14 state that foreign affairs and defense are the responsiblity of the central government. Article 15 clearly stipulates that HKSAR's Chief Executive and principal executive officials are to be appointed by the central government. Although Para. 1 of Article 17 vests the HKSAR with legislative power, Para. 3 immediately restricts it, particularly regarding the relationship between the SAR and the central authorities. The latter can invalidate any HKSAR law which is not in conformity with the national law in this regard. Similarly, Para. 1 of Article 19 grants the HKSAR independent judicial power but Para. 3 of the same article immediately restricts it particularly in the areas of foreign affairs and defence. Chapter IV of the Basic Law deals with 'political structure'. Article 43 declares that the Chief Executive, while representing the HKSAR, is accountable to the central people's government. He is to be selected 'by election or through consultations held locally and then be appointed by the central people's government' (Art. 45). It has been this stipulation for consultation that makes Hong Kong people greatly concerned about China's future domination. Beijing clearly expects the future Chief Executive to be as powerful as the British governor has been in the last some 150 years. This 'administration-guided structure of power' clearly limits the elected legislative council which, under the Basic Law, also can be dissolved by the Chief Executive over matters of budget and other laws if consensus does not emerge after some consultation between the executive and the legislature (Art. 50). The most knowledgeable critics of the draft Basic Law were the two draft delegates, Martin Lee and Szeto Hua, who both had been outvoted repeatedly during the drafting. They published a pamphlet to inform the residents during the period of popular consultation. A few of their own comments are cited below.[16] (1988/May print and our translation).

1. General analysis on the relations between the central government and the HKSAR: The Sino-British Joint Declaration promises 'a high degree of autonomy'. This is the foundation of the Hong Kong–central government relation by which the success or failure of the 'one country, two systems' will be determined. In quite a

few ways the draft Basic Law has failed to reflect the Joint Declaration. The examples are:

(1) The delineation between 'defense and foreign affairs' and all other affairs is not clear. The national government seems to be able to extend its authority beyond strict 'defence and foreign affairs'.

(2) The Draft Basic Law (Article 16) gives authority to the Standing Committee of the National People's Congress to nullify an SAR law if it sees a conflict between the Basic Law and an SAR law. In Hong Kong, according to common law practice, such conflict can only be decided by an independent judicial court.

(3) Article 17 allows national laws to be extended into Hong Kong if national unification and territorial integrity are concerned. This clearly contradicts the Joint Declaration.

(4) The Hong Kong Affairs Committee of the National People's Congress is responsible for overseeing relations between the central government and Hong Kong. However, the structure and procedures of this committee have not been clearly written down. If this committee fails to protect Hong Kong's interests, then, the 'high degree of autonomy' set forth in the Joint Declaration will be denied.

2. On the political system of the Hong Kong SAR: Generally speaking, the powers of the future SAR government differ little from those of the current authoritarian colonial government. The new system under the Basic Law is not democratic enough to accomplish the goal of the Joint Declaration, which requires the popularly elected legislative council to hold the chief executive accountable to the electorate. For example, SAR legislative power under the Basic Law is sadly limited and also administratively checked whenever exercised. On budget and other policy making matters, legislators enjoy little initiative. If laws are unacceptable to the Chief Executive, he can refuse to sign and to engage in consultation until the Chief Executive singly chooses to dissolve the legislature. Moreover, when a Hong Kong law is unacceptable because the Standing Committee of the National People's Congress judges it to be in

conflict with the Basic Law, the law is either immediately nullified by Beijing or is returned to Hong Kong for revision. On matters of defense or foreign affairs or matters concerning national unification and territorial integrity, the Standing Committee from Beijing can order the Hong Kong legislature to adopt whatever laws it deems or it can simply decree a new law on Hong Kong's behalf. Under the Basic Law, the legislature cannot investigate the conduct of the executive branch; nor can it request administrative officials to serve as witnesses. The legislature, therefore, will have no power to investigate high level officials on their official conduct. This powerlessness to bring charges against the official conduct of the Chief Executive is too inadequate to be practical (see Articles 73, 75, 49, 50, 16, 17 and 72). In short, the legislature cannot sufficiently function as a check on the executive branch by requiring executive accountability to the legislature. Mr Martin Lee and Mr Szeto Hua, in their severe criticism, voiced disappointment over the methods by which the Chief Executive and legislative members are to be chosen. They objected to both the 'electoral committee' and 'functional constituencies' because both can be dominated by a few powerful executive individuals. The Basic Law does not specify who can vote in which functional group through prior assignment. Such methods for selecting the Chief Executive by a nominating committee is not significantly different from 'outright appointment at the top'. Many fear that the first group of SAR officials in both executive and legislative branches can create future harm if they simply follow direction from above without popular or institutional checking. After all, the policies and laws they put into practice will have long-lasting effects until such time as Hong Kong can have universal popular elections for both branches. Mr Lee and Mr Szeto prefer that all legislative council members be directly elected by the people as soon as possible. In particular, they advocate direct popular election of the chief executive who must be made accountable to the legislature. In short, they want instant direct democracy. Many people think Lee and

Szeto are too radical because they do not believe the people of Hong Kong are ready for a system of political parties yet. If true wisdom can prevail on all sides, Hong Kong is, indeed, the best place to experiment in true democracy after some 150 years of foreign rule. Neither Taiwan nor mainland China are as roundly prepared for democracy as Hong Kong is.

Popular discontent with the Basic Law

After five long years in subgroup debates and plenary sessions, the National People's Congress approved in April 1990 the final version of the Basic Law. Different groups in Hong Kong reacted quite differently. Those influenced by *Ta Kung Bao, Wenhui Bao*, or the local New China News Agency or the *Mirror Monthly* hailed it as a victory for 'one country, two systems'. The majority of its residents were poorly informed and remained silent. Highly educated professionals of the new middle class since the 1970s and 1980s were disappointed. They were the ones planning on emigration since 1984. They felt that the Joint Declaration itself had been betrayed by the majority drafters of the Basic Law in conspiracy with the rich and powerful businessmen of Hong Kong. There had never been a real opportunity for the individual Hong Kong liberal drafters, as educators, lawyers, religious leaders or medical doctors, to win sympathy from the mainland drafters. Hong Kong readers of *South China Morning Post*, the *Far Eastern Economic Review, Cheng Ming Monthly* and the *Nineties* felt cheated by local intellectuals and the media for not having forcefully advanced a debate publicly for the protection of the existing free life-style and self-government in Hong Kong. Many feared changes to come because they did not trust the Beijing regime. Privately it is still often said by some that 'we love China, but we hate the communists'. The British, too, shared some blame in local resentment for failing to secure in detail a carefully defined Joint Declaration preventing China from unilateral exercise of sovereign authority in making the Basic Law. Others in large numbers simply accepted the inevitability because Hong Kong must depend, in the long run, on mainland China for prosperity and stability after the British withdrawal.[17] The only way open to them was to seek emigration and British citizenship.

By and large, among the majority residents, a strong 'local pride in Hong Kong is more widespread than outsiders may think'. This comment is often made to us during interviews. Confidence about their future has declined among many interviewees. They fear the communist influence will permeate local life. Older residents dread the return of the scene of cultural revolution of 1966–76 or a possible worse future after Deng Xiaoping's death. Quite a number of respondents expressed distrust in local politicians who hold office seeking personal fame or other advantages.[18] There is a comprehensive self-image among the new middle class and younger residents who are sophisticated, self-confident, energetic and proud of their reward for hard work. They often express mixed feelings of uncertainty in their future. Such self-reliant professionals are contemplating ways to secure foreign passports but refusing to depart from Hong Kong forever. This trend was a retreat from the early 1980s when optimism was often expressed in the Joint Declaration. When the Basic Law was finally available for all to reflect upon, criticism against the British government was not uncommon. Governor David Wilson, too, received the following harsh comment:

> The governor, Sir David Wilson, has not lived up to expectations in his first year's work. A scholar and diplomat by training, who gets on well with the Chinese in Beijing, he has increasingly appeared to be a careerist, interested in pleasing London and Beijing but weak and aimless in his attention to Hong Kong's situation. His public statements, few as they are, are vacuous. He is not backed up by a strong team either, and the public is disgusted by toleration of the shifting of retiring senior servants to the business sector while what and whom they know can still be put to advantage.[19]

Perhaps, the most obvious concern for many was their possible loss of human and civil rights. Not through legal guarantee under the British but well implemented in the court of law in Hong Kong, there have been such basic civil liberties and human rights. The majority of the Hong Kong people 'feel free and happy about life here, largely because their rights are tactfully guaranteed by Britain's excellent liberal tradition of government. . . . Thus in Hong Kong freedom remains a gratuity from a nonviolent administration rather than a right enshrined by law.'[20] In 1991 the Hong Kong government accepted through adoption by the LEGCO the 1986 rights charters of the United Nations as binding and enforceable. However, the practice of such human, civil, political and economic rights will be in doubt after 1997.

Popular disappointment with the British postponement of election and reform

Since the early 1980s under Governor M.C. MacLehose political and institutional reform had begun at the district level. In actuality, from the end of 1968 the Hong Kong government was exploring for a broad and unified approach to undertake a systemic administrative reform. There were a number of areas in need of improvement, such as political-administrative corruption and waste, rising crime-rate, housing shortage, school reform, economic development and industrial diversification. The town level and urban units of government were totally inadequate to support a society increasing in wealth and in diverse social conditions. After the Red Guard riot in 1968, the British government became conscious of the need for consultation between all governmental agencies and the civilians in both rural and urban sectors. In order to make such progress in areas of social welfare, transportation, environmental health, control, of illegal drugs and administrative efficiency, Governor MacLehose initiated a comprehensive reform plan in the machinery of government: district council and district administration were streamlined. Civilian consultation committees came into existence in the New Territories. In the urban region some ten civil affairs councils were created to link voluntary agencies and private clubs. Several hundreds of such mutual aid committees came into existence throughout the entire colony. Thus, the 19 district boards and councils came to be known as the lower tier of government. At the urban level, the Municipal Council-Administration and the Urban Regional Council-Administration were both overhauled for efficiency and cooperation through different voluntary neighborhood committees. At the highest level an Independent Commission Against Corruption (ICAC) was created to fight all kinds of illegal or inefficient practices. In short, the people and government in Hong Kong worked together in a system of voluntary consultation to make Hong Kong a viable place to live and to work. It was this idealism accompanied with rapid economic growth and commercial expansion that made Hong Kong an experimenting democracy.[21] This three-tier system of government has functioned well under an authoritarian colonial governor. The people have had few complaints because the government is open through a system of consultation. There are about 430 such consultation groups appointed formally by the government. However, politically conscious leaders and interest groups still look forward to greater participation by way of direct election. One way to facilitate direct election is to develop political parties. However, there had been no well-organized political parties in Hong Kong until the time of 1991 legislative election.

The British government in 1984 declared its intention to continue with its political reform by formally instituting a representative government in spite of the return of Hong Kong to China in July 1997. At that time there were still 13 long years ahead. The scheduled 1988 LEGCO partial election was postponed as a result of Beijing's objection. After the Tiananmen Incident in 1989, the entire population in Hong Kong was galvanized by the consciousness of their own future political uncertainty after 1997. The British government, thus, could not remain blind to popular unrest in Hong Kong.

The Tiananmen Incident made the draft Basic Law much less acceptable to the Hong Kong people and to the British government. A new crisis was on hand for all parties: Beijing feared foreign conspiracy would attempt to sabotage the 1997 transfer; London favored rapid democratization before 1997. The local liberal forces in Hong Kong were engaged in anti-Beijing street demonstrations.[22] A new sense of urgency pressured Britain and Hong Kong in several areas, including the number of directly elected LEGCO members, and the method of selecting the future Chief Executive. Many proposals were discussed but none was fully acceptable either to the mainland drafters or to the three major groups from Hong Kong: the conservative 'group of 89' headed by Vincent Lo, S.Y. Chung, and T.S. Lo; the moderate group supporting the government position under the leadership of Executive Council member Lydia Dunn, and the liberal group headed by the LEGCO member Martin Lee and Szeto Hua. For example, Louis Cha's earliest conservative proposal before the 4 June incident was discussed fully and supported by Xu Jiatun but defeated eventually.[23] In Britain after the Tiananmen Incident, new demands were presented to the Foreign Affairs Select Committee for British passports for the 3.3 million Hong Kong-born residents. An 11-member group of the Committee arrived for an inspection tour in Hong Kong. When the Chinese students were fasting in Tiananmen Square in Beijing, a million Hong Kong residents were pouring into the street in support of the pro-democracy movement in China. Even the leftist *Wen Hui Bao* published a lamenting four-word editorial: 'Deep Grief, Bitter Hatred'. The Basic Law Consultative Committee in June 1989 terminated its work with an announcement: 'We are temporarily unable to carry out our work as planned.' At the highest official level, members of the Executive and the Legislative Council met during the Beijing crisis to discuss what steps should be taken about the Joint Declaration and the draft Basic Law. This gave legislator Martin Lee the best opportunity to insist on speedier democratization. He suggested that half of the 60-member LEGCO should be popularly elected in 1991 and that all should be directly elected in 1997. When they met in response to Lydia Dunn's persistence for a consensus proposal two days later, they agreed that: 'half of the legislature should be elected by universal suffrage and half by indirect functional constituencies in 1997 and that the entire legislature should be elected by universal suffrage in 2003.'

When Chinese troops moved into Tiananmen Square and people began dying, demonstrators in Hong Kong were shocked with emotion. Some shouted, 'Chinese butchers step down.' Some cried, 'We do not recognize the Chinese government.' Others screamed 'Blood for blood.' Still many demonstrators seriously announced, 'Protect Hong Kong. If Hong Kong collapses, no one will be left to fight for democracy.'[24] Martin Lee 'called on Britain to renegotiate the Joint Declaration to make Hong Kong a part of the Chinese confederation, independent in all but name'. Other activists demanded a fully elected government by 1997. By far the loudest cries were for Britain to provide a place of refuge for her subjects. Eventually, Hong Kong's pro-democracy forces organized themselves into a permanent organization – Alliance in Support of the Patriotic Democratic Movement in China (ASPDMC). It still functions today under Szeto Hua's leadership.[25]

Meanwhile, the British public was equally shocked by the bloodshed in Beijing. The upshot was the recommendation on British policy direction from the Foreign Affairs Committee of Parliament. The recommended changes include: (1) rapid democratization in Hong Kong before 1997; (2) half of the LEGCO to be elected by universal suffrage in 1991 and all to be popularly elected by 1995; (3) the first post-1997 Chief Executive to be elected by a democratically chosen electoral college.[26] The Thatcher government, however, failed to adhere to these suggestions. Prime Minister Thatcher's government agreed at long last, as mentioned earlier, to allow 50 000 family heads and their dependants to enter and acquire the right of abode in Britain. However, preference to enter Britain will be primarily given to police officers and government officials in sensitive posts.

In Hong Kong, the Tiananmen Incident deeply affected the senior Executive Council leader Lydia Dunn. She called a meeting on 26 July 1989 of both councils to seek their views on changes in the draft Basic Law. She easily won full support from all participants. After some debate, they agreed to elect by universal suffrage 20 members to the 60-member legislature in 1991 and no less than half in the 1995 election. Later, there were many other proposals to change the Basic Law, one of which was suggested by a pro-Beijing education union leader, Cheng Kai-nan (Gary Cheng). His proposal recommended that 40 per cent of the legislative members represent the functional constituencies, 40 per cent represent the moderate groups, and the last 20 per cent be elected by universal balloting. All these suggested changes in July and August of 1989 would be submitted to the next working session to be convened in Guangzhou in December 1989, half a year after the Tiananmen Incident.

When these and all other recommended proposals were also presented to the Thatcher government for a last-ditch struggle to revise the Basic Law on behalf of the six million residents in Hong Kong, again Margaret Thatcher ignored the 'crisis for change'. She accepted the views of Percy Cradock who felt it 'useless to force the pace of reform'.[27] On 16 February 1990, the Basic Law drafters met in Beijing and voted to accept no revisions not agreeable with Beijing's views.

THE NEW BRITISH PATH OF ELECTION REFORM AND THE TRANSITION IMPLEMENTATION

From 1989 to 1991, as political factions and parties in Hong Kong began their preparations for the 1991 election, pressure was put on the British government concerning British citizenship and the right of abode in Britain. Among the 18 seats to be elected by direct popular votes, all but two were captured by Hong Kong United Democrats headed by Martin Lee. This was the very first direct election for the Legislative Council in Hong Kong's history. The result clearly demonstrated the determined popular preference for democracy in Hong Kong. In Britain, a new prime minister would soon choose a powerful politician, not a China expert or anyone who had served in Hong Kong, to be the new Hong Kong governor. Chris Patten was a populist advocate of immense self-confidence. As the former head of the Conservative Party and a close personal friend of Prime Minister Major, Chris Patten had his own strong influence in the parliament and was well-known to the British public.

A new British policy and a new stage in Sino-American relations began to emerge in July 1992. Governor Patten was to confront criticism from those China experts in the British Foreign Ministry, especially the former personal adviser of Margaret Thatcher, Percy Cradock. Patten had to convince those suspicious members of the parliament and his antagonists among the British public, especially those in the media.

Back in Hong Kong the new governor realized he had to campaign to maximize his popular support and to map out his reform strategy to keep the vocal public on his side and to skillfully confront Beijing's counter measures against his election reform proposals. However, first of all, he had to know the situation well in Hong Kong and know how the people were divided politically. It took him three months to get his reform package in order. The battle with Beijing began on 7 October 1992, when he unveiled his proposal in a speech to the Legislative Council.[28]

Governor Patten's reform package and strategy

Upon his arrival in Hong Kong, the young and energetic new governor took no interest in the traditional ceremonial trappings of his office. He casually rode and walked on the streets, visiting with people and kissing babies. He initiated a new political style and was an overnight hit. However, the people in Hong Kong had long lost trust in Britain and resented the Thatcher-Cradock defeatist approach to dealing with China. That old disappointment could not easily be replaced. During his first five weeks in Hong Kong Patten made no official move to visit with Zhou Nan, the leader of the New China News Agency (NCNA) who replaced Xu Jiatun in 1989. One of the authors of this book was doing interviews in Hong Kong when Patten and Zhou Nan finally met on 20 August 1992. It was a prearranged courtesy call for exchange of greetings. They stressed the need for cooperation on 'smooth transition' and on the new airport construction and agreed that Hong Kong's 'prosperity and stability' depended on Sino-British adherence to the Joint Declaration.

A sudden shock came on 7 October when the Governor presented his proposal for the 1994–5 election reform of the district boards and the municipal-urban and legislative councils.[29] Beijing and the pro-China media reacted instantly with anger. The battle for 'hearts and minds' in Hong Kong between Britain and China would continue through the media and by secret diplomacy. Initially, Patten had the support of the people and the media in Hong Kong itself. He was attacked, however, on his home front in Britain by Sir Percy Cradock and former Hong Kong governors M.C. MacLehose and David Wilson. He depended comfortably on the loyalty of the Hong Kong civil servants to keep the government machinery running smoothly. The cooperation of the Legislative Council, in particular, was essential. But the LEGCO was divided among different factions: pro-China, neutral, or in favor of democratic reform. During the first few months Patten's popularity remained very high in the opinion poll. From Beijing, however, came the demand that he must abandon the 'reform package' and return to the convergence with the Joint Declaration, the Basic Law and the seven letters of diplomatic exchange between the two foreign ministers. Beijing would not talk to him when he bravely made his visit to the Chinese capital on 21–24 October 1992. The top officials refused to see him. Only the director of the Hong Kong and Macao Affairs Office, Lu Ping, played his host.[30] Without Beijing's cooperation, he would continue to delay implementation of his own reform. Daily attack and support appeared in the media war for the next five months within Hong Kong and between Britain and China until 22 April 1993, when the first diplomatic round began in Beijing. The 17 rounds of talks were kept secret. Tension and continuing harsh exchanges through the media made concessions even more impossible.

What was Patten's strategy and what was in his reform package? It appeared that Britain placed the best man in the field to seek China's cooperation, for smooth transition if possible, or, if not possible, to proceed with election reform unilaterally. Patten was to reverse the trend of continuous British concessions since 1984 when the Joint Declaration was being negotiated. The bloody Tiananmen Incident, the Hong Kong people's support for pro-democracy movement in China and the 1991 election victory against the pro-China candidates in Hong Kong were all positive indicators in his favor. Moreover, this was the last British opportunity for moral redemption and for withdrawal with dignity and pride in 1997. His strategy was to create a *fait accompli* from which Beijing could not escape without openly betraying the interests and demands of the six million residents of Hong Kong. And China could not succeed in achieving 'smooth transition' without making concessions to win sufficient support from the voters of Hong Kong. Besides, Hong Kong's prosperity and stability were critically important to China's own economic development. If Patten's ability and popular support could rise to meet the challenge, China would either have to make concessions or accept British unilateral implementation of Hong Kong's democratization. Britain had nothing to lose by not trying this strategy venture. Governor Patten's strategic performance seems to have confirmed this line of argument. The potential price to Britain was loss of China as a future market for trade and investment, as we suggested in Chapter 1, where we considered why Britain had traded Hong Kong for better relations with China beyond 1997. However, China surprised Britain and preferred the 'second stove' to concession.[31]

Patten's package of reform includes, in essence, the following major areas:[32]

1. Single candidate and single vote. Whether one votes as a member of a functionary constituency of a trade union or a civil service union, one casts one's vote for a single candidate only. There were 30 such functional constituencies. Nine of them were newly formed in his reform proposal.

2. Direct popular election of constituencies. There were 20 such seats in the 60-seat legislature. The colony was divided accordingly so that all parties and candidates could compete, each party deciding where it wished to offer a candidate to compete against candidates of other parties which also made the same strategic choice of whether or not to run a candidate.

3. 'Electoral Committee' at the district level for the rural districts in the New Territories. Some 300 members of the 19 rural District Boards together chose 10 members for the Legislative Council. Today there are three types of representatives in the LEGCO: functional, direct or collegial in nature.

4. 'Abolition of appointment' at all levels of the District, urban-municipal and legislative councils. Thus, the Governor, representing the central leadership as chief executive would no longer be able to dominate. As a result, the three-level councils would truly function as the people's democratic policy-making branch of government.

5. Lowering of voting age from age 21 to 18 to expand participation.
6. 'Need for enabling legislation' from the LEGCO to put his package proposal into practice. This voluntary surrender of his own authority to the LEGCO is a generous act legitimizing his reform through democratic process. The voters, the LEGCO members, the political parties and the media were all naturally ready for such a progressive practice.

Another aspect of Patten's reform for a representative government since 1992 can be termed a 'quiet process of localization'. This process did not require 'enabling legislation' from the LEGCO. It has been almost unobtrusively carried out by administrative actions, the more obvious ones being as follows:

1. Clear separation of legislative from executive powers. The Governor is no longer the president or presiding head of the LEGCO. Currently the 60 members of the LEGCO select their council president.
2. Monthly question–answer hour. Governor Patten is now available in person to respond to questions from the LEGCO members on a regular basis. This is one of the standard accountability practices in parliamentary systems of government.
3. Elimination of ex-officio members in the LEGCO. In the past, not only were there appointed 'unofficial' members, there were also three executive council members regularly voting and attending the LEGCO meeting as a matter of right: the head of civil service, the attorney-general and the finance secretary of the Governor's cabinet.
4. Private bill practice. Individual legislators now can introduce a personal bill on public matters concerning government policy-making. This new practice will increase the scope of legislative authority, although Patten can veto any bill so introduced.
5. Policy role of the LEGCO. The legislature now functions as a series of smaller committees, each specialized in a function. This is a departure from the previous practice of doing business in plenary session.

These examples help illustrate Patten's fresh democratic division of power allowing the legislature to grow in strength, in leadership and in responsible behavior. The voters in Hong Kong can immediately recognize the process of democratization and localization. This abdication in executive power and leadership in favor of empowerment of the LEGCO has no precedent. Beijing, for example, does not acknowledge such transitions as legal and thus regards them as a violation of the Joint Declaration and the Basic Law. In Chapter 6 we will discuss the Chinese path of 'second stove' and many other Chinese objections to Patten's 'violations'.

Governor Patten has opened up appointments, at the highest administrative level of the executive branch, for those of Chinese descent. For example, the positions of the Finance Secretary and the Chief Secretary of the Civil Service are now occupied by the Chinese for the first time. This level was formerly reserved for European appointees. More positions at the second highest level are now easily available to Chinese descendants. As many British civil servants of high positions are gradually retiring, Patten continues to have greater opportunity to localize his administration.[33]

What has been the popular sentiment about Patten because of his confrontation with China and his unilateral implementation of reform? We shall simply summarize popular reaction by the polling results. He arrived in 9 July 1992. The following 12 months were designated 'the year of Christopher Patten'[34] in terms of public attention, to be followed by 'the year of constitutional debate' in Hong Kong. As China saw him, 'Patten was the invisible hand behind the entire battle between China and Britain over Hong Kong's constitutional development'. However, the general public in Hong Kong who watched with frustration and uncertainty about their own future, saw the 17 rounds of diplomatic scuffle was merely the spectacle of two sovereign powers pursuing their own self-interests. Only after the end of the seventeenth round of the talks on 27 November 1993 did Governor Patten proceed with his unilateral implementation. The legislative council and the governor worked together to pass two major pieces of law in election reform, one for the District Board election in 1994 and the other

for the LEGCO election in 1995. The political campaign
and election outcome will be discussed in Chapter 7.

Of Governor Patten's popularity, the director of the Social
Science Research Center (SSRC) of the University of Hong
Kong wrote, 'In 1992–1993, Governor Patten was such an
unprecedented personality in capturing public attention that
the SSRC had to track his popularity first on a daily basis,
and then on a weekly basis.' As a result, almost 60 polls
were conducted in that year to measure his popularity alone.[35]
His second year was 'less active' and the SSRC rating was
done on a monthly basis. Hong Kong is quite advanced in
media polling by research agencies. We shall limit our cita-
tions on Patten's popularity only to sources then available
to the SSRC.[36] His weekly popularity in response to his policy
speech is summarized below:

1. Target size for questionnaire distribution is each time
   around 1200 and the return response about 57–54 per
   cent on average.
2. Raw data are 'very satisfied', 'just satisfied', 'neutral', 'just
   dissatisfied', 'very dissatisfied' and 'do not know'. The
   total was divided among these six categories. 'Very satisfied' response for the 52 weekly rating falls between 2
   and 3.4 percent. 'Just satisfied' fluctuated between the
   highest of 37.4 per cent and the lowest of 12.1 per cent.
   The 'neutral' response from the highest 12.4 to 5.0 per
   cent. 'Just dissatisfied' was from 13.1 per cent high to
   4.2 per cent. 'Very dissatisfied' was the most ignorable
   in a high of 2.9 per cent to the lowest of 0.8 per cent.
   Our conclusion is that the general public simply refused
   to judge the Governor's policy speeches while he was still
   attracting weekly attention. The supportive category of
   'just satisfied' was very high.[37]

The Governor's monthly rating on his 'policy speech satisfaction' during the first 12 months fluctuated between the
highest of 70 per cent in October 1992, when he delivered
the 'reform package' speech, to the lowest of 52 per cent
in September 1993. His second year 'monthly satisfaction'
approval rate began in October 1993 with 60 per cent and
ended in June at 47 per cent. This was a clear decline when
the failure of the 17 rounds of diplomatic talk ended on

27 November 1993. On the other hand, Governor Patten lived daily with an acrimonious media barrage from the pro-China papers. At the same time, he was evaluated highly on many issues by the liberal pro-Hong Kong papers. Despite his own concentration on it, his election reform was never at the center of popular concern. Economic stability and social harmony for the immediate future worried most of the six million people in Hong Kong. The Governor, too, had been very concerned about economic stability and progress. For example, he came to Washington to plead for 'Most Favored Nation' status for China, so that Hong Kong would not be adversely affected without it.

Either to protect his supporting base in London or to unite the liberal forces in Hong Kong behind him as he faced Beijing's media barrage against him personally, Governor Patten has so far been successful and reasonable in managing Hong Kong's transfer to China in 1997.

Democratization has gone a long way since Patten's arrival in July 1992. His task has been a typical one in British colonial history of 'honorable' retreat. There has always been, for example, a responsible and peaceful British retreat, whether from India in 1947, Burma in 1948 or Malaya in 1957. India received independence by an Act of parliament, handing over the country to Mr Nehru. Burma was peacefully delivered to General U Sang. For Malaya, the British even fought and defeated internal communist guerrilla revolt before withdrawal. In 1963 London handed over the strategic colony of Singapore to unite with the Federation of Malaysia. Hong Kong, however, has been a uniquely frustrating experience for Britain and for her last governor to manage. For example, Britain built up stability and prosperity in Hong Kong during decades of poor development in China.

Governor Patten's performance seems to have made the best use of the last five years to institutionalize the unusual British colonial legacy in Hong Kong. He has tried to redeem Britain from the reputation of 'betrayal' by Sir Percy Cradock, Lord David Wilson and Lord MacLehose. During the last four years of governorship, many economic, political and diplomatic issues have required Patten's skillful leadership:

1. As a professional politician, he cheerfully accepted the humiliating reception shown him on his 1992 trip to Beijing. His reform technically violated the Joint Declaration by sidestepping consultation with China or with the Joint Liaison Group (JLG) before his reform speech.[38]
2. He kept pressuring China for Chinese concessions. Thus, he repeatedly delayed the submission of his reform draft bill to the LEGCO until January 1994 after the talks had collapsed.[39]
3. Patten skillfully used and welcomed the LEGCO to constantly put pressure on Beijing. Beijing was hysterical about Patten's unilateral action at China's expense.[40]
4. By the middle of June 1993, Patten himself was under pressure from both supporters and critics. He flew to London to attend a cabinet meeting and saw Prime Minister Major in private. He thus avoided isolation from London and gathered more support from Britain. Meanwhile, he had to tone down well-intentioned criticism, from the United Democrats in Hong Kong, of his deliberate delay of legislative action. Frequently caught in the middle, he responded skillfully.[41]
5. To keep the Hong Kong pro-democracy forces united, the British Ambassador Robin MacLaren in Beijing insisted on the 'through train' principle to allow all elected LEGCO members to serve out their full terms to September 1999. On the other hand, Beijing had declared its determination to dissolve the LEGCO on 1 July 1997 and to create its own provisional legislative council. LEGCO was divided on this issue but Patten was able to sway it in his favor.[42]
6. Pressure was mounting on Patten by early October 1993. No progress was being made in the Beijing negotiation. When would Britain decide to call off the deadlocked negotiation? The people of Hong Kong would not wait any longer. They were losing confidence in Patten and the British government. There was no time for further delay for the 1994 election arrangement.[43] Patten's personal popularity rating was plummeting. In his LEGCO Question and Answer time, the governor was asked to explain how he could improve his personal credibility with China to ensure 'smooth transition' by 1997. He said that in the absence of concrete results from the Beijing

talks, Britain and his government would make certain new arrangements which should be acceptable to the people and to members in the legislature. He declared that Britain and his government would not allow Beijing to dictate. He revealed that certain arrangements, in fact, had been made. But he wished to see progress in Beijing within weeks, not months.[44] In short, he was, as media commentary later referred to him, skillful and statesmanlike.

7. In early 1994, Patten's popularity declined further. His second part of the election draft bill was in danger of being defeated in the LEGCO, which itself then was badly divided. Beijing at this time attempted to lure Patten back to Sino-British negotiation to delay preparation for the 1995 LEGCO election.[45] By early March 1994 his second election draft bill reached the LEGCO and was soon passed by a small margin. Thus the September 1995 LEGCO election could be fully implemented. More than half of the population were therefore legally enfranchised to vote directly for their own candidate under the single candidate/single vote system. Because of the multiple party competition, only the most popular party candidate can win. Meanwhile, the most popular new Democratic Party came into existence.[46]

The crowning popularity of the John Major cabinet, with Governor Patten as field commander to guide and maneuver through the divided jungle of confused political loyalties in Hong Kong, has resulted in the overall delivery of election victories in 1994–95 at the district board, municipal-urban and the legislative council levels. These victories were won under new laws devised by Patten. Their fulfillment testifies to the accuracy of his judgment that the Hong Kong people will embrace democracy if given choice. The 1994–95 election victories further proved that China might have been the loser also if Britain had not postponed the 1988 election.

What was the result of the 1995 LEGCO election? Only a few comments are made below. The campaign was open and peaceful. One pro-Taiwan candidate and several independent candidates were elected.[47] The sad returns were gracefully accepted by the defeated pro-Beijing candidates. In specific figures, under Martin Lee the Democratic Party, formerly known as Hong Kong United Democrats, received 12 out of 20 seats in direct popular polling and seven through the Electoral Committee, which was constituted by about 300 district board voting members. There were 10 to 12 seats won by small pro-democracy parties which have pledged to vote in the LEGCO with the Democratic party. Thus, the Democratic Party is now the strongest single party in the LEGCO, with a majority of 29–31 seats out of 60. The Liberal Party won the second largest number of seats. As a party of business people under Lee Pengfei's pro-China leadership, it will often cooperate with other leftist council members. What shocked many observers most was the crushing defeat of the pro-China Democratic Alliance for the Betterment of Hong Kong (DAB). The Beijing government forces had been fully mobilized in their support to the DAB. Under the leadership of the NCNA, all Chinese company leaders and their employees in Hong Kong were told to vote for the DAB. Unfortunately for the DAB, the election returns gave it only six seats. Actually four of these were from the safe functionary constituencies with lesser competition. The election proved that the DAB so far has little or no voter support from open districts allowing direct popular votes. During a month-long campaign, the pro-China candidates had hammered out the theme that their close contacts with China would bring more benefit to the voters if they were elected. DAB's Chairman and Vice Chairman, Tsang Yok-sing and Cheng Kai-nan jointly admitted, 'We are soundly defeated by the Democratic Party candidates.'[48] Chairman Tsang said further, 'Why do we run at all? ... This is the first time that LEGCO is totally elected. We have good connections with China. We try to use our channels to communicate with China. The result of these elections are bound to have a big impact on things here on how China sees us.'[49] And according to Cheng Kai-nan: 'Hong Kong will have to pay for this. We warned them that it would be better to see different voices.'

Many other people offered their comments either on the defeat for China or the victory for Governor Patten. From Beijing, first of all, came the announcement from the Hong Kong and Macao Affairs Office that the new 'Legislative Council would be disbanded on 1 July 1997'. The Office of the NCNA in Hong Kong reiterated Beijing's determination to dissolve the newly elected legislature. China clearly seems to regard the Democratic Party as a 'subversive organization'.[50] Its Chairman, Martin Lee, on the other hand, proudly acknowledged:

> This election makes clear the will of Hong Kong . . . This election is a referendum on the aspiration of the people of Hong Kong . . . The Hong Kong people voted with their hearts and minds for freedom and genuine democracy. The election is, in short, a mandate for democratic government and real constitution, legal and human rights reform to ensure basic freedoms in Hong Kong after 1997.[51]

It was ironic that China officially denounced the election as a violation of the Joint Declaration and the Basic Law and yet still openly participated in it and supported the pro-China candidates. As Professor Lo Shui-Hing (Sunny Lo) commented: 'The most important significance of this election is the participation of pro-China forces . . . The extent of the participation of pro-China forces is unprecedented.'[52]

Recent Sino-British conflicts and resolutions

In the few months before 1 July 1997 'separate and unilateral' implementations of the major agreements and of the Basic Law have been unavoidable. For the British, much has been accomplished except for one major project: the new airport construction. For the Beijing regime, its own unilateral implementation of the Basic Law is currently moving forward rapidly. At the same time, Beijing is encountering new problems from people who are asking for the promised 'high degree of autonomy' and preferring universal election to superficial consultation. Especially the very vocal residents and politicians in Hong Kong want to keep their legislature, universally elected since September 1955, intact till 1999.[53]

The British want an honorable withdrawal. But the London government and Governor Patten are determined to avoid becoming a 'lame duck' government before the actual transfer takes place. Several concerns of Sino-British cooperation have been discussed because both sides wish to ensure that the transfer is likely to be a harmonious event.[54] For example, only three weeks after the September 1995 election the Governor declared his 'full cooperation on transfer'.[55] He is ready to welcome communication with the Preparatory Committee (PC) which was to be established to replace the Preparatory Working Committee (PWC). The PWC was created in July 1993 as Beijing's 'second stove' machinery to undertake studies and to make policy research reports to the Hong Kong and Macao Affairs Office under Lu Ping. The PWC was divided into five study groups, each focusing on various topics in one of the following areas: political, legal, social, economic and cultural. Madame Chan Fang On-sang (Anson), Secretary for Civil Service, and acting governor whenever Patten was absent, has been in close contact with Lu Ping's office in Beijing. She welcomed the formal establishment of the Preparatory Committee in January 1996. She herself has been reported as a possible candidate, together with several others, for the first post-transfer Chief Executive.[56] On 4 February 1996, the Governor further reaffirmed his full cooperation with both the PC and the LEGCO. He made a major TV broadcast speech in which he pleaded for cooperation with all sides. He also pledged to carry out his duty not as a 'lame duck' but as a conscientious departing leader.[57] However, the Governor always seems determined to advance arguments on behalf of the Hong Kong people for their self-government in accordance with the British interpretation of the Joint Declaration.

On what might be his last visit to Hong Kong after a formal meeting with Chinese Premier Li Peng, Prime Minister Major came to Hong Kong on 2 March 1996 and pledged repeatedly that Britain's interest in and contact with Hong Kong will continue beyond the transfer in 1997.[58] At their Bangkok meeting on 1 March 1996 Premier Li Peng likewise expressed China's Hong Kong policy of 'tax exemption and administrative hands-off'. He affirmed that the post-1997 Chief Executive will follow the will of the people.[59]

The real focus in late 1996 and early 1997 would be on who was the first Chief Executive and the degree of his or her acceptability to the general public. A second critical issue surrounds the number of current LEGCO members to become members of the future Provisional Legislative Council.

Currently political groups and business leaders are in consultation with the Beijing authority on such issues. Some Hong Kong people, on the other hand, are currently protesting the dissolution of their popularly elected legislature, whose term does not end until 1999.

In conclusion, we stress that the Joint Declaration and the Basic Law have been misinterpreted by both China and Britain to meet unilateral convenience in separate implementation. China was confident and able, before the Tiananmen Incident, to promise Hong Kong a 'high degree of autonomy'. Since 1989, China has depended on a more strict interpretation of the Basic Law to ensure stability and control for peaceful transition. Britain's initial neglect of Hong Kong's interests in the early 1980s was totally unintended. Unfortunately Hong Kong was the 'absent third party' to the Sino-British secret negotiation for transfer. Governor Patten's presence on the scene has, indeed, converted the seeming 'betrayal' into a surprise struggle for democratic self-government. When, beginning in 1992, Governor Patten was on the offensive to implement the new British policy of democratic election reform, China was understandably angry and began stonewalling. Since early 1996, when China began to implement her 'second-stove' approach, she encountered certain unexpected difficulties – for example, the protests of people who insisted on keeping their elected officials in 1994 and 1995. Both Britain and China are culpable for having failed to utilize the Joint Liaison Group, which had been designed originally to prevent unilateralism and the problems it generates.

6 Chinese Implementation of the Joint Declaration and the Basic Law

In our last chapter, we described Governor Patten's dilemmas and difficulties in introducing a representative form of political system, given the complexities among conflicting groups in Hong Kong and the opposition from China. In this chapter, we shall consider how the Chinese government has all along expected the British to cooperate on the basis of the Joint Declaration, the Basic Law and other exchanges of understanding in 1990 when the Basic Law was being finalized. For the common purposes of 'stability and prosperity' in Hong Kong and for 'smooth transition' in 1997, the Sino-British Joint Liaison Group (JLG) was originally set up in 1985 to help resolve any unexpected difficulties.

The British government in London and in Hong Kong did much to cooperate. However, in less than five years, perhaps under pressure from liberal forces in Hong Kong and from Britain's own rebellion against treaty agreements, Governor Chris Patten arrived in Hong Kong in July 1992 with a reform package: to introduce democracy in Hong Kong. He did not even consult China or go through the JLG. Instead he unilaterally announced the reform package and created a new crisis in Sino-British relations over Hong Kong. China did not expect Britain to suddenly change Hong Kong's political status quo from what it had been in the past 150 years of colonial rule. Much less did China expect Britain to violate the three agreements on what was to happen or not to happen during the transition years. Britain, on the other hand, apparently thought it had the full legal right to introduce more democracy as its legacy before departure in 1997.

For Beijing, much was at stake. It could not allow Western 'spiritual pollution' to destabilize the communist system of government. It was eager to preserve Hong Kong's prosperity and stability to the economic advantage of both Hong Kong and China. Moreover, Hong Kong was only the forerunner. After it, Macao and Taiwan would be unified with the mainland of China. Thus, China realized, a way must be found to accommodate the different conditions in Taiwan, in Macao and in Hong Kong. That way, of course, is what we know as 'one country, two systems', a long-term formula of 'unity with diversity' or the coexistence of two political systems under the single roof of 'Chinese national sovereignty and territorial integrity'. This formula was conceived by the paramount reform leader Deng Xiaoping and was considered to be a 'generous concession framework' through which to bring back, in stages, Hong Kong, Macao and Taiwan. In essence, the formula will grant 50 years of self-government to each such Special Administrative Region (SAR). All three are exempted from taxation to the central government but will be defended by the national forces.[1] In practice, this somewhat resembles the American federalist system except that the residual powers are reserved to the national government and that this is merely a temporary necessity to achieve eventual integration. Britain accepted this formula through the Joint Declaration. The Chinese government would provide a mini-constitution, or Basic Law, as it is officially called, to govern Hong Kong and to maintain its defense.[2] There was not much left for Britain to do for Hong Kong that Britain had never wanted to do since the 1840s. This, indeed, was why the Beijing government accused Britain of treaty violations and bad faith. Besides, more important than Hong Kong is China's determination to make the 'one country, two systems' work.

We shall focus in this chapter on China's unilateral preparation – or second stove approach – in case the diplomatic renegotiation should fail. China wanted to get Britain to abandon the Patten package. It did not succeed. Both Britain and China have, since 1993, been implementing those agreements unilaterally as they saw fit to interpret the treaties. We shall quote from Deng Xiaoping's speeches to develop his theory of 'one country, two systems', the Preparatory Working Committee for unilateral preparation, the Preparatory Committee which was officially set up in January 1996 to implement the Basic Law, the popular consultation in the spring of 1996 in Hong Kong to prepare for establishing a Provisional Legislature (PL) or Provisional Legislative Council (PLC) to replace the LEGCO which was elected in 1995 under the Patten reform package, and comment on the selection of the first Chief Executive before the end of 1996. The difficulties of creating a temporary legislature are also briefly discussed later.

DENG'S THEORY OF 'ONE COUNTRY, TWO SYSTEMS'

From the Chinese point of view since 1949, Hong Kong was to be taken back whenever Beijing was ready to take such steps, and the British would simply have to give up the land at that time. How to achieve this goal and what specific methods would be considered appropriate were, as Beijing saw it, purely Chinese domestic affairs.[3] No foreign interference in this matter, *vis-à-vis* Hong Kong, Macao or Taiwan, would be tolerated. Such a legalistic approach was publicly indicated in 1972 when the Beijing delegation to the United Nations told the world body not to classify Hong Kong as a regular 'dependent territory' to be handled by the Trusteeship Council of the United Nations. It should be noted that 'Chinese nationalism' at home unquestionably supports such an official approach. Britain in 1972 did not register any strong protest against Beijing's sovereign assertion over Hong Kong's future disposition. In the 1970s China was more concerned about getting American military and diplomatic forces out of Taiwan and was also eager to secure Washington's formal treaty acknowledgement that 'there is but one China', and 'Taiwan is a part of China'.[4] This acknowledgement was achieved by the Shanghai Communiqué which President Richard M. Nixon signed in February 1972. By the early 1980s, while diplomatic negotiation was in progress over Hong Kong's sovereign transfer, Beijing offered the same theoretical framework of 'one country, two systems' to Taiwan for a peaceful unification and full integration in 50 years. Little Macao, connected with China by a footbridge, was offered the identical proposition for sovereign transfer to take place in 1999. In short, 'one country, two systems' was Deng Xiaoping's theoretical invention of a peaceful solution to achieve Chinese territorial recovery and national integration to undo the historical humiliation of Western and Japanese aggression in China in 1841 and 1895.[5]

Just how the originator of this theory, Deng Xiaoping, articulated the theory's justification and applicability requires analysis in terms of Chinese historical 'change and continuity'. The long history of governing experience in China's systemic institutional continuity is quite relevant to Deng's perceptions in revolutionary transition and in modernizing China toward reinstitutionalization. In an attempt to explain Deng's thinking, we would like to remind our readers that China, unlike Japan, has had a very painful debate since the 1870s on whether to accept the 'wholesale adoption' in Western learning or to restrict Western learning to 'scientific-technological practice only'. The early official conclusion before the 1911 revolution had been a reaffirmation in 'Chinese learning as the foundation and Western learning in practicability'.[6] Sun Yat-sen again did not want to undermine Chinese political and cultural values. He invented a political-institutional 'five-power theory' of government. He was committed to democratizing China gradually. His doctrine is in official practice in Taiwan, which utilizes the five-power theory. Mao Zedong, on the other hand, immediately turned to Marxist institutional dictatorship in his socialist revolution of 1949. But he is condemned for what he did. Both experiments of democracy and socialism under Sun and Mao collapsed on mainland China. Deng Xiaoping's new experiment since Mao's death has been the 'third grand innovation', which he calls 'socialism with Chinese characteristics'.[7] This recent mixture of market economy and communist dictatorship calls for opening China up to the international interaction of trade and investment. On the other hand, Deng advocates domestic, political and economic 'deepening in reforms'. This peaceful approach is a long-term strategy of a 'non-violent domestic revolution' to transform China to a new stage of modernity.

The Deng era of a 'third grand innovation' requires peaceful change at home and absence of war along China's borderlands. During this expected long peaceful period ahead China must achieve peaceful territorial reunification, and hence the emergence of 'one country, two systems' and later the conclusion of the Sino-British Joint Declaration on Hong Kong.

How to define the precise contents and dynamics of its application in delineating central and regional relations is theoretically important. How has Deng Xiaoping himself explained and interpreted the new Hong Kong–China relations between socialist China and capitalist Hong Kong in the long 50 years after the transfer? We quote here from his own addresses to a visiting delegation from Hong Kong[8] and to the Basic Law drafters (the translation is our own):

> I am glad to talk to you as visitors to witness our signing of the Joint Declaration. We know we have a common goal – to love China, to love Hong Kong, and to protect Hong Kong's prosperity and stability during the next 13 years before transfer . . . Many friends fear policy changes after my generation's deaths. Let me emphasize that our policy will not change. The central government, our characteristics as a long-enduring nation and our country's tradition have all displayed our firm standards for self-respect and self-honor to fulfill our obligations under an international treaty. We do not change policies in 50 years or in the next few generations. On the other hand, not all economic and social changes are bad. For example, our sovereign political recovery of Hong Kong is a change. A change for better is a good change. It is beneficial to Hong Kong.
>
> Please do not believe that there will be no change at all. I am sure you welcome change if it is good for Hong Kong . . . We change in China too. Rural change and urban reform are big changes. 'One country, two systems' is a big change. There is good change and there is bad change. We cannot reject changes altogether. Some people in Hong Kong fear meddling from the central government. You must distinguish whether a meddling is good or not for Hong Kong's stability and prosperity . . . In the next 13 years and 50 years after that I am quite sure of law and order in Hong Kong. Please never forget destructive forces in Hong Kong which can come from different directions. If there is turmoil, Beijing will act to restore order. Such meddling should be welcome. The central govern-

ment will practice 'Hong Kong people governing Hong Kong'. Beijing will refuse to govern Hong Kong directly. During the later part of transition and during changes in personnel, there is bound to be general confusion. You must still govern yourself. There is only one condition in self-governing. That is to love China and to love Hong Kong. I can assure you 'Hong Kong people governing Hong Kong', as a policy will never change... The only central presence in Hong Kong is the stationing of a small number of troops to prevent turmoil... Finally I ask you to visit different parts of China to witness changes for the better...

So long as you love our nation and its unity, you can advocate your political views, including condemning the Communist Party...

Three years later in 1987 when addressing the Basic Law drafters, Deng had the following to say:

The Basic Law promises 50 years without change. There will also be no policy change for 50 years after agreement with Taiwan under our scheme of 'one country, two systems'. Our policy of 'reform at home and opening to the outside world' will not change. Our living standard and national wealth will take more than 50 years to reach the medium level in living standard. Our nation needs political stability. From a broad perspective for unity, we need 'one country, two systems' to assure stability and to assure regional administrative self-governing in Hong Kong and Taiwan. There will be no change in our 'four cardinal principles' of government – socialist system, communist party leadership, socialist legality and democratic centralism. If policy remains unchanged, these cardinal principles must not change either. Who else can lead China if there is no communist party? 'One country, two systems' is not a Russian innovation, nor a Japanese or an American invention. It is a new Chinese approach – a Chinese characteristic. If we change our 'socialism with Chinese characteristics', what will happen to Hong Kong? There will, then, be no stability and prosperity for Hong Kong. We oppose 'capitalist pollution' for the purpose of protecting our socialistic system...[9]

Toward the end of his speech, he objected to blind imitation of the West. Democracy, in his mind, might bring division and chaos to Hong Kong. If so, the central government would not stand by idly. Deng was firmly convinced that in mainland China the people are not ready for direct election above county level and that a multiple-party system would not yet be suitable for China. In short, Deng clearly set the limits against introducing too much democracy prematurely to Hong Kong.[10]

As we analyze his seven speeches on Hong Kong and his pet theory of 'one country, two systems', we are convinced that the paramount leader was truly afraid of chaos and turmoil in post-1997 Hong Kong. Deng could not afford to allow the experiment to fail in Hong Kong. Such failure would instantly discourage Taiwan's willingness to negotiate toward national unification. We are persuaded to conclude that Deng's conviction that China and Hong Kong are mutually in need of each other appears to have wide support. China must pursue economic reform in the mainland and socio-political stability in Hong Kong, which will help provide trade, investment and management experience. In case of large-scale turmoil, China's troops stationed in Hong Kong will act to restore order. Its token presence in Hong Kong after 1997 will serve to minimize any such large-scale turmoil from being contemplated. We are further convinced that Deng, as the last powerful revolutionary leader in twentieth-century China, is himself thoroughly aware that Sun Yat-sen's democratic revolution of 1911 could not survive in mainland China in the next half-century if it were soon reintroduced. The only alternative is Deng's 'socialism with Chinese characteristics' – which puts emphasis on capitalistic market economy and communist party leadership at the central level while direct electoral democracy is being slowly and experimentally introduced at the lower level. Thus, we believe Deng's 'peaceful revolution' or reform will eventually lead to a new polity of 'democracy with Chinese characteristics', which will resemble, in the end, what Sun Yat-sen's revolution 'of the people, by the people and for the people' has fought for.

Our study of Deng's 'peaceful revolution' convinces us that he is a leader of enormous practical experience with no time to debate theory. He appears guided by traditional political strategy: utilizing the balancing function of statesmanship to achieve national consensus. Given the internal conflict of factional competition inside the Communist Party, Deng would want to insulate Hong Kong from China. His concept of 'Hong Kong people governing Hong Kong' is therefore the foundation of the Basic Law. Secondly, he must be sure that in Hong Kong the absence of turmoil comes from the stationing of Chinese troops in Hong Kong. Deng and the Chinese government, therefore, could not understand Governor Patten's drastic reform package aimed at undoing the treaty agreements. China experts in Britain, including Sir Percy Cradock, former governors Edward Youde, Murray MacLehose and David Wilson, have all been quite outspoken against Patten's election reform since 1992. In fact, as sitting governor, David Wilson once said publicly that people ought to have confidence in the Sino-British agreement on Hong Kong's future and that China has had a good reputation on treaty enforcement. He said:

> The Chinese really had no need to sign a very detailed arrangement of this sort for a territory which was going to be theirs, but they did, they put an immense amount of effort into it. Internally, their policies have changed year by year, and they have changed very dramatically sometimes, but if you look at their international record for sticking to their treaties I think they would want to keep their reputation.[11]

He continued that every effort should be made to make sure that the 'one country, two systems' concept did work, that it was not something that was merely casually put down 'on a piece of paper', and that many practical conditions were taken into account to ensure the two systems would work in convergent mutual satisfaction between China and Hong Kong for 50 years after 1997. Governor Wilson added that 'the Chinese leadership realize that giving a separate system in Hong Kong is what is going to make sure Hong Kong really is useful to China as well as being what most people in Hong Kong actually want . . . If you look at the situation from the Hong Kong point of view, we have to deal with China. China is our next door neighbor, China is involved in so much of what we are trying to build for the future, we need contacts, we need to be in touch with the leadership.'

Realistically, beyond 1997, Hong Kong's continuity in 'prosperity and stability' is far more dependent on China than the other way around. The business tycoons and middle-level majority merchants seem far more practical than those advocating human rights and universal elections. There seems a greater long-term understanding between Sir Percy Cradock and Governor David Wilson on the British side and paramount leader Deng Xiaoping and Xu Jiatun on the Chinese side. Deng, in addition, has had to guide the Beijing government to ensure that post-1997 Hong Kong will not in any way threaten the continuity of the socialist political system in China. His 'one country, two systems' has been designed to insulate against 'coming spiritual pollution'. Indeed it is a wise and genuine stopgap instrument superior to instant full integration with its attendant danger and instability. This gradual accommodation in time will allow much to happen in the fifty years following 1997.

CHINA'S REACTION TO PATTEN'S REFORM AND THE 17 ROUNDS OF TALK

The Chinese government was not oblivious to hostile developments in Hong Kong after the Tiananmen Incident in June 1989. Anti-government Chinese students and intellectuals were secretly assisted to escape through Hong Kong. Anti-China liberal candidates of the United Democrats won handsomely in Hong Kong's first popular election in 1991. The legislature in Hong Kong adopted in 1991 the human, civil and political rights covenants of the United Nations. On 9 July 1992, Chris Patten was sworn in, to assume the position of governorship. He vowed to fight 'for the interests of the people' and to 'build trust with China'. Yet 14 days later, Governor Patten declined to accept the invitation from Lu Ping to visit China. The Chinese government was even more surprised to learn that the International Commission of Jurists suggested that local organizations in Hong Kong monitor the human rights record after 1997.

Even the United States House of Representatives in August 1992 passed the US–Hong Kong Act in spite of Beijing's immediate protest of interference. Governor Patten started a series of unusual meetings with political groups in late August, only five days after Zhou Nan's courtesy call at Government House. This was the first meeting between the new governor and the head of New China News agency in Hong Kong. Conscious of politically adverse moves on the governor's part, Lu Ping, the head of the Hong Kong and Macao Affairs Office of the State Council in Beijing warned, on 27 August 1992, that: 'China will dissolve the Legislative Council in 1997 if it does not comply with the Basic Law.'[12] Five days later, Lu Ping again reminded publicly that: 'failure to align Hong Kong political reforms with the Basic Law will breach the Sino-British Joint Declaration.'[13] A week later in Hong Kong the pro-British Group of 89, the Cooperative Resources Centre (CRC) reversed its allegiance in support of the Beijing position. The new governor had, indeed, divided Hong Kong into hostile camps in two months.

The air was filled with gathering tension. Beijing criticized the Hong Kong government for violating the Sino-British Memorandum of Understanding on financing the new airport construction. Toward the end of September 1992, Lu Ping warned his Hong Kong counterpart that 'the Basic Law cannot be amended before 1997'.[14] One week before Patten's reform speech, the NCNA urged the Governor to work through his China experts to 'make all policies conform with the spirit of the three Sino-British agreements on the future of Hong Kong'.[15] One day before the Governor's LEGCO speech, the deputy director of the local NCNA delivered another serious warning that: 'in tabling the electoral arrangements for 1994–95 without China's blessing, Patten will be breaching the principle of convergence and hampering Sino-British cooperation.'[16] However, China's worst fear in months came when Patten announced his 1994–95 electoral reform package in the LEGCO. This bombshell enraged Beijing. The breakdown of communication was, therefore, complete after his 17 October 1992 speech.

Naturally, the content of Patten's reform package was quite comprehensive. We have detailed it in Chapter 5. The explosive impact of it was, of course, difficult for China to swallow. The reform issue divided the Hong Kong community into pro-British, pro-China, and pro-Hong Kong factions among activists and elite leaders, while the largest majority of the Hong Kong residents did not care and did not have a basis to choose sides. China, after 17 October 1992, formally accused the British of legal 'breach of the three agreements'. Normal channels of Sino-British communication, such as the Joint Liaison Group and semi-annual meetings of both foreign ministers, were all adversely affected. Suddenly, China was confronted with the possibility of unilateral British democratization by surgical reforms. Governor Patten was counting on cooperation of the LEGCO where he planned to work up a majority to pass his proposals. If fully successful, Hong Kong would have a three-tier government elected by a huge number of no less than 3.2 million new voters. This was more than half of Hong Kong's total population and clearly violated the target percentages of the elected members in the LEGCO as designated by the Basic Law.[17] From the very start, Beijing stood firm on two major positions. First, Governor Patten should withdraw his proposal. If not, any violation of the three Sino-British agreements would result in dissolution of the elected bodies, including the LEGCO after 1997. Additionally, China decided never to acknowledge the reform package and not to undertake any discussion on it. Second, Beijing let it be known that China might be compelled to invalidate Patten's reform results and might complete the sovereign transfer in 1997 without British participation.

Bickering went on with added dimensions. The local NCNA accused Patten 'of masquerading as a saviour' of Hong Kong by democratizing the political system. He was further attacked repeatedly for violations of the 1991 new airport construction memorandum. China was afraid that the cost of the new airport construction would go beyond Hong Kong's ability to pay after 1997. Premier Li Peng joined the airport debate while Beijing's delegate demanded changes in Britain's funding proposals.[18] Four days before his trip to Beijing, Patten's supporters in the LEGCO backed a motion to create a district electoral committee to choose ten members in the 1995 election. This led to China's Basic Law drafter expert and Lu Ping's adviser, Professor Xiao Weiyun, to declare that Patten's cabinet members and his policy-making secretaries would not be allowed to serve in the Hong Kong government beyond 30 June 1997. This was announced in addition to Beijing's earlier declaration to dissolve the LEGCO as elected in 1995. Thus, there was no through train for the legislative and the executive policy-making officials to remain in government. The most embarrassing message for Patten came at Lu Ping's press conference when the governor was still in Beijing. Lu declared, for the first time, that: 'China will form the SAR legislature, judiciary and government (executive) unilaterally if Britain reneges on its previous commitment to policy convergence on the Basic Law.'[19]

The Sino-British crisis over divergent views on the implementation of the three agreements was even more aggravated when the British Foreign Office jumped the gun on Beijing by releasing the Hurd–Qian correspondence of 1990 concerning drafting the Basic Law with regard to the electoral arrangements for 1995. Britain insisted that the seven exchanges of correspondence were not policy commitments. They were exchanges of discussion only. They could not be considered together as a formal agreement as claimed by Beijing. However, Britain itself was divided on this. For example, while the former British Chief Secretary of Civil Service in Hong Kong publicly condemned Patten's reform package, Foreign Secretary Douglas Hurd announced his full backing of Patten and revealed that there had been prior 'full discussion' of the reform proposals in Cabinet before Patten's announcement on 7 October 1992.[20] The overseas edition of the *People's Daily* in Beijing mounted another blistering attack on the governor and alleged his conspiracy with foreign powers 'to destabilize Hong Kong and China'.[21] Beijing even threatened to cancel all current and future Hong Kong government contracts beyond 1 July 1997.[22] In short, there was a stalemate. The bitter exchange between Beijing, London and Hong Kong went on for months. Patten had the majority support in the LEGCO. On 13 January 1993, pro-China legislator Philip Wong moved to block the introduction of Patten's reform bill. He was heavily defeated by 35 to 2 in the motion debate.[23] At long last and to the pleasant surprise of the six million residents in Hong Kong, Britain and China both announced their forthcoming talks on the

electoral arrangement. Governor Patten called the announcement 'a victory for common sense'.[24] However, China declared two days later that it would reserve the right to veto
the result of the 1995 election and that the coming talks
would not be open to the media.

During the six months before Sino-British talks began in
Beijing, popular reaction was hopeful of positive results in
the negotiation concerning Governor Patten's electoral reform. Other than the pro-China media, other daily reporting in Hong Kong was generally neutral. The people in Hong
Kong were, by and large, reserved in their comments. The
new governor, however, was the center of popular conversation and weekly polling as we described in Chapter 5. The
vocal elite of pro-democracy groups in Hong Kong and their
agents in the LEGCO were ready to cooperate with the
governor. On the other hand, the anti-Patten, pro-China
papers followed the Beijing line closely. Generally they attacked the governor as being irresponsible and not seriously
concerned about 'stability and prosperity' and 'smooth transfer'. They held him responsible for political confusion and
for creating popular uncertainty in their future. Some members in the LEGCO often confronted the governor after his
October trip to Beijing. Some asked him to explain why he
had failed in his October trip. Supporters asked him to submit
his reform draft proposals for the LEGCO to discuss. Certain academic pro-China voices accused him of creating anti-
Beijing hostility among the population. Some feared that
Governor Patten would soon use the LEGCO as a scape-
goat to cover his own failure in reform.

Officially the local NCNA consistently maintained that the
LEGCO, as a subordinate 'advisory body' to Patten, had no
constitutional authority to change the understanding and
decisions between Britain and China in implementing the
Joint Declaration and the Basic Law. The spokesman of the
NCNA further commented on the recent discussions in
the LEGCO primarily as a result of pressure from the
governor's office. This behavior of the LEGCO was labeled
'irresponsible'.[25] Pro-China *Wen Hui Bao* in Hong Kong made
the following points against the governor: (1) The LEGCO
has no legal status to act; (2) it has no power to act on
matters of sovereign transfer; (3) Britain is an independent

sovereign country, is held responsible for all its international treaties and agreements, and therefore should not and cannot allow a subunit of the government to discharge its own obligation under international law; (4) Governor Patten 'has divided the Hong Kong people into factions', and hence new conditions of political unrest 'are not conducive to economic development' between the people of Hong Kong and the people of China.[26] In short, the divided media in Hong Kong was more and more polarized, while Governor Patten was waiting strategically for news from the forthcoming talks. The informed public in Hong Kong was speculating about the strategy behind China's concept of 'second stove' and about whether China would take unilateral action. Toward the middle of February 1993, the 'second stove' concept still had no firm definition. Some among the Hong Kong Affairs Advisers suggested it should merely be 'an advisory body of people to engage in future transfer policy research'.[27] In our judgment, Beijing was using the 'second stove' tactic to prevent Governor Patten from advancing his reform proposals through the LEGCO. It was a form of damage control intended to deny validity to the governor's 1994–95 electoral reform package. By denying cooperation with Patten and by stonewalling against his patience, Beijing would gain sufficient time to influence the people of Hong Kong.

Before the first round of talks began, China insisted that no local Chinese official from Hong Kong should act as a delegate representing the people of Hong Kong. This was to Beijing a matter of principle because Beijing could not logically negotiate with its own people. The talk was strictly between Britain and China as two sovereign states.[28] Political leaders in Hong Kong were disappointed with Beijing's 'artificial argument' in not allowing local Chinese delegates to be included in the British delegation. They detected hypocrisy in Beijing's 'legal alibi', and they were afraid of another betrayal if the talks were kept secret.[29] When the Hong Kong government gazetted the draft reform bill, Beijing was angry. The anger led to more attacks against Patten among pro-China business leaders who echoed China's complaints over gazetting the reform draft. They therefore declared publicly their support of China's position and insisted that the coming talks would be restricted to only three agreements: he Joint Declaration, the Basic Law, and the Sino-British understanding through the Seven Letters in 1990. Hence, the governor's strategy calculated to influence the coming talks failed. Premier Li Peng took advantage of the situation to delay the talks and accused Britain of bad faith in the governor's reform package. Two days later, Lu Ping declared at an urgently called news conference China's decision to formally organize a 'second stove' approach to implement the three agreements unilaterally – to fulfill the Basic Law's purpose.[30]

Lu Ping held Britain constantly responsible for the breakdown of communication. Whether China would take over Hong Kong before 1 July 1997 would depend on whether Britain fully adhered to the Joint Declaration. He made clear that China's consistent position had always been in favor of cooperation and against confrontation. 'If the governor fails to cooperate, China will be forced to follow the Basic Law and to prepare for the first post-97 SAR government and legislature . . . Democracy in Hong Kong will be implemented gradually . . .'[31]

Reports from Beijing soon revealed that Deng Xiaoping was concerned over possible 'unexpected small British traps'. On 12 March 1993, the Hong Kong government suddenly published Patten's draft reform bill in the official gazette. The publication caught the Chinese government by surprise and antagonized the communist leaders into 'explosive anger' shortly before the start of the diplomatic talks. The next day the Standing Committee of the Political Bureau of the Communist Party held an emergency meeting on Hong Kong. Chairman Jiang Zemin told them: 'never to hold any false hope from Britain. China must begin to organize our own stove.'[32] During the meeting these few top leaders, whether influenced by Deng's warning or not, agreed that Governor Patten had deliberately created this obstacle to influence the coming Sino-British talks. They agreed further to bring the matter before the meetings of the National People's Congress and the Chinese People's Political Consultative Conference. Both were being held simultaneously at that moment in Beijing. Premier Li Peng therefore quickly reversed China's position on the coming talks in his prepared text of Government Work Report to the NPC and CPPCC.

The two 'representative' bodies, in turn, passed resolutions in unanimous support of the government. In short, the Chinese government was resolved to harden its negotiating position and to make nationwide propaganda against Governor Patten's 'future traps'. With nationwide support, China could apply pressure in future contact with both London and its Hong Kong government. It was clear that China took great advantage of Patten's 'small step on 12 March' and made a little crisis of it. The episode, however, helped to explain Deng Xiaoping's earlier suspicion or insight in his dealing with Britain in the early 1980s. He was reported to watch closely the daily developments in Hong Kong's experiment with his 'one country, two systems'. It is known that he hoped to see the transfer in person in 1997.

The first of the diplomatic talks took place on 22 April 1993. Little was agreed upon in the early rounds. Refusing to discuss it, the Chinese side never officially acknowledged the existence of Patten's reform package. Beijing's chief negotiator was Vice Foreign Minister Jiang Enzhu, who repeatedly warned that a confrontational approach with China would achieve nothing and that Patten's unilateral reform would not last long. Britain's chief delegate was Ambassador Robin MacLaren. When the rounds of talk continued, accomplishing nothing at all, the LEGCO in Hong Kong passed the bill on Boundaries and Electoral Commission. China immediately criticized the 'unilateral action as a new obstacle to Sino-British talks on electoral arrangement'.[33]

By early June 1993, Patten was pessimistic about the progress of the talks in relation to the legislation timetable for his reform bills through the LEGCO. The fifth talk was scheduled two weeks later on 14 June. Clearly, the governor was being forced to renege on his legislative timetable. Beijing 'rebutted any and every attempt to introduce any part of the Patten package into the discussions'.[34] The Chinese side did later show some interest in presenting their alternative proposal in coming talks. Britain suddenly became optimistic while the governor was still frustrated at being unable to go it alone. On the other hand, the local community in Hong Kong was neither optimistic nor pessimistic, for they had lost trust in both sides. Patten's personal popularity was now on the decline because of his 'untimely step' in publishing his draft reform bill in the *Gazette* on 12 March. He was held responsible for causing the Chinese to harden their position. Beijing was all along able to remain in full control of the talks.

China expected people in Hong Kong to lose confidence in Governor Patten, and those favoring China would therefore gather in momentum. Both London and Patten, as before, proved to have no power at all, unless by unilateral reform, to confront China's unilateral 'second stove' counteraction. However, what contributed to self-constraint on both sides was their fear over popular reproach and media criticism in Hong Kong. On 16 June 1993, to attempt to break up the stalemate, Prime Minister John Major called for a summit meeting in Hong Kong on 1 July. At the end of the fifth talk, nothing of substance relevant to the 1994–95 election arrangement had yet been mentioned.[35] Jiang Enzhu blamed the British for lack of good faith because of the little progress made in the talks. Ambassador MacLaren acknowledged, on the contrary, that some progress had been made. On 14 June 1993, a serious episode occurred: the British announced in Hong Kong that the 'exchange of seven letters in early 1990 between the two foreign ministers had no force of constraint'.[36] On the same day Beijing countered and demanded good faith on diplomatic agreement.[37] Britain had earlier agreed on 13 April 1993 that the talks would be based on the three valid agreements: the Joint Declaration, the Basic Law and the Seven Letters.

The seventh round of talks took place on 5–6 July. British Foreign Secretary Douglas Hurd flew to Beijing on 8–9 July to meet Foreign Minister Qian Qichen to jointly review the progress of the discussions and probably to convey whatever was useful for China to know.[38] Hurd's visit to Beijing and Hong Kong boosted Hong Kong's optimism on the talks. For example, among 511 telephone interviews on 6–7 July, 72.8 per cent of those interviewed considered Foreign Secretary Hurd's visit helpful to the talks, 44.5 per cent were optimistic about future sessions, while fewer than 20 per cent were pessimistic. The survey indicated a strong 66 per cent disappointment over the seven talks in the past two and a half months since 22 April.[39] In addition, before the eighth round of talks, Beijing began to assure various visiting delegations from Hong Kong that China was determined to carry out 'one country, two systems' and was able to guarantee Hong Kong's stability and prosperity under any adverse influence; and, secondly, that China would fully carry out the three Sino-British agreements. This was the assurance what Hong Kong visitors sought.[40]

The eighth round of talk focused on Mr Hurd's guidelines concerning the electoral committee, functional constituencies, and the criterion of the 'through train'. The talks concentrated on nine new professions or occupational groups which should be given representation in the 1995 LEGCO election. Other new issues were raised by the British side. However, the Chinese side considered these new issues within her internal sovereign domain, and thus, they did not come under discussion. These issues, from the British point of view, were closely related to 'smooth transition' in 1997. They included British participation in the preparatory committee of 1996, the direct universal election for the LEGCO in 2007, and agreement upon the methods used to establish the Nominations Committee for the Chief Executive. Because both sides made their positions clear to each other for the first time at the eighth session, they reached a 'new stage of talk'.[41] Nothing was agreed upon during the next several rounds of talks until 2 October when the two foreign ministers met in New York. They both admitted that the Beijing talks had been stalemated over issues which they raised at the eighth round. Both pledged their willingness to continue the Beijing talks, with the focus on political reform, new airport financing and the 'through train' for the LEGCO members to serve their full term to 1999. For Britain the bottom line was then either a 'through train' agreement or breakdown of the talks leading to Britain's unilateral implementation of the Patten reform package.[42] For the Chinese side, the bottom line was British return to the three documents, the Joint Declaration, the Basic Law and the Seven Letters of Sino-British Understanding of 1990. Short of this, China, too, could allow the Beijing talks to drag on, aware of Governor Patten's timetable to implement his constitutional reform in Hong Kong. When Britain hinted at a possible deadline for the talks, the Chinese government responded with a counter action:

For Hong Kong, the die was cast for the year when, on 9 July 1993, Governor Christopher Patten said it was better for Britain to take unilateral action on constitutional reform in the territory than to surrender on principles. One week later, Chinese Foreign Minister Qian Qichen, formally inaugurated a 57 member Preparatory Working Committee for the Hong Kong Special Administrative Region Preparatory Committee, although its implementation was suspended until its second plenary meeting later in December. This was an obvious move by China to further discredit the Patten-led Hong Kong government and implicitly, to marginalize the partially democratized Legislative Council, which in any event it did not recognize as a legitimate body.[43]

In early October, Patten's popularity reached its nadir. It came down to 56 per cent from 65 per cent a year earlier. His annual government report satisfaction rating went down from 42 per cent in October 1992 to 22 per cent in 1993. Popular satisfaction rating on his constitutional reform remained at about 26 per cent and 10 per cent of the respondents expressed dissatisfaction. However, an overwhelming 65 per cent of them had no opinion on his reform.[44] Much of his difficulty with the public was related to his adverse relations with China which had no trust in him at all. The advisability of setting a deadline to the fruitless Beijing talks was to be the major topic of the next British cabinet meeting on 10 November 1993, at which Patten would give his evaluation of the talks and plead for undivided support.

The thirteenth round took place on 11–12 October, again with no result achieved. China, however, was willing this time to separate the 1994 district and the municipal-urban regional election arrangements in 1994 from those concerning the LEGCO election in 1995. Governor Patten, too, supported Foreign Minister Qian Qichen's suggestion to discuss the 1994 local election separately at the fourteenth round of talks. Furthermore, on 15 October 1993, one of the vice chairmen of the National People's Congress revealed to members of the Hong Kong visiting municipal delegation that the 1994-elected members of the District Boards and the Municipal Councils would have fewer difficulties riding the 'through train' beyond 1997. However, he also said that Mr Patten should not create more changes such as unilaterally abolishing the appointed council members and suddenly increasing the elected members in the LEGCO to 30, or increasing the number of foreign judges of the Court of Final Appeal after 1997. If Britain did not make these sudden changes, in clear violation of the Basic Law, all other minor matters could be solved easily. Lu Ping was ready to talk about the 1994 election voting age, the 'single vote and single member constituency', and whether or not to keep the 'appointed seats'. The British, in response, suddenly were prepared to cooperate and to accept the power of the Preparatory Committee 'to confirm' later on the 'through train' for the 1995 elected members of the LEGCO.[45]

The issue that divided them, in the last analysis, was Britain's rejection of the Chinese claim of its violation of the three agreements. Legal experts of the British Foreign Office testified in Parliament in November 1993 against Beijing's claim. China could not abandon its demand that Britain return to all three agreements. Without such 'claim of violation' Beijing could not later have the legal right to condemn Britain and to dissolve the LEGCO on 1 July 1997. Therefore, the last several rounds of talks were again a sheer waste of time. To spare Governor Patten's timetable for reform, Britain gave up the talks after the seventeenth round. The termination was later described as follows:

> China so far has been able to sit back and let Britain water down its own proposals while giving nothing in return . . . If there is no through-train beyond 1997 and no cooperation on practical matters in the Joint Liaison Group the chances of a smooth transition to Chinese rule are drastically diminished. Stability and prosperity in Hong Kong will be undermined.[46]

On 25 November 1993, three days before the termination of the talks, China's *Wen Hui Bao* in Hong Kong summarized the blame in its editorial as follows:

1. Governor Patten had no right to interfere in Sino-British negotiation. He now demanded termination of the talks.

This is sheer confrontation ... Smooth transition is
sacrificed in his official gamble.

2. Governor Patten 'has no right' to terminate the talk
   on behalf of the British government which alone has
   dealt legally with China.
3. He has claimed 'in the name of the people' to stop
   appointing members to district boards. However, we
   all know that 18 out of 19 district boards are on record
   opposed to his action. More than 100 district board
   members have signed the petition to express their
   opposition.
4. Many people have supported the Chinese suggestion
   to make arrangements first for the 1994 district-muni-
   cipal election. Now Governor Patten is threatening to
   terminate the Beijing talks; he claimed a lack of time
   to talk further, even to settle minor problems.[47]

On the eve of the seventeenth round of talks, Deputy
Director Wang Qiren told a visiting delegation from Hong
Kong on 24 November that, without convergence on the
three agreements, he did not know how they could be as-
sured that sovereign transfer would be certain to take place
on 1 July 1997. If the Basic Law is violated, he said, how
can there be a through train? If the mutually agreed Sino-
British understanding set forth in the seven letters is abandoned, what can be the purpose of meaningful negotiation?
Mr Wang finally asked Britain to negotiate faithfully at the
seventeenth round.[48] To China's disappointment, Governor
Patten declared his intention to submit a portion of his election draft bill on reform to the LEGCO and thus both sides
called off the talks on 27 November. Some of the Hong
Kong delegates to the National People's Congress and members of the Preparatory Working Committee were angry and
condemned Governor Patten's action. They held him responsible for breaking up the talks in Beijing. *Wen Hui Bao*
in its editorial blamed the governor:

> Britain was determined not be constrained by the diplo-
> matic talks. Diplomatic talks were designed to deceive China
> and to prolong the time to deceive the Hong Kong me-
> dia ... Patten yet still pretends he does not abandon the
> negotiation.[49]

The *People's Daily* described in detail how China had gone round after round to persuade the British to return to the three agreements. For many days, pro-China media attacked Patten for his deception of the people. And yet the governor still insisted he was committed to the talks. Lu Ping reminded Qian Gufung, a visiting Executive Council member of the Hong Kong government, that Britain was fully aware that whenever Patten's draft bill on reform was introduced in the LEGCO, it would signal Britain's unilateral termination of the negotiation. However, we believe that Beijing's own strategy was to procrastinate in order to force Britain to compromise under pressure of time. Patten understood this well, as is evident from his remark in July about China's immovable position on the governor's unilateral timetable. On the other hand, Michael Sze, Constitutional Affairs Director of the Patten administration, a frequent attendant at the talks in Beijing and a participant at the November cabinet meeting in London, was genuinely optimistic on the resumption of the talks. There was still enough time for diplomatic maneuver by either side before Patten formally introduced his draft bill on reform 15 December. However, neither side moved.

UNILATERAL ESTABLISHMENT OF THE 'SECOND STOVE'

The day after Governor Patten's 1992 reform speech, Lu Ping began to warn repeatedly about China's unilateral implementation of the three agreements. However, Beijing proceeded rather timidly and in measured pace. It recruited in stages three types of pro-China Hong Kong leaders: members of the newly created Preparatory Working Committee, Hong Kong Affairs Advisers, and District Affairs Advisers. In addition, the New China News Agency seemed to have become the commanding headquarters, or Beijing's 'shadow government'. The PWC, formally called into existence in July 1993, consisted of 27 members from China and 30 from Hong Kong. Foreign Minister Qian Qichen was appointed its chairman. It was not 'the second stove' nor 'the second authority' in Hong Kong, as clearly declared by the National

People's Congress. Beijing justified PWC's necessity on the grounds of British violation of treaties and the lack of co-operation from Britain. The PWC was to work diligently on policy study, on methods of selecting the first Chief Executive before 1 July 1997, and on the need to create a Provisional Legislative Council to replace the LEGCO. Upon the formation of the Preparatory Committee in early 1996 as called for by the Basic Law, the PWC, which had no standing in either the Joint Declaration or the Basic Law, would be dissolved. Director Zhou Nan of the NCNA in Hong Kong, who is also a member of the Standing Committee of the National People's Congress, made clear that the PWC would deal with different transfer issues and that its creation should in no way affect the Sino-British talks after April 1993.[50] The mainland members of the PWC were heads or deputy heads and high level policy-making and policy-implementing leaders in the following categories:

Foreign Ministry	4
Hong Kong and Macao Affairs Office	4
NCNA Hong Kong Office	4
Standing Committee of the NPC	2
Former Mainland Basic Law drafters	6

PWC members from Hong Kong are:

Representing Hong Kong at the eight NPC	5
Representing Hong Kong at the CPPCC	10
Former Basic Law Drafters	12
Newly named Hong Kong Affairs Advisers	4
Current members from the LEGCO (pro-China)	4
Former members of both LEGCO and Executive Council	6
Representing farm population	1[51]

Many of them wore several hats, but the total was still 57 and those from Hong Kong were also Hong Kong Affairs Advisers.

None were included from the United Democrats. The then Vice Chancellor (head) of the University of Hong Kong was excluded because he once voted against Premier Li Peng at the National People's Congress. The Preparatory Working Committee has had great influence in Beijing and among

the Hong Kong population. All members of the PWC (Preparatory Working Committee) were also appointed, in December 1995, members of the Preparatory Committee, which
is authorized by the Basic Law to organize the first SAR
Government before 1 July 1997. Upon their appointment
Lu Ping immediately declared that Britain should not meddle
in the PWC's activities, to avoid interfering in China's future
domestic affairs. Any such interference would be totally ineffective. At the same time, the Chinese Foreign Ministry announced that the PWC would not interfere in Hong Kong
affairs. The PWC held its first meeting in Beijing on 15 July
1993. Labor leader Tam Y. Chang (also a member of the
LEGCO) asked for a policy to define the criteria for elected
and appointed officials to ride the 'through train' beyond
1997. On the other hand, Li Fook-sean (Simon Li) revealed
before the meeting that four current LEGCO members would
not be permitted to ride the 'through train': Martin Lee,
Szeto Hua, Christine Loh Kung-wai and Emily Lau.[52] The
next day the PWC announced the formation of five sub-
groups, each focusing on a different one of the following
five areas: political, economic, legal, cultural, and social and
security. Each subgroup had two co-chairpersons, one from
Hong Kong and the other from China. Some members, such
as Liberal Party leader Allen Lee, were eager to see the PWC
work with a high degree of openness. He was, of course,
disappointed. On 1 September 1993, the political subgroup
met to discuss the creation of the PC in 1996, the organization of the Provisional Legislative Council to replace the
LEGCO, and the need to maintain Hong Kong's 'executive-
directed government'. The cultural subgroup met on 16
September and agreed, first of all, to maintain the existing
liberal-plural existing cultural tradition in Hong Kong. After
all, an ideological socialist culture, under 'one country, two
systems', cannot be introduced to Hong Kong. The pro-China
leader of the Democratic Alliance for the Betterment of Hong
Kong frankly admitted at the meeting that in theory 'human rights' concerns should take precedence over domestic
constitutional matters, because these were serious problems
in the relation between human rights and the Basic Law
and also between current Hong Kong law and the Human
Rights Covenant. These problems would require earnest

discussion.[53] Together, these study groups were watching to see if the Sino-British diplomatic talks would succeed or fail. What transpired would instantly influence their study and their reports at the future plenary meeting. Indeed, the serious work began with new momentum only after the breakdown of the diplomatic talks. On 9 December 1993, the PWC members at their second plenary meeting listened to an analysis from its Chairman Qian Qichen on their future work. He cited the need to follow the *Selected Works of Deng Xiaoping*, Volume 3, on how to deal with Hong Kong before and after 1997. He urged them to work to ensure 'smooth transition' and to 'take to heart' the concerns of the Hong Kong people.[54]

In short, all these second-stove appointees at each of the three tiers were carefully selected. Many, probably, worked hard behind the scenes to get such appointments. The jobs conferred new status, new influence and fresh promise for future promotions. All are working explicitly or implicitly under the local NCNA, which itself has been a huge well-organized bureaucracy of more than a thousand salaried Beijing appointees, divided into dozens of departments and subunits. Without this elaborate 'shadow system', there is no way for Beijing to achieve 'smooth transition' after the seventeenth round of talks.

On the other hand, this 'non-second power center', as claimed in Beijing, has been an effective reminder that the Chinese population in Hong Kong would remain divided and acrimonious, manipulated and frustrated as they went through the 1994–95 major elections. The majority of the people in Hong Kong had always been privately governed by their own sense of fair play and balance. They acknowledge themselves as Chinese or Cantonese who have millions of close relatives on the other side of the border. The British did not always treat them as real equals for the 150 years, or let them enjoy the degree of democracy and human rights that Governor Patten claims to be fighting for on their behalf. Optimistically, the Hong Kong people hope to receive the best of both worlds from London and Beijing. But they were disappointed in 1984, 1988, and 1990 when the direct election postponement and the many ambiguous provisions in the Basic Law were making their destiny less certain. Most of the people could not afford to emigrate. Britain would not give them new citizenship and the right of abode. Some emigrated elsewhere on their own but have since returned for better opportunities still existing only in Hong Kong. They have suffered and felt betrayed. The irony of such betrayal has been that both Britain and China have fought for 'the hearts and minds' of the Hong Kong people. Britain has now reached its sundown. What does the sunrise promise?[55]

THE PREPARATORY COMMITTEE AND EARLY 'SECOND STOVE' IMPLEMENTATION BY THE HONG KONG AND MACAO OFFICE

In Chapter 5, we described the British frustration at complying with the Joint Declaration and the Basic Law. We can condense our description here of Beijing's similar unilateral frustration and performance. During the 17 rounds of talks, China was ignoring Patten and stonewalling his reform. Since the spring of 1996, Beijing has been requesting cooperation from the Hong Kong government for assistance in media time, meeting space, and so on. We find that the Patten government was merely providing China with whatever it deemed minimally necessary. Two great nations are playing politics unilaterally at the Hong Kong people's expense. The Hong Kong people are currently rating and judging the promises of high autonomy, preservation of lifestyle, and 'Hong Kong people governing Hong Kong' for 50 years without changes under 'one country, two systems', which are not yet fully charted.

China's unilateral implementation is being carried out by the Preparatory Committee established by the National People's Congress. The PC exercises its authority under the NPC and its major task is to establish the first HKSAR government. This includes the responsibility to form a Selection Committee which in turn is to recommend (no election) a candidate for the future Chief Executive to the central government for appointment; and to prescribe the specific method for forming the first Legislative Council. Due to the stalemate in political reform negotiations between China and

Britain, the NPC is giving the PC the additional responsibility for creating a temporary legislative council. The latter, as mentioned above, is not mentioned in any previous agreements or understanding between China and Britain.

The PC is also dealing with other outstanding issues relating to Hong Kong. As it now stands, 'the through train'[56] is likely to carry the District Board members and other officials to 1999. It also seems less controversial to carry the urban and municipal elected members by the through train to 1999 and beyond. It is, however, at the 'high tier' level, that we see greater conflicts of interest including issues of loyalty, right of permanent residency, HKSAR passport after 1997, foreign civil service officials and their localization, and so on.[57] These issues too, are slowly receiving answers from China.[58] Here we will focus on the politics of the selection methods for members of the Selection Committee to be established by the PC. In April 1996 Director Lu Ping of the Hong Kong and Macao Office (HKMAO) came to Hong Kong to consult personally and to conduct the group-by-group consultation on issues relating to future Chief Executive and Provisional Legislative Council selection. These tasks had to be completed in 1996 to enable, for example, the Chief executive to prepare his team for takeover on 1 July 1997. The following pages will describe Beijing's unilateral process and the difficulties it encountered.

After the 17 September 1995 LEGCO election, the bulk of Patten's implementation was largely completed. Beijing had the advantage of deciding what to reject and what to compromise with. By November 1995 word was out that the PC would have 90 members from Hong Kong and 60 from China. All 70 PWC members would be included. The PC would be more liberal than the PWC by including many elected LEGCO liberal members. Widely separated political parties would be invited to join the PC to placate internal conflicts in Hong Kong.[59] One week later, in December 1995, it was learned that Beijing no longer required the practice of collective responsibility on PC decision-making. That is, negative voices were allowed and unanimity was not necessary. Frederick Fung Kin-kee (Frederick Fun) was invited to be a PC member. Head of the Alliance for Democracy and the People's Livelihood (ADPL), Mr Fung insisted that he would join only if the PC (1) invited all parties; (2) allowed ADPL members in the PC to speak and vote their own judgment; and (3) operated in high transparency to allow citizens to read and hear what the PC was doing. On the other hand, there were small groups of people in Hong Kong protesting against not using popular election to determine PC members. On 21 December 1995, the National People's Congress received a list of 150 names (94 from Hong Kong and 56 from China) for approval, which it granted a week later. Among those from Hong Kong, business and industry took 34; professional and educators 33; religion, rural affairs, and so on, 16; and for those in the political field, 11.[60] On 26 December, Beijing made public both the entire rostrum and Qian Qichen's PWC work report. The list was not received in Hong Kong with accolades. Complaints were registered against heavy representation by rich merchants. Meanwhile, Premier Li Peng and Foreign Minister Qian, who is also the chairman of the PC, urged all 150 members to carry out 'one country, two systems'. All must at all times remember to 'love China and love Hong Kong'. Their speeches were echoed at the conclusion of the first PC meeting in Beijing.[61] Three weeks later when complaints continued against the 'black box secrecy' of the PC deliberations, Lu Ping finally gave in and the PC proceedings have since become open to the media.[62]

Since Beijing has ruled out elections in Hong Kong, Beijing depends now on a wide scope of popular consultation to select members of the temporary legislature and chief administrators. Such consultations did not get off the ground until April 1996. Lu Ping and his deputy director, Wang Qiren, came to Hong Kong for them. The people of Hong Kong have been, of course, long divided over the issue of popular election versus prearranged consultation. Genuine 'Hong Kong people governing Hong Kong', as promised in the Sino-British agreement and the Basic Law, has been accepted literally by many. Some of them in April 1996 were protesting at every place where Lu Ping went. They were waiting at the airport when his plane arrived. A brawl between protesters and policemen took place around his automobile. While consultation was under way later inside a huge hall, protesters were shouting in the street outside. They waited for his departure at the airport only to find that he had left by other means.

In direct contrast were those Chinese patriots who welcomed the opportunity for consultation to speak out in favor of Hong Kong and for China against Governor Patten and Britain. For many of them Hong Kong's return to China after more than a century and a half was exciting. In less than ten months they would be able to practice self-government as a part of China. For many other people the return to China would be full of reflection in personal memory no matter what 'the two systems' will eventually become.

As a general trend, as time draws near for the transfer, there are popular signs of emotional-psychological shifts in the favor shown by the general population toward China. According to polling by Baptist University's 'Transition Project', the result is as follows. Among 628 interviewees:

1. Forty-six per cent were happy to see Hong Kong as a part of China. Compared with the results of the past three years, this was the first time those who wished to return constituted a majority. In 1993, 42 per cent were willing to join China.
2. Those wishing Hong Kong to be independent were 14 per cent, compared with 25 per cent for 1993. This was a big decline.
3. Those who considered themselves 'Chinese of China' amounted to 33 per cent, an increase of 11 per cent compared with 1993.
4. Those who considered themselves 'Hong Kong Chinese' equaled 28 per cent, a decline of 8 per cent, compared with 1993.
5. Those calling themselves simply 'Hong Kongese' equaled 35 per cent, the same as in 1993.
6. Those ethnic Chinese calling themselves 'Hong Kong British' were 5 per cent, down from 12 per cent in 1994.[63]

In addition, Hong Kong is now thought more safe and secure than before by foreign companies. According to the Industrial Commission statistics of the Hong Kong government, overseas (foreign) companies continued to set up Asian-Pacific regional offices here in 1995. More local offices for

Southeast Asia were established in 1995 than in 1994. More foreign investors or company administrators have greater confidence in Hong Kong's future prosperity after 1997 than at any previous time.[64] Peaceful transition and China's own continuing investment in Hong Kong, and the expected future strong Chief Executive with unified support from Hong Kong business tycoons will, no doubt, encourage investors everywhere. There is today a 'reduced' British governor and a liberal 'fighting' LEGCO. Both of them hope to block the establishment of a provisional legislature. They hope a pro-democratic and popular Chief Executive will soon emerge to protect Hong Kong's interest.

In short, among the population, especially with younger people, there is an increase in shared 'common Chinese national consciousness'. Youth groups in Hong Kong in the spring of 1996 requested the Chinese University in the New Territories to conduct a survey. The result of 1034 telephone interviews by random samples of people from age 18 to 40 indicates that respondents were able to point out the ethnic characteristics of the Chinese nations. China's long history and culture got positive accolades. Seventy-three per cent of the interviewees are proud of being Chinese; 85 per cent acknowledge the Chinese people's industriousness and economic competitive capacity; 63 per cent believed that problems concerning unification with Macao, Taiwan and Hong Kong are purely within China's domestic sovereignty and should be left for the Chinese to decide themselves. Finally, 87.6 per cent asked for increased curriculum in education to allow youth to know more Chinese history and culture.[65]

In conclusion, in spite of small crowds demonstrating on the street in April 1996 in Hong Kong, the general atmosphere and popular trends, as we have been able to observe, have been positive toward Beijing-guided unilateral implementation. More such protests may occur whenever a liberal-democratic cause can be advanced. No one is able to anticipate what may happen during the early decades after 1997. However, nothing will be allowed to disrupt the basic stability and prosperity of Hong Kong.

THE PROVISIONAL LEGISLATURE AND ITS CONSULTATION

On procedure, the Preparatory Committee must first decide whether or not to adopt the PWC recommendation to create a Provisional Legislature (PL). Attorney Lau Yaochu, an NPC member from Hong Kong, warned in March 1996 that if the PC adopted the PWC recommendation to create a PL, it would constitute an act worse than violating the Basic Law. It would have 'burned the Basic Law'. Miss Lau acknowledges the constitutional power of the PC to adopt the PWC recommendation. However, to do so is a misuse of its power because when the NPC established the PWC in 1993 it mentioned nothing about creating a Provisional Legislature in 1997. If the PC is now eager to adopt the PWC recommendation, the PC must also make laws to delineate the structure, working procedure and scope of its power. She argued that the Provisional Legislature cannot legislate for itself. Neither the PC nor the NPC has power to legislate for the Hong Kong Special Administrative Region.[66]

On 20 March, the PC's temporary legislative subgroup in Beijing met and adopted the PWC's recommendation. Thus, legally this decision converged with the decision made by the Standing Committee of the NPC of August 1994, which says that the three-tier government in Hong Kong should cease to exist on 30 June 1997. According to the PWC, the PL will have 60 members, who will be recommended by the new 400-member Selection Committee. Questions may arise over the PL's legality, representativeness and authority. Such questions were, indeed, raised during the consultation. On 25 March 1996, the overseas edition of the *People's Daily* provided the full official legal defense for the PL.[67]

Foreign Minister Qian Qichen, who is also the Chairman of the PC and a Vice Premier of the Central Government, spoke on 24 March at the PC meeting. He said that the Western model of democracy does not meet the interests of classes in Hong Kong. Western democracy is 'not conducive to stability and prosperity'. Therefore, it should not be 'blindly applied'.[68] One week later, 26 members of the LEGCO from downtown Hong Kong marched to the head office of the NCNA in opposition to creating a Provisional Legislature and delivered a signed letter to Chairman Qian Qichen of the PC. Among the 26 members, 19 were from the Democratic Party. Others included veteran legislator Emily Lau, Christine Loh, and Vice-Chairman Yeung Sum of the Democratic Party, who spoke for the group and complained that the creation of a PL by non-elective method is a 'violation of the Joint Declaration, and the Basic Law . . . an insult to "Hong Kong people governing Hong Kong" and to a "high degree of autonomy"'.[69] On 2 April 1996 Governor Patten, in response to the PC request for full cooperation, spoke of his government's complete cooperation on three conditions, namely, (1) cooperation be based on the Joint Declaration and the Basic Law; (2) no harm be done to the morale and integrity of the civil servants; and (3) until 1 July 1997, only his government be in charge of Hong Kong.[70] The governor further declared that he would not do anything 'to undermine the legality and authority of the LEGCO'. Because the LEGCO was elected by the people, to abolish it, Beijing should provide convincing explanations to the people. Whether Beijing, too, has committed 'three violations' of the Joint Declaration, the Basic Law and the authority of the National People's Congress is now a popular topic of conversation in Hong Kong. One well-known author writing in *World Journal* on 7 April 1996, explained in detail that Basic Law Articles 66, 68 and 69, were compromised. Beijing, he explained, over-extended NPC's power in violation of Articles 70 and 71 of the Chinese Constitution.[71] Governor Patten, speaking on 11 April from London said that Prime Minister Major was opposed to the PL and his government would resist such a body for the next 400 days.[72] Current developments in Hong Kong confirm that the people in the street, officials in the civil service, political parties and legislators have all been involved in the debate over creation of the PL.

There were different voices eager to be invited during the 13 and 14 April consultation on two topics: the organization of the provisional legislature and the organization of the Selection Committee. Participation was by invitation only. Each person was allowed only three to five minutes to state his/her position. Such consultations took place at various places and were attended by over 600 delegates representing various organizations. These speakers were eager to compete for seats on the 400-member Selection Committee. They realized that competition would be keen, because the number invited from a given profession depended on the total number of people in that field. The most controversial comments were made in the area of politics and administration in government. Serious disagreements were voiced. For example, Allen Lee of the Liberal Party preferred to 'compress and narrow' the number of people to be invited to speak. He suggested that speakers should be limited to 'former unofficials' of both Executive-Legislative Councils. The huge number of civil servants, therefore, would be excluded. Speakers from education and human resources areas, however, were opposed to denying invitations to former civil servants as soon as they have left office. Most speakers on the first day came from the huge commercial organizations, local Chambers of Commerce, realty groups, construction units, the import-export trade, wholesale-retail associations and the tourist industry. Speakers from the financial and industrial area insisted that a much larger list than 400 names must be nominated by the PC for competition in the selection process. It was ironic that no one was invited to speak from the Democratic Party or from other liberal groups of the so-called politics-administration field. However, among only a few hundred 'Hong Kong Affairs Advisers', 88 were invited to participate on the first day of consultation. Current and former officials of both Executive and Legislative branches of all three tiers had only 18 invited participants. When speakers at the consultation asked why members of the Democratic Party and other current leaders in the LEGCO and other groups had not been invited, no one replied. By inference, the list of invitations had been prearranged and consented to by the PC long in advance.[73]

At the end of the second consultation day, the nominations committee subgroup of the PC met at the Hong Kong NCNA office to hold a discussion. They wished to hear from members who represented Hong Kong in the NPC and the Chinese People's Political Consultative Conference (CPPCC) in Beijing on how to organize the 400-member committee to produce the future Chief Executive and future members of the provisional legislature. From the performance of the two-day 'democratic' consultation, it is not difficult for any observer to conclude that the prospect for Hong Kong's autonomy after 1997 is not very optimistic. One media commentator made the following evaluation:

> The Preparatory Committee's two-day public consultation game play was not satisfactory at all. The game play did not receive a good score from the general public. Nor did it succeed to isolate the opponents. It simply ended in a dull performance which has further galvanized the public into greater dissatisfaction. From all random street opinion polls, not a single interviewee supported the creation of a provisional legislature to replace the elected LEGCO ... The Communist government insisted on public consultation game play and yet refused to provide a fair hearing to their opponents ... Even the appearance of Hong Kong people governing Hong Kong will disappear.[74]

When university students were not allowed to speak and were forced out of the room, they quickly called it 'false consultation, true dictatorship'. Outside the room, members of the teacher's union simply quietly conducted a sit-in. Meanwhile, Governor Patten came to the aid of the protesters. He emphasized that Hong Kong is a 'free and open society'. He was concerned that the pro-democracy leaders who represent 70 per cent of the Hong Kong people were not invited to participate in consultation. For 50 hours there were some twenty 'fasting protesters' including three LEGCO members who were carried by automobile to wherever Lu Ping was. To the PC's ten requests for cooperation, the Patten government responded that it would 'cooperate well on most of the ten requested areas. However, the Hong Kong government would not, in principle, allow the provisional legislature to function in Hong Kong before 1 July 1997 ... Hong Kong has its elected LEGCO, and to do otherwise would violate paragraph 4 of the Joint declaration'.[75] Patten's government insisted that two legislatures at the same time would lead to instability and confusion among the civil servants.

Responding to Patten's concern, PC chairman Qian Qichen said three weeks later that the provisional legislature had to start to work before 1 July and that its laws would not be applied until after the transfer. The NCNA deputy director

Zhang Junsheng insisted that the Hong Kong government should keep its promise of cooperation, including providing a place for the provisional legislature to meet. Beijing will, no doubt, retain the British legal system but not those controversial political by-laws which had not been part of the past British practice in the court of law in Hong Kong. This includes, for example, Hong Kong's eleventh-hour adoption of the United Nations Human Rights covenant in 1991. Many party leaders and legislators in Hong Kong are aware that, in the final analysis, Patten only wishes to be very certain of the Beijing promise not to create a second power center before the transfer. Lately messages out of Beijing confirm that Lu Ping has decided that the Provisional Legislature can still be postponed and many of the current LEGCO members will soon be invited to join the new legislature.[76] This is a fresh policy compromise that all in Hong Kong hope to see officially confirmed in Beijing.

We conclude this discussion by emphasizing that the PL has become a symbolic provocation which hurts, humiliates and antagonizes some 80 per cent of Hong Kong's population. To replace a popularly elected LEGCO violates their minimal degree of autonomy. Beijing has been caught in the dilemma of getting rid of anti-Beijing forces on the one hand, and expanding popular support on the other. On the PL issue, all Hong Kong professionals are united in opposition. Lu Ping's 'consultation trip' to Hong Kong should be an eye-opener for him. It is time for China to act in accord with the true feeling of the majority of the people who have never so determinedly opposed any other issue. All said, we tend to believe that the transition will be relatively smooth. Beijing will make more genuine concessions to win back popular support for the historic change on 1 July 1997. For example, more new promises on the 'through train' will be made to civil servants.[77] The new PL is not likely to be so different in personnel from the current LEGCO. And Lu Ping appears ready to make the PL more acceptable to the majority of people once the British are gone.[78] PC Chairman Qian Qichen has often reaffirmed his commitment to carry out Deng Xiaoping's broad policy goals not to change Hong Kong's internal system. Again, Lu Ping announced recently that after 1997 Hong Kong Chinese will find traveling abroad much easier than at present and that all Chinese in Hong Kong holding foreign passports will still be legally considered Chinese if they so desire.[79] When Britain is effectively neutralized by the approaching date of transfer, the Beijing leadership and the Hong Kong people will probably find a new spirit of cooperation. After all, they are committed to a common purpose: the continuation of stability and the growth of prosperity. One professor of the Economics Department of the Beijing University recently proclaimed a list of '10 new opportunities' for economic expansion in Hong Kong after the transfer in 1997.[80] All Chinese people in Hong Kong are likely to be excited about these ten new opportunities that may transform Hong Kong into an even stronger economic power. Lately Beijing has increasingly dealt directly with official Hong Kong representatives. For example, Chief Secretary Chan Fang On-Sang's official visit to Beijing in April 1996 was a clear indication of China's abandonment of its strategy of downplaying Hong Kong's official status in direct Beijing–Hong Kong negotiation. From now on there will be more such new 'Sino-Hong Kong' internal contacts for harmony under 'one country, two systems'.

POLITICS OF CHIEF EXECUTIVE SELECTION

Article 43 of the Basic Law makes the Chief Executive the head of the government accountable to the central government. Article 45 describes the Chief Executive's selection 'by election or through consultations held locally and . . . appointed by the Central People's Government'. Article 45 goes on to say: 'the method of selecting the Chief Executive shall be specified in the light of the actual situation . . . and in accordance with the principle of gradual and orderly progress. The ultimate aim is the selection of the Chief Executive by universal suffrage upon nomination by a broadly representative nominating committee in accordance with democratic procedures.'

Who the first Chief Executive will be has been the subject of profound interest among all groups and political parties. Beijing has intentionally dropped hints about possible candidates in order to stimulate the media to make guesses. Chief Secretary of Civil Service Chan Fang On-Sang was the first to be labeled as a potential contender. By December 1995, business tycoons were quite open in talking about their favorite. President Jiang Zemin of China met several potential contenders to learn their views on the '97 transition'. The HKMAO director, Lu Ping, hinted at a dark-horse appointee. Well-informed recent sources from Beijing indicated that Chan Fang On-Sang 'is not likely' to be the first Chief Executive. China has since early 1994 made it known that who the future Chief Executive will be would be relevant to the Sino-British cooperation and Hong Kong–Beijing relations after the transfer. Business tycoons now publicly support candidates from their own ranks because, as they see the future, Hong Kong will 'not be a political city. It will be an economic city.' On candidate's qualifications, Lu Ping has suggested, among others: 'attractive personality, moral integrity, unsuspiciousness, and ability to serve the people'. Two of the wealthy potential candidates suggested have been Dong Jianhua and Wu Kuang-Zheng, son-in-law of the late Y.K. Pai of Shanghai.[81] Wu graduated from Columbia University and has wide contacts in Washington, DC.

Dong Jianhua has since January 1996 remained the consistent front runner for the Chief Executive's post. His close relations with Taiwan are considered a critical factor in his favor. Dong is a member of the Executive Council of Patten's government, a member from the Hong Kong area in the CPPCC and a PC member. He has almost exactly the same qualifications as Wu Guang-Zheng.[82] Dong was born in 1938 in Shanghai. His father was a shipping industry tycoon. Young Jianhua was educated in Britain. In 1992 he was tapped by Governor Patten to enter the Executive Council. He is the only leader who has good working experience with Taiwan and Beijing, as well as inside the Hong Kong government. Besides the above three contenders so far, a heavyweight PC member, S.Y. Chung, recently leaked the information that there may be eight contenders being considered. All may be recommended by the 400-member Selection Committee.[83] Allen Lee, Chairman of the Liberal Party with a strong business background, suggested in April 1996 that not until September or later will the decision on the first

Chief Executive be made. He said also that the Provisional Legislature would not be organized before December 1996. More recently the Overseas Edition of the Beijing *People's Daily* gave Dong Jianhua a publicity boost in all major foreign languages. However, a great deal still depends on how peaceful and stable the transition will be between now and early 1997. All three candidates so far mentioned will undoubtedly play a major role after 1997.

CONCLUSION

We must give credit to the British for leaving behind a fairly good system of government, a free press, a competitive experience of free enterprise, and a strong tradition of law and order. We still may raise the question of why Britain had felt it necessary to introduce a representative form of government. If reforms had been absolutely needed, why did the British Hong Kong government fail to pursue election reforms harder in the 1970s and 1980s? These questions are raised because we believe Britain's weakness in dealing diplomatically with China in the 1980s should have warned London to restrain its ambition in the 1990s by not pursuing at that time what it had not wanted to achieve in preceding decades. London should have gone along in the 1990s with whatever the Hong Kong Chinese people could or could not do for themselves. However, it failed to pursue this sensible course expected of it by Beijing. As a result, China became angry and suspicious of the British because of Patten's perceived arrogance and his strategy which left no room for negotiation. Governor Patten should have realized that China would not permit his reform to succeed at Beijing's expense. China went along with the 17 rounds of talks because it did not wish to antagonize the Hong Kong people further. It is clear, then, that what Britain achieved between 1992 and 1995 could easily be lost after 1997, given the nature of leadership in Beijing and the control of local politics under the Basic Law. We are, therefore, much inclined to conclude that former governors Murray MacLehose, David Wilson and Percy Cradock were more realistic and accurate in their effort to secure as much for democracy as they possibly could without creating a scene of crisis or a diplomatic breakdown.

The price China paid for not cooperating with Governor Patten was to raise grave doubts about the likelihood of 'smooth transition'. A new spirit of cooperation, however, is now being rapidly developed between the people of Hong Kong and the government of Beijing. The passage of time will gradually cure the unnecessary wounds inflicted between 1992 and 1997.

Beijing had no apology for its unilateralism. Ironically it now has a much freer hand and a better excuse to pursue policy goals than before. There are many realistic politicians and businesspeople in Hong Kong who will cooperate with Beijing. Indeed, the victims of Patten's reform have been several individuals and the Democratic Party under Martin Lee, Yeung Sum and Cheung Bing-Leung. Beijing is punishing them today for their cooperation with Patten and their strong stands on democracy and human rights.

Other Hong Kong leaders and most of the people had realized earlier that Beijing could not afford to let Patten succeed and to allow democracy in Hong Kong to be a challenge to communist survival in China. Hong Kong people's support of the pro-democracy movement in China in 1989 taught Beijing not to underestimate any potential threat. Beijing, therefore, has reasons to harden its anti-democratic position in order to prevent future 'turmoil' in Hong Kong. In short, Hong Kong's long-term dependency on its existence as a part of China has given Beijing much more freedom and flexibility in dealing with Patten. On the other hand, post-1997, Britain will still have good relations with the people of Hong Kong, who will, by a large majority, want to retain several of Britain's beneficial legacies, such as the English language, the cultural tradition, the Civil Service efficiency, and, most practical of all, the commercial relations and goodwill with all the Commonwealth nations of the United Kingdom. Beijing will still welcome British trade and investment in both Hong Kong and all parts of China.

All sides must have learned a valuable new lesson. The Patten reform taught all sides what can and cannot be done in a particular political environment. The power to control ensures the ability to bargain successfully. Ever since 1984

Britain has displayed skill in diplomacy, but she did not have the enduring power to control the political environment surrounding Hong Kong. The Patten reform has lifted popular political consciousness in Hong Kong and among its politicians. From now on, the communist leadership must learn how to deal with a well-educated population in Hong Kong.

7 Political Developments in Hong Kong

INTRODUCTION

The modern history of Hong Kong is full of irony and uniqueness.[1] Throughout Hong Kong, many Chinese were encouraged to go to the United States to become railroad builders and mining workers. As soon as the continental transpacific railroads had been completed, the United States government passed a Chinese Exclusion Act in 1882 to bar them from acquiring American citizenship. Today, the United States champions Hong Kong's human rights: the Congress passed a Hong Kong Act in 1991 against future human rights violations after 1997. Britain as colonial master was never able to win popular gratitude or even average respect from the Chinese population in Hong Kong. Today, Britain fights earnestly to leave an enduring democratic legacy before the return of sovereignty to the Chinese communist government.[2] There have been many such examples of irony. On the other hand, the Chinese and the British in Hong Kong can remember other unique and positive contributions that British Hong Kong has made toward twentieth-century revolutionary transformation in China. For example, Sun Yat-sen was educated in Hong Kong, where his secret bases for the 1911 revolution were allowed by the British government. During the Sino-Japanese war in late 1930s many patriotic Chinese intellectuals made their safe haven in Hong Kong. On the eve of the communist takeover in 1949 many communists and pro-communist intellectuals made the colony their temporary refuge from Nationalist persecution. Today's Hong Kong has emerged economically strong under the British, thanks to significant contributions from anti-communist Chinese from Kuangdong province and from the Shanghai coastal region. The colony's population in 1945 was barely half a million. Prosperity and stability in Hong Kong since the 1960s has clearly been the result of both the British

130

success in the art of good governing and the work ethic of the new emerging population in Hong Kong. The unique border security arrangement since 1949 between British Hong Kong and revolutionary China has been appreciated by both sides. The Sino-British bickering in the 1990s, in contrast to the continuing economic miracle of growth and prosperity in Hong Kong, cannot be correctly or fully understood and adequately appreciated unless its many-faceted aspects are investigated and explained. Such an explanation may help to reduce misunderstanding and misplaced blame over Hong Kong's return to China and over the unique handling of the transfer since 1982 and especially after 1989.[3]

The people of Hong Kong have not been able to acquire a voice on their own behalf. They were never given a fair opportunity to develop experience in political participation and self-government. Today they suffer from lack of self-identity as an 'autonomous' new political community. The historical factors that have contributed to this unique phenomenon of transition can be quickly reviewed. Such a review may provide a balanced perspective on the on-going changes affecting Hong Kong in recent years.[4]

To begin with the history in the 1840s, Hong Kong was not 'a fishing village' as British historians often preferred to call it when Britain first occupied it. The entire area, on the contrary, was quite well-developed in population density and local government control. Later, in 1898, Britain forced China to lease to her the New Territories. By then the Manchu government in Beijing and the Chinese people in the area finally came to realize that the 'gunboat diplomacy' of 'British Imperialism' had succeeded at China's expense. Without the New Territories and Kowloon, Hong Kong would probably have been no more significant than little Macao, under Portuguese control since the 1530s. There was never an amiable relation between the Chinese and the British imperialists, who governed Hong Kong with a strong tint of racial superiority. The Chinese people, on the other hand, never lost their feeling of patriotic Chinese identity. In the 1920s and 1930s anti-British strikes were quite frequent. Not until 1967, when the 'Red Guard turmoil' in Hong Kong became a threat to British law and order, did the Hong Kong government realize the need to consult the local people for stronger community development. Not until the early 1980s was there a new and cooperative spirit between the local residents and their local level of government. This was the successful and well-known practice of 'government by consultation' under Governor Murray MacLehose. Britain did not allow meaningful election at any level of the colonial administration. The so-called 'un-officials' were generally the Chinese 'appointees' unilaterally chosen by the governor to window-dress the system. This practice was not eliminated until Governor Chris Patten's election reform in 1994–95. The point here is that the people of Hong Kong were never given a genuine chance to practice self-government. They did not, until recently, organize political parties or functional groups to compete in elections.

Why did the Chinese people, who were so highly educated, so willingly accept the British rule of autocracy? The answer is that there were often wars, droughts and revolutionary chaos in mainland China. Many people from Guangdong came to Hong Kong to escape poverty. Hong Kong was a good outlet to reach the outside world. Through Hong Kong the people from Guangdong left for America or Southeast Asia. Just to be able to come to Hong Kong was for many a rare opportunity for a better life. After the revolution of 1911, China again went through civil wars and warlordism. Hong Kong was again a safe place in the 1940s to escape to. However, the Japanese occupation of Hong Kong at that time forced patriotic Chinese to return to China to fight against Japanese aggression. The years following World War II found China in the renewed chaos of bitter civil war. Many Chinese, rich and poor alike, came to Hong Kong before 1949, and again after the Great Leap Forward in the 1950s. In short, British Hong Kong never escaped the misfortunes in China. The new wealth and prosperity in Hong Kong in the 1970s and 1980s are traceable to the influx of new refugees from the People's Republic of China. Without the efficient British control of the borders, many more millions of Chinese refugees would have crossed into Hong Kong. Had Britain failed to prevent the tides of incoming refugees, there would have been no standing space in Hong Kong. The remarkable ability of the British to use cheap labor and to manufacture for export trade was responsible for economic growth in Hong Kong. Maintaining law and order was in itself an unprecedented achievement. Britain governed well and made prosperity and stability possible in Hong Kong.[5]

This success story is the source of new problems now that the British must depart and Hong Kong Chinese must be governed under Chinese sovereignty. On the other hand, the communist government in China also has a great problem: it must now find a successful way to preserve Hong Kong's prosperity and stability and at the same time insulate itself from capitalist 'spiritual pollution' which, if not properly controlled, may spread anti-regime sentiment all over China. Therefore, all three, the British, the Communists and the Hong Kong people, must face the new reality. China wanted Hong Kong's economic investment and modern skill so it could reform itself. Unfortunately, the people of Hong Kong feared communism. And again, unfortunately, they were denied a direct voice in the negotiation in the 1980s and again in the 1990s. They trusted both Britain and China but were unable politically to demand anything from them. They were politically powerless even to express their feelings until the Tiananmen Square Incident in 1989 when they protested all over Hong Kong in support of democracy in China. Only after such demonstrations of 'people power' did the British and the Chinese government realize their own misjudgment and underestimation of what the Hong Kong people wanted and could do for themselves after 1997. Clearly, careful measures had to be taken to ensure a 'high degree of autonomy' and 'free life-style' as enshrined in the Joint Declaration of 1984. On the other hand, after the Tiananmen Incident, Britain, China and the international community were confronted with a new circumstance of crisis proportion. Mutual trust disappeared between Britain, China and the people of Hong Kong. Nearly all the major powers of the world condemned China for its military crackdown on student demonstrations in Beijing.[6] Suddenly a great many Western nations and Japan were very concerned about Hong Kong's future and human rights climate after 1997. Political developments there and the implementation of the Joint Declaration in Hong Kong became headline news in many countries. Under such watchful pressure, what could Britain

do? How should China respond? What really could be done
by the combined efforts of all the countries on behalf of
Hong Kong? Of course none could or would do much except Britain, China, and the people of Hong Kong themselves. Only they could avoid a transition crisis in Hong Kong:

1. The British. Did Britain seriously intend to introduce
   representative government to Hong Kong when the negotiation on sovereign transfer took place? Why was democratic reform not well specified in the Joint Declaration
   of 1984? Why did Britain renege on the scheduled 1988
   LEGCO election as promised in the earlier White Paper?
   Was Britain unduly encouraged by the Tiananmen crackdown and by the 1991 LEGCO election victory of the
   United Democrats of Hong Kong under Martin C.M. Lee?
   Why was Chris Patten authorized to implement an election plan without Beijing's prior agreement? The answers
   to these questions were not difficult to discover. Governor Patten's populist statesmanship changed much of
   the political climate in Hong Kong. On the other hand,
   his personal success immensely damaged Sino-British
   relations at Britain's expense. All in all, however, his
   positive contribution to democratic political development in Hong Kong is unquestionable.[7]
2. The Chinese. Why did Beijing deny the people of Hong
   Kong a direct voice in the early negotiation in 1982–4
   and during the 17 talks in 1993? The people resented
   both Beijing and London for excluding them. Why did
   China fail to learn later from opinion polls on what
   the people in Hong Kong thought and feared after
   the Tiananmen Incident? Why did Beijing prefer consultation, instead of popular referendum, on the Basic
   Law and popular election of the Chief Executive? Ex-
   cessive harshness in China's revenge against British
   unilateralism seems to have cost the people dearly in
   Hong Kong. Whatever the answers to such questions,
   China's own failure over convergence between the Joint
   Declaration and the Basic Law will still hurt the people
   in Hong Kong. Political interest groups and party development were deeply affected by the Sino-British
   stalemate.

3. The people of Hong Kong. They have always been, like other Chinese people all over the country, realistic and resigned to destiny. However, in the case of sovereignty transfer, they erred by misplacing their faith in the benevolence of Britain and China. Both have fought to win their hearts and minds. Neither appeared to have understood or even cared how they truly felt.

In 150 years, Britain had not prepared the people of Hong Kong to be self-governing. People were taught to be more concerned about 'stability and prosperity' than about politics and democracy, except for the rich few and the political activists who make up a small but influential minority. For a number of reasons, the Hong Kong people regret the British departure. However, they have not protested against reunification with China.[8] Because of this, external pressure for the rule of law, human rights and democracy in Hong Kong after 1997 may not have much impact on what will actually come to pass in Hong Kong after 1997. The majority of Hong Kong people will focus more on how China is transforming itself in relation to Hong Kong's quality of life and personal wealth. Politics may be the last thing in their minds. Those who cannot afford to emigrate will be prepared to endure whatever destiny brings to them. This philosophy of resignation, along with the influence of the deep-rooted Chinese cultural values and the pro-China patriotic nationalism endemic to Hong Kong, will work in China's favor.

Changes in political development in Hong Kong will largely depend on the degree to which Beijing organizes and guides and trusts the Hong Kong government. The support of business tycoons and the efficiency of the strong British civil service tradition will cooperate to retain 'life as usual'. Once the Hong Kong and Beijing governments have acquired a high degree of self- and mutual confidence, there will likely be greater autonomy and more freedom to make the co-existence of 'two systems' more acceptable to the people. This chapter will focus on discussions of political parties and individual leaders, the problems of political culture and political identity, the polling of public opinion, and finally the economic integration and democratization in Hong Kong.

POLITICAL PARTIES AND PARTY LEADERS

The goal of political parties is to win popular elections and to govern by making and implementing public policies. Britain never introduced popular elections and political parties in Hong Kong.[9] The people in Hong Kong never gave any thought to being independent after the British withdrew. They have lived in transition from one kind of crisis to another and have expected to return to their original homes in China.[10] For most people, politics and public life under the British were far removed from their day-to-day lives. Political parties might have started emerging had the British not canceled the 1988 popular election for the LEGCO. Other previous elections were local ones or, by law, allowed only those candidates representing functional constituencies.[11] For example, Martin Lee won a seat in the LEGCO to represent the legal profession. Others were invited by the governor to be appointed at various levels in the 'three tiers' of government, from district boards to regional and urban councils to, at the highest level, the LEGCO. In a real sense, all those appointees merely acted as pro-government advisers. Their majority decisions could be totally ignored by the governor, who alone acted legally and authoritatively on behalf of the Queen and her government in Britain.

The return of Hong Kong to China under the Joint Declaration is the new beginning of real politics and real party politics. The first political party in Hong Kong was organized in 1990 to compete in the first partial popular LEGCO election in the following year. It was formally named United Democrats of Hong Kong (UDHK) and remained under this name until May 1994, when the new name, Democratic Party (DP) was adopted after the merger with Meeting Point (MP). The DP has operated under the leadership of Martin Lee, Yeung Sum and Cheung Bing-leung, who are seriously committed to long-term democracy in Hong Kong in conjunction with gradual democratization in mainland China. Chairman Martin Lee and Szeto Hua of the DP are the best-known leaders among the public.[12] A more detailed introduction to the DP and its popular leaders may help illustrate the political mode and prospect in Hong Kong.

Martin Chu-min Lee (or Martin Lee or Martin C.M. Lee) was born in Hong Kong in 1938 during his parents' trip to the colony. At age 11 in 1949 he and his parents escaped to Hong Kong when the Communists took over China. Young Lee became a devoted Catholic while attending a parish school at age 14. He was later educated in Britain for a legal career. For three years he was the Hong Kong Bar president and its elected LEGCO member in 1985. In the same year Martin Lee was chosen by Beijing as a Basic Law drafter. His straight talk earned many trusted followers of his political position. He symbolizes democratic hope for Hong Kong and encourages his followers, many of whom are very religious, to be politically active citizens. Martin Lee seems possessed by his unshakeable faith in the rule of law to protect human liberty and free media. He views the rule of law as the only dependable sinew capable of binding the infrastructure of human relations in a well-organized society to which each citizen owes certain obligations. In a speech in 1986 he declared that Britain 'no longer can secure democracy for Hong Kong because to do so would invite Beijing's suspicion. We in Hong Kong must fight for our future. The present government is afraid and unwilling to take a stand on sensitive issues . . .'. He anchors his strength on support from public opinion through a free media in Hong Kong. Direct popular election for genuine democracy in Hong Kong is the 'bottom line' definition of 'one country, two systems'. This, to him, is the only guarantee for a 'high degree of autonomy'.[13] Lee's commitment to democracy is immitigable. He uses his legal practice income to pay his staff for political activities. Back in the 1980s he decided to remain in Hong Kong even though he has a British (BDTC) passport. However, he is not afraid to continue to fight for democracy after 1997. In an interview in 1994, he said:

> The imprisonment of Martin Lee by China could give the democratic movement a vital focus . . . If they were to lock me up that won't even be a bad thing for the cause. It might be an initial setback, but it may be a good thing. I am mentally prepared if that were to happen. My philosophy of life is that so long as I am still fighting for something, I have not failed. It is only when I give up

that I have failed. When I am fighting for democracy and human rights, these are universal values, I cannot be on the wrong side. This fight may not be over even when I die, but it does not mean I have failed. Other people will take over. Democracy will come to China.[14]

By early 1994, Martin Lee concluded that 'China wants to rule Hong Kong'. Under his leadership in the 1991 LEGCO election, his UDHK won 12 out of 18 seats in the popular vote. In the 1995 election, his Democratic Party won the largest number of seats, 20, in the 60-seat LEGCO, while most other candidates competed only in functional constituencies. With support from new members of the small parties and from independents, Lee's party is in control of 29–31 seats in the LEGCO.[15] He is considered 'the lightning rod of democracy in Hong Kong'. His future after the 1997 takeover by China is not easy to predict. In an interview he said of his future: 'It is not going to be my problem. It is going to be their problem. I shall stay here, and they will have to think of ways to get rid of me. I do not believe I will be put into prison, but the possibility is there.'[16]

The Vice Chairman, Yeung Sum, is a university lecturer and a former social work specialist. In the early 1990s, he was a member of the LEGCO. As a writer on social, political and cultural issues, he has been well known to common readers. Yeung explains in his book why he has entered politics. As a member of the newly educated elite at a time of 'decolonization of 150 years', he wants to seize this historic moment to dedicate himself to the mobilization of people to implement 'Hong Kong people governing Hong Kong' as promised in the Joint Declaration of 1984. He admits that his 'social conscience' compels him to devote himself to 'competitive democratic development in Hong Kong'. He believes in 'open politics and open competition among parties and concerning policy alternative'.[17]

The second Vice Chairman of the Democratic Party is Professor Cheung Bing-leung (Anthony Cheung), the Chairman of Meeting Point before and since the merger in May 1994 with the UDHK.[18] Meeting Point (MP) was one of the first parties in 1992 to echo Governor Patten's election reform, after being quite neutral in the Sino-British conflict on representative reform before the transfer in 1997. Anthony Cheung's enthusiasm in support of the Patten reform caused many MP senior members to withdraw their membership because of their personal opposition to this reform. Like the former UDHK and the current DP, MP was organized in 1983, in response to Beijing's proposition of 'one country, two systems', to work for a genuine emergence of democracy in Hong Kong after 1997. However, Cheung soon realized that democracy in Hong Kong could not easily be achieved and balanced, given the anti-democracy crackdown in 1989 and China's opposition to the Patten reform. Maintaining good working relations with China became progressively more difficult. By early 1994, MP was accused of being a 'subversive' party against China. This charge apparently contributed to the MP decision to merge with UDKH in order to become a new Democratic Party in May 1994.[19] Like Yeung Sum, Anthony Cheung has been an articulate politician who truly believes in post-colonial democracy in Hong Kong without much interference from China in Hong Kong's internal local affairs.

A fourth powerful individual of the new DP is Szeto Hua, who is equally supported and respected by voters and the media in general. An educator by profession, a former drafter of the Basic Law, and one of the ten popular members of the LEGCO, he has long been well known in Hong Kong. His political power and support have come from his Teachers' Union which he helped to organize and over which he has presided for many years. His popularity emerged in part from his leadership role in 1989 during the Tiananmen Square pro-democracy movement. Szeto organized the Hong Kong patriotic pro-student demonstrators into a permanent structure, Hong Kong People in Support of Patriotic Pro-democracy Movement in China (HKPSPPM). Since the spring of 1989, this organization has annually demonstrated in front of China's NCNA office against a variety of issues the group is opposed to. His movement group and the teachers' union, which has nearly 55 000 members, are both committed, under his firm leadership, to democracy in Hong Kong and in China as well.[20] He was ousted as a Basic Law drafter in 1989 because of his support of the anti-Beijing movement. As a third-term LEGCO member, Szeto Hua has a large listening audience when he speaks. He was born in Hong Kong in 1931. His family left there to return to Kuangdong when Japan occupied Hong Kong in 1942. After the war Szeto returned to Hong Kong in 1951 to become a school teacher. After 40 years in teaching, he retired in 1992 to devote all his time to social and political movements in Hong Kong. Because he has his own power base and is also an inspiring leader and legislator of the Democratic Party, he will remain powerful in the political life of Hong Kong.

These four top leaders of the largest party in Hong Kong, however, may find life after 1997 very difficult for them even though their party emphatically and truly represents the 'hearts and minds' of many voters. The party has stood firm, since its 1991 platform, on its long-term commitment to democracy in Hong Kong. It is committed to 'full accountability of all governmental units to the LEGCO'[21] and 'full popular universal elections' at all three levels as soon as possible. On the issue of Hong Kong–China relations, the party has urged that Hong Kong must retain 'the final decision-making power' on any question relating to the 'internal affairs of Hong Kong'. Internationally, the party urges all countries to 'formulate separate and comprehensive policies regarding their relations with Hong Kong'. Its position is firm on extensive 'human rights enjoyment' as enshrined in the Human Rights Charter and other rights covenants of the United Nations. In short, if Beijing is willing, Martin Lee's party can make a democratic contribution during and after the 1997 sovereignty transfer. This party and its leaders can make Hong Kong 'an experiment of democracy with Chinese characteristics'.

Recent reports have indicated that Beijing may not be willing. It has kept the Democratic Party out of its transition team. Martin Lee has tried and failed to persuade the Beijing leadership for cooperation. All DP members will be forced to get off the 'through train' in July 1997. Since January 1996, when Beijing began its unilateral implementation of the Sino-British agreements and its own Basic Law, it has become increasingly clear that the DP leadership must begin, as it already has, planning its own survival strategy after 1997. The Beijing leadership, however, may not be able to eliminate the deep-rooted popular support of the voters as demonstrated in the 1991 and 1995 elections.[22] The party's policy platform in 1995 was even more appealing to the voters regarding the promotion of human rights and the interests of the lower working class. In January 1996, Vice Chairman Anthony Cheung declared the party's strategy would be to confront Beijing's harsh and untrue charge of 'Anti-China, Pro-Britain disruption in Hong Kong'.[23] There will clearly be no retreat from parliamentary struggle because of the party's strength in the urban, municipal and district councils. It has been rumored that Beijing is eager to drive the party leaders out of Hong Kong. But party leaders in the LEGCO have expressed their determination to return to street demonstration and to confrontation if they are dismissed from the LEGCO.[24] Many voters in Hong Kong are now opposed to the formation of a 'provisional legislative council' by appointment to replace the elected LEGCO of September 1995, according to a poll conducted on the 26–27 March by the Democratic Party. All things considered, it is too early to assume that Beijing would not revise its harsh policy toward the Democratic Party between now and July 1997. In anticipation of difficult days ahead, party Chairman Martin Lee and Vice Chairman Yeung Sum toured North America to enlist support from the United States government and from the overseas Chinese communities in San Francisco, Washington DC and New York. They met groups in Congress and saw officials in the Department of State in April 1996. They were invited to brief the media people in the United Nations.[25]

Britain, in short, is packing to leave. The struggle for high autonomy and freedom has begun between political parties of the Hong Kong people and the communist leadership in Beijing. It is up to China to redefine the 'one country, two systems'. Beijing will either win the hearts and minds of the people or make them victims by betrayal. Martin Lee's party fears either of these alternatives.

Next to MP-UDHK, the second political grouping which merged in 1994 was originally called the Cooperative Resources Centre (CRC). It happened to be the first in 1993 to reorganize and now calls itself the Liberal Party. The word 'party' had never been used before by any existing political grouping. No other political party, up to February 1993, had ever declared its ambition to compete after 1997 for the post of Chief Executive and 'to retain in close communication' with the Beijing government. This Liberal Party's Preparatory Committee Chairman, Lee Peng-fei (Allen Lee), announced on 28 February 1993 that such was exactly his party's objective. In early 1993 the CRC had a larger number of seats in the LEGCO than any other group. The formation of the Liberal Party was announced shortly before the Sino-British talks took place in Beijing. The CRC politicians expected success from the Beijing talks. It was, therefore, good timing to look toward smooth transition in 1997 and party victory beyond. However, as became evident before the end of 1993, the politicians of the new Liberal Party were engaging in wishful thinking and soon experienced deep disappointment.

A careful examination of its members indicates that this new party was not new at all. It is like a chamber of commerce of professional people whose leaders are lawyers, medical doctors, public accountants, engineers, bankers and insurance men. Together, they represent a new class of professional and managerial people who want stability and prosperity for Hong Kong in general and for their own personal success in particular. Their approach has been to seek Beijing's early acceptance of their party in order to be better prepared to take over in 1997. Unlike the United Democrats or the current Democratic Party in 1994, which has a political agenda of commitment to pursue, and unlike the Alliance for Democracy and People's Livelihood (ADPL), which is fighting for the livelihood of the lower income class, the Liberal Party seems more concerned about capturing political power in 1997.

The Party's Preparatory Committee of 44 members came into existence on 28 February 1993. More than 70 per cent of them were business people or corporation presidents. Allen Lee, however, made a promise to recruit support from as many classes as possible. Not merely emphasizing commerce and industry, the party would focus, Lee declared, on 'the interest of the whole society' and 'in pursuit of the creation of wealth'. The party believes in 'Hongkongese self-government, positive participation in the LEGCO, and serious concern over future executive structure in the post 1997 government'.[26] Twenty of the 44 members of the Preparatory Committee were either LEGCO Members (14) or district board councilors (6). Allen Lee emphasized protection of personal freedoms and freedom for free enterprise. He eagerly stressed cooperation not confrontation with Beijing. Without cooperation 'from the sovereign center, no party can succeed'. We can therefore conclude that this is a party of the ambitious new middle and upper middle class. It has no well-known participants from the group of rich business tycoons who had already established close relations with Beijing.

As we have said, Britain had never prepared the Hong Kong people for political leadership and for the vigorous competition of party politics. The Liberal Party was the first local party of wider representation. Its formation was generously welcomed by other politicians. Martin Lee welcomed philosophically all political competition among parties, as should anyone in an open society with free speech. He said that 'the existence of different voices is an indication of greater choices for the public'. However, political parties should operate with complete transparency as a sign of fairness to the voters. Professor Anthony Cheung, head of Meeting Point within the DP, emphasized that multipartyism in Hong Kong was a proper and healthy phenomenon: 'Political participation space is still open for more people to contribute.' Fung Kin-kee (Frederick Fung) of the ADPL had long anticipated formation of a liberal party. Its birth 'could stimulate other political groups to do likewise for electoral competition in 1994–95'. He was doubtful, however, whether the new party could represent other classes beyond those with commercial-industrial interests. Cheng Kai-nan (Gary Cheng) of the Democratic Alliance for the Betterment of Hong Kong, however, believed that, given the current political environment in Hong Kong, no political party could fully exercise its normal function. The Liberal Party seemed too ambitious.[27]

On 6 June 1993, the Liberal Party leaders were officially parading in the streets on the party's first open appearance. Several local offices were established for recruitment. Allen Lee declared his intention to compete for party leadership through later election. Meanwhile, Sino-British diplomatic talks had reached their fifth round with no positive result. China did not wish to encourage the formation of political parties. The people of Hong Kong 'can enjoy freedom without democracy', commented the Vice President of the Chinese University in Hong Kong, Dr Ambrose King. In spite of Beijing's discouragement of it, politicization in Hong Kong had been accelerating since the 1991 LEGCO election, although no one saw any sign for optimism beyond 1997. One reason for this lack of optimism is that more than 70 per cent of Hong Kong residents usually support China, a clear expression of their political heritage. No political parties can operate successfully in Hong Kong without reaching a certain understanding with Beijing. Only the United Democrats and the Democratic Party have so far come into open confrontation with Beijing. Within the Liberal Party strong criticism was soon heard against its leadership. The public accused the Liberal Party's position for being inconsistent. When it was formed eight months earlier, some of its members perceived it as 'not radical, not conservative, not even pro-China. It was supposed to remain moderate'.[28] Allen Lee responded, 'but now the circumstances have changed. Society is more polarized, our moderate position is no longer possible.' He pledged to review the party's policy line soon and admitted further that the policy line eight months previously had been biased about 'inevitable success of the Sino-British talks'. The failure of the talks meant 'no through train' for many party members in the LEGCO and on the district boards. Allen Lee's failure to remain consistent on the issue of Patten's reform even caused Zhou Nan of NCNA to label him 'unstable on policy stand'.[29] It became clear for critics that the Liberal Party was an opportunist federation of 'unprincipled interest groups' which saw great advantage in associating with Beijing. However, it will remain flexible enough to gain recognition from Beijing as well as from Hong Kong.

Among other political parties that offered candidates for elective offices are the Liberal Democratic Federation, the Hong Kong Democratic Foundations, the ADPL and the MP as mentioned before, the New Hong Kong Alliance, and the dormant Kuomingtang and Chinese Communist Party.[30] Shortly before the September 1994 elections there were some twelve parties, including such small parties as the '1, 2, 3, Democratic Alliance' (pro-Taiwan), and the 'Federation for the Stability of Hong Kong' (pro-Beijing). The better known Democratic Alliance for the Betterment of Hong Kong has had genuine and openly enthusiastic support from Beijing and the NCNA in Hong Kong. Tsang Yam-kuen is its Chairman and Cheng Kai-nan is the Secretary-General. Both are articulate and well known and are playing a major role in various capacities as empowered by appointment from Beijing. The DAB appears to have a reasonable future in the long run. With campaign signs all over the colony in 1994, Hong Kong 'has become openly and decisively political'. Voter registration has achieved its highest record in years. As Professor Michael E. DeGolyer said: 'Voting is a socially acceptable behaviour: of 636 surveyed in February 1994, 54 per cent indicated they were registered voters, and 73 per cent of those registered intended to vote. Some 17 per cent were unsure and 10 per cent had no plans to vote. The breakdown of the Sino-British talks has had a dampening effect on participation.'[31]

Had it not been for the crisis of transition caused by the Tiananmen crackdown and Britain's change of mind about imposing the Patten reform, Hong Kong would most likely have been returned to China peacefully. The Beijing regime would have implemented the Basic Law with sufficient British cooperation and quiet acceptance by a less fearful and less anxious people. The Tiananmen Incident, unfortunately, provided a good excuse for Britain to challenge China by creating a new reform crisis in 1992, which suddenly destroyed the early original trust prior to 1989 between China, Britain and the people of Hong Kong. The Chinese people since 1984, and especially after 1989, have had to worry about their personal freedom and economic uncertainties beyond 1997. They were driven to suffer from political polarization and from fear of the disintegration of social harmony. Therefore, an increase in interest in politics and political parties became unavoidable among the people. They had not the confidence after 1984 to presume on a hands-off policy by China or any significant effort by Britain or even from their own parties and politicians. Thus, political parties were not at first trusted and could not develop properly so long as

Britain and China remained in stalemate. Besides, other more personal and important issues for policy discussions were emerging: for example, new issues of the brain drain, the right of abode in Britain, the 'through train' for career politicians after 1997, and compensation for expatriates in the civil service. But on these issues political parties were not empowered to deal. They were for Sino-British diplomacy to settle. Therefore, many sensitive issues must wait until after 1997 when Britain is no longer a player, and challenge and response will then develop directly between China and Hong Kong. Currently, no one can really say much yet, except Beijing, perhaps, about what 'one country, two systems' will be, certainly not Hong Kong politicians.

POLITICAL CULTURE AND POLITICAL IDENTITY

Politics deals with human interaction in certain given social environments. Human interactions lead to problems and their solutions. Politics leads ultimately to public policy debates and majoritarian consent, depending on the institutional and dynamic structure of the political system. In British Hong Kong, more than 90 per cent of the land is leased from China. Ninety-eight per cent of the people are Chinese who have never cut their strong ties with the southeastern part of China. Their language, culture and sense of nationhood are all Chinese. The common history between Hong Kong and China binds the two places into one unique psychology. Local politics in Hong Kong, indeed, emerges only through this historical reality. The British episode of colonialism in Hong Kong has been a short moment of 150 chaotic years. However, the British legal system, values of personal freedom, the operation of economic free enterprise, and so on, have influenced the upper echelon of the new local elites. This legacy sharply affects current political culture and political identity, to some degree driving China and Hong Kong apart.

In order to understand Hong Kong people's political culture and their political identity, we must understand how the British and the Chinese in the past have thought of each other. Common experiences, some better and some worse, have affected both the foreign rulers and the ruled. We here need only to mention a few highlights that may continue to influence future policies pursued by Hong Kong in conflict with Beijing in the decades to come. Much has occurred in China since 1949, and more immediately since the Tiananmen Incident in 1989, that has seriously changed the fundamental attitudes of China and Hong Kong toward one another in the early 1990s. Fear and anxiety is not new in Hong Kong and may continue after July 1997. Despite the shared long history, Hong Kong's story of both bitterness and success under the British government has always meant a series of challenges and adjustments. Culturally and politically the people of Hong Kong have developed a somewhat separate identity or self-consciousness. Economic affluence and international recognition of their success may soon be modified by an uncertain future after the transfer of sovereignty to China. We will trace their political attitudes through a few major changes since the 1950s that have inculcated in Hong Kong this new political/cultural identity.

Today in Hong Kong, the intellectuals, the politicians and the people seek to identify their own cultural and political characteristics more urgently and more seriously than Chinese people elsewhere because of their uncertainty in their own future. How should they, after 1997, relate to Britain and China? What does their own central core of values consist of? How have political changes, over which they have had no control, affected their deep psychological feelings? Their cherished core values, despite transition and current transformation around them, consist of 'need for prosperity and stability, for law and order, and for the Hong Kong way of life . . .'.[32] These political and social values are in danger because of the British departure and the unpredictability surrounding the change of sovereignty in 1997. Their own sense of pride and respect is being continuously undermined by the 'laughable bickering' between Beijing and London, both of which characteristically still claim to have Hong Kong's interests at heart. This decade of bickering has imposed upon Hong Kong people a love-hate attitude toward those who have together made their way of life less certain. The Patten era is disappearing and the politician's through train for a career has jumped the track. Thus, the people's identity and loyalty remain in a state of confusion, demanding urgent reorientation. Britain has stayed too long and will leave too little behind. China is their future hope but generates instant fear. Thus, Hong Kong's identity in culture and in politics may be appropriately expressed as follows:

> The general survey of the Hong Kong cultural scene might begin with the recognition that, at heart, Hong Kong is by and large devoid of a unifying cultural foundation. Three socio-ideological specters haunt her like so many layers of structural strait jacket, namely, modernism, colonialism, and Chinese traditionalism. The combined and respective impacts of these, at different levels of tangibility, made up the sociocultural labyrinth that the "Hong Kong folks" have learned to live with. For these Hong Kong folks, this unlikely amalgamation, being part and parcel of the fabric of every day life, has been largely assumed and "normalized". Yet others observing from the wider perspective of social and historical development can immediately see the complexity, the schism that must entail for the formation of culture concerned, and all the more marvel at the vibrant sociocultural order being sustained in spite of all.[33]

Without a unified culture and tradition of its own, the people of Hong Kong are easily swept by values of contemporary or popular culture, globally as well as regionally, that can intoxicate everyday life through movies, television and comic reading. In an ultimate deep sense, and like the small city state of Singapore, the Hong Kong people's value focus, in an apolitical manner, is on wealth accumulation and the struggle for survival through competition in the commercial world. But unlike Singapore, which is an independent and confident republic, the Hong Kong people, with affluence and success, still cannot deliver themselves to the 'promised land' of liberty and autonomy.[34] Politicians and parties without deep ideological or value commitments will inevitably emerge to join the promises of new opportunity that come with the transition in sovereignty. Others in the opposite camp will not easily surrender without a real struggle for democratic values in the political development in Hong Kong. Who are those popular leaders in politics today?

Public opinion polling did not become an evaluation barometer until the 1991 election. Politicians in the LEGCO received no personal attention from voters before 1990. Only after Governor Chris Patten's arrival in 1992 did the opinion polling industry participate in daily political development. The governor, for example, received polling reports, from weekly to monthly intervals, in his first year in office. Of dozens of members in the LEGCO, only the ten most popular members were reported in each bimonthly polling survey. Among the ten, some were elected by functional constituents. A few were appointed by the governor. They were, however, mostly very liberal: for example, supporting women's rights. Only one of the ten was a former British citizen, Elsie Tu. She was not affiliated with any political party but was consistently opposed to Patten's election reform. Unlike Elsie Tu, Loh Kung-wai (Christine Loh), although an appointed member, was in the forefront in favor of representative and election reform and human rights. Often competing with Elsie Tu for the top place was Lau Wai-hing (Emily Lau) who took a consistent progressive stand on democratic values and reform. Among the male members of the ten, Martin Lee was more often the first among three or four men in the rating. He is usually followed closely by Lau Chin-shek, Szeto Hua, Yeung Sum or Selina Chow, and occasionally by Allen Lee of the Cooperative Resources Centre. Tam Yiu-chung was occasionally among the top ten but with a lower ranking. He represented the huge Federation of Trade Unions and often associated with Allen Lee who usually took a moderate to neutral or pro-Beijing stand on Patten's election reform. What they did or said in the LEGCO was fully reported. According to polling records by Robert Chung Ting-yiu of the Social Science Research Center of the University of Hong Kong in his twelve bimonthly polls of 1993–4, some ranking examples are as follows.

Popular Polling 8–10 February 1993:
    1 Elsie Tu
    2 Emily Lau
    3 Lau Chin-shek
    4 Fung Kin-kee
    5 Martin Lee

  6 Szeto Hua
  7 Andrew Wong
  8 Tam Yiu-chung
  9 Selina Chow
 10 Allen Lee.
Popular Polling 17–18 June 1993:
  1 Elsie Tu
  2 Emily Lau
  3 Martin Lee
  4 Lau Chin-shek
  5 Yeung Sum
  6 Szeto Hua
  7 Allen Lee
  8 Andrew Wong
  9 Selina Chow
 10 Lau Wong-fat.
Popular Polling 1–7 February 1994:
  1 Elsie Tu
  2 Emily Lau
  3 Martin Lee
  4 Lau Chin-shek
  5 Yeung Sum
  6 Szeto Hua
  7 Selina Chow
  8 Tam Yiu-chung
  9 Andrew Wong
 10 Allen Lee.
Popular Polling 31 May–1 June 1994:
  1 Emily Lau
  2 Martin Lee
  3 Lau Chin-shek
  4 Szeto Hua
  5 Christine Loh
  6 Fung Kin-kee
  7 Selina Chow
  8 Allen Lee
  9 Andrew Wong
 10 Lau Wong-fat.[35]

Daily newspapers associated their names as symbolic leaders with what they did each day in the LEGCO or in other

political activities. Emily Lau, Christine Loh and Elsie Tu, who exceeded most others in recognition, were all non-partisan independent legislators. On the other hand, Martin Lee, Yeung Sum, Lau Chin-shek and Szeto Hua had all been leaders of the United Democrats or later the top leaders of the Democratic Party since 1994. They have long been well recognized, even before the 1989 Tiananmen Incident, as eager supporters of the pro-democracy movement in China. For each of the rankings cited above, the SSRC carefully chose about 500–600 pollees, who were asked to rank all the LEGCO members and select the top ten, instead of re-ranking the ten from the previous polling. The distance between the top five and the lower five was an average of about 3–4 percentage points. In short, individuals in Hong Kong politics are respected or trusted more than political parties in terms of platform or policy stands.

Political parties in Hong Kong have been seriously handicapped for a number of reasons. First of all, Britain previously and China more recently discouraged party development for their own selfish interests. Second, professional-occupational direct representation in the LEGCO has rendered unnecessary the need for parties and party endorsement for nomination for the legislative seats. The Executive Council has never been open to election. The governor appoints members to his personal cabinet, which is not responsible collectively or individually to the LEGCO. There was, up to 1991, simply no room for democratic parties to be developed. However, since 1991 and 1994, political parties have suddenly come into formal existence to compete for some seats by popular election. Thus, the mushroom growth of new parties has created a state of confusion for the average resident in Hong Kong. Many new and little-known parties have no real organization, leadership, discipline, grass-roots support or comprehensive campaign platforms. Most of them are protest groups without broad appeal. In 1993 the SSRC of the University of Hong Kong, under Robert Chung Ting-yiu, started polling people to discover their recognition of and support for political groups (or parties as some later used the word) at bimonthly intervals. 530–630 well-chosen pollees were asked to rank the top five of the nine groups. We quote below several of the

12 bimonthly polling results.[36] Party names, first in abbreviation and then in full are as follows:

ADPL   Hong Kong Alliance for Democracy and People's Livelihood
CRC   Cooperative Resources Centre (prior to LP)
DABHK   Democratic Alliance for the Betterment of Hong Kong
DP   Democratic Party
FTU   Hong Kong Federation of Trade Unions
LDFHK   Liberal Democratic Federation of Hong Kong
LP   Liberal Party
MP   Meeting Point (before merger with UDKH to be DP)
UDHK   United Democrats of Hong Kong.

Popular Polling, 23–24 February 1993, total sample 631:
   1 UDHK
   2 ADPL
   3 MP
   4 CRC
   5 DABHK
Popular Polling, 27–28 April 1993, total sample 622:
   1 UDHK
   2 FTU
   3 MP
   4 CRC
   5 DABHK
Popular Polling, 25–26 August 1993, total sample 513:
   1 UDHK
   2 MP
   3 FTU
   4 LP
   5 LDF
Popular Polling, 28–30 December 1993, total sample 502:
   1 UDHK
   2 MP
   3 LP
   4 FTU
   5 DABHK
Popular Polling, 24–28 February 1994, total sample 524:
   1 UDHK

2 FTU
3 MP
4 LP
5 DABHK

Popular Polling, 22–23 June 1994, total sample 602:
1 UDHK
2 MP
3 ADPL
4 LP
5 DABHK

Popular Polling, 19–20 December 1994, total sample 577:
1 DP (merger of UD/MP)
2 FTU
3 ADPL
4 LP
5 DABHK

Clearly, the new DP remained (as UDHK) on top at all times because of its commitment to popular democracy. The DABHK, a pro-Beijing party organized in 1992 under Tsang Yam-kuen (Donald Tsang), consistently scored worst among the top five. While both the FTU and the DABHK were included in the top five, neither the Liberal Democratic Federation nor the Conservative CRC made it. They were later merged and replaced by the new Liberal Party under Allen Lee. All other marginal parties will probably be absorbed by those among the top five in the early years following 1997. An important question is whether or not the Democratic Party, under Martin Lee, Yeung Sum, Anthony Cheung and educator Szeto Hua will be tolerated after 1997. During our interviews we were repeatedly told that if these leaders should ever travel abroad, they would probably be barred from returning to Hong Kong. The party is fully aware of its uncertain future in the early years after 1997. Its leadership will patiently wait for changes in Beijing. Support for the policies of the Democratic Party seem likely to continue among highly educated local elites, young university students, and the media professionals. Other parties among the top five will certainly continue to compete and come to terms with the post-1997 leadership in Hong Kong.

Politicians, parties, and all the serious voters in Hong Kong are generally full of anxiety and uncertainty, and they have good reason to be. But not many people are willing to express their political views frankly. The media are voluntarily prepared to exercise self-censorship. The rich tycoons are speaking out against the premature rush to enhance democratic process, although the Basic Law promises universal suffrage for the election of the Chief Executive.[37] Deep down in the community, the people of Hong Kong are divided. Many vividly recall painful memories under the British and the Chinese. Some are filled with anxiety, some with hope, as they wait to find out how 'one country, two systems' will work after 1997.[38] What painfully affects the Hong Kong Chinese most seems to have come from three directions: 'the British version' of Hong Kong's political history, 'the PRC version', and 'a Hong Kong version'. Professor M.E. DeGolyer explains these three versions as follows:

The British Version, according to DeGolyer, is that Hong Kong, the 'barren rock' of the 1840s, is modern today whereas the barbarous 'laws of China' remain essentially unchanged. Beginning in 1989 Britain realized that it had to be concerned with the human rights record in China and in Hong Kong after 1997. Britain was sure the Hong Kong people were 'strictly non-political', and deported out of Hong Kong those who were 'subversives'. Britain gave Hong Kong an efficient government, a rule of law, and a 'better life in peaceful circumstances'. Instead of participatory politics and election, Britain 'consulted the proper people' for advice after 1982. She believed that the people preferred always to live under the colonial form of government. Unfortunately, recent research proved this assumption to be false.[39]

The Chinese Version of Hong Kong's political history is that 'Western force' often drove 'better people' out of Hong Kong 'at a great cost to China'. Thus, Hong Kong symbolizes an 'imposed trade', 'unequal treaties', and legal asylum extended to those who are 'not honest businessmen' but 'rapacious drug dealers' seeking a haven from legitimate Chinese control. Hong Kong has been a 'hotbed of subversion', drug smuggling, trials, prying into China's affairs, burning of the Basic Law, calling 'for the overthrow of the Beijing Government', and encouraging the 4 June protestors.[40] The Beijing version continues that there have been many past protests against British colonial rule, expulsion, and repression. Through the Basic Law, eventually, Hong Kong and China 'will be one'. Until after 2047, China will help protect Hong Kong's prosperity and stability for the benefit of all before ultimate full integration occurs.

A Hong Kong Version of its Political History is that the real history supports neither the British view nor the Beijing claim. 'Until December 1990 membership in a political party was illegal, and not until September 1991 could people even vote directly for a small portion of the LEGCO.' Government was corrupt in favoritism; local elites sought influences through consultancy by invitation. Britain chose a minimalist role for governing so long as the economy prospered and people were obedient to British decrees. People are well informed but powerless to change anything. From 1884 to 1949, history shows many anti-British political revolts, strikes and demonstrations. Political expressions were forbidden up to the 1980s. The people were anti-colonial and patriotic toward China but opposed to communism.[41] Now, on the eve of return, their political options are still limited. Political participation is likely to grow if good faith is displayed in the implementation of the Basic Law and if general democratization in China takes place as well. Fundamental self-identity among the people remains divided into 'Hong Kong Chinese' or 'Hong Kong person'. A good 20 per cent simply call themselves 'Chinese'. M.E. DeGolyer concludes: 'Hong Kong politics, in fact, seem to be increasingly in search of an identity and a focus . . . Already a nationalistic identity is being forged in Hong Kong, but it differs significantly from that on the mainland.'[42]

So far, we have focused on politicians and parties who are popularly recognized with respect and support in public opinion and who share with and fight for some political values and convictions of the electorate. The pro-China politicians and parties have enjoyed little or no respect and support in the media and at the opinion polls. Their identity and image are not well known and have not acquired legitimate recognition. However, they will loyally support and contribute to the post-1997 SAR government. Their strength and public recognition will grow as the transition date draws nearer. It is necessary to summarize the politics of pro-Beijing groups.[43]

THE PRO-BEIJING GROUPS AND POLITICAL DEVELOPMENT IN HONG KONG

Not all pro-Beijing groups operate in the open. These groups include the strong control of the Federation of Trade Unions (FTU), the newly organized women's association, such as the Hong Kong Federation of Women organized in 1993 (HKFW). The Association of Chinese Enterprises (ACE) includes mainly economic entities operated by mainland people with investments in various fields in Hong Kong. Young students with merely secondary school education have organized into the Association of Post-Secondary Students (APSS) which is Beijing's vehicle to enroll young people with 'strong nationalistic sentiment'.[44] The Federation for the Stability of Hong Kong (FSHK) has members and politicians from all levels in the government and among many advisers on 'Hong Kong Affairs'. These pro-Beijing individuals and groups may currently remain less active or politically neutral. Some do not want to associate openly with official Beijing representatives in Hong Kong. The New China News Agency has been quite busy in recruiting pro-China residents in Hong Kong over the last decade.

According to Lo Shiu-hing (Sunny Lo) and Donald Hugh McMillen in their joint authorship,[45] pro-China local elite have a serious image problem with the voters and with the general public in Hong Kong. Their excellent analysis divides 'pro-China elite' in Hong Kong into five basic groups. The 'Loyalist group' enthusiastically embraces Beijing's policies toward Hong Kong. The 'moderate group' includes Hong Kong's liberal-intellectuals whose independent thought and policy suggestions are often acceptable to Beijing and thus lead them closer to Beijing. The 'unstable nationalists and patriots' in Hong Kong are interested in a 'greater and unified China'. They despise opportunists who seek new connections for their fame and influence in the future. 'The former pro-British appointees' have lately shifted their loyalty to Beijing. Finally, the 'low-key individuals' prefer to be silent players so as not to lose favor or opportunity in their business deals with Beijing. These five distinct pro-China groups demonstrate clearly the real and potential differences among themselves with certain regard to their purposes or motives in connection with Beijing. Because they are not coherent or homogeneous groups it is not easy for Beijing to coordinate them into united support against pro-Hong Kong groups, parties or individuals.[46] The 'uncritical stances' and 'unstable commitments' of these groups naturally come into certain conflict with the 'pro-Hong Kong' elite members who are defenders of British Hong Kong whether they are in the LEGCO or elsewhere. Those who have eagerly supported Governor Patten in political reform development are generally considered 'pro-Hong Kong'. They are mostly concerned about personal freedom, free press, the 'high degree of autonomy' and genuine self-government by the Hong Kong people as promised in the Basic Law.[47]

The identity or image crisis divides Hong Kong elite members into degrees of inclination toward slower or rapid integration under Chinese sovereignty. Both elite groups have, no doubt, accepted the transfer of sovereignty but not the pace of integration through threatening 'indirect control' from Beijing. This is, in truth, the fear commonly shared by all the pro-Hong Kong elite. Professor Donald Hugh McMillen in his writing associates the fear of the pro-Hong Kong elite with his factional analysis of the current leadership structure in Beijing.[48] Which faction will come to govern China is difficult to foresee. Given China's deep penetration since early 1980s into the infrastructure of Hong Kong's society, the local fear of 'indirect domination' after 1997 is real and deplorable in view of the lack of trust in 'one country, two systems'. In addition, political development in Hong Kong has been deeply eroded by the presence of the New China News Agency as we have described before. The 'less visible' group associated with other organizations cannot be easily observed. Unfortunately, the breakdown of Sino-British cooperation since 1992 has given justification to China's unilateral strategy to implement the Joint Declaration and the Basic Law in a more restrictive application of treaty interpretation. For example, the extra-constitutional body, the Preparatory Working Committee (PWC), was organized in

1993 to draw up a blueprint for the sovereignty transfer. Beijing has so far tapped more than 600 individuals as officially appointed Hong Kong Affairs Advisers and District Affairs Advisers. Thirdly, Beijing decided to sponsor pro-China candidates to participate in the 1994 district and municipal elections and the LEGCO election in the following year. Together, these activities contribute significantly to 'dual political developments': one scored for Governor Patten and the other helped China to test its pre-transfer strength. Thus, although still under Britain, divided political development implicitly separates Hong Kong into two camps of politics. There is no denying that the majority of residents in Hong Kong have to 'bend with the wind'. Those with self-identity as 'Hong Kong Chinese' (36 per cent to 40 per cent in 1994) will likely increase gradually at the expense of 'Hong Kong person' (37 per cent to 30 per cent). The simple identity of just 'Chinese' (19 per cent to 20 per cent) will be guided by changes in future political development in Hong Kong.[49] The recent public mood is moving toward 'smooth transition'. We are inclined to believe that, as Britain retreats and disappears, China will graciously make greater efforts to ameliorate its policy-making in order to win changes in public confidence. If the well-known hard liners Lu Ping in Beijing and Zhou Nan in Hong Kong were to leave office, it would reflect the rise of a moderate top leader to take over after Deng Xiaoping's departure from the scene. That would be good for Hong Kong. Political development there will be inseparable from political development in China. 'Democratization with Chinese characteristics' is still slow or impossible in China yet. However, no matter who emerges to govern China, a certain degree of political decentralization in policy leadership to the provincial level will accelerate. Such expectation among politicians and economic-managerial experts is being heard in all parts of the country. Technological and professional bureaucrats have already emerged at non-central level to share greater policy-making authority. There has been too much imbalance between economic-management reform and deplorable stalemate in political and systemic reform. In China during the last fifteen years progress has been made in transportation, communication, education and social development. These advances have put pressure on demand for political leadership restructure in the Communist Party.

Hong Kong will benefit automatically from such liberalization and democratization in China, provided no foreign meddling interferes in political development in Hong Kong and Taiwan. The communist leadership in China will forcefully react and has been very suspicious of foreign subversive and conspiratory interference in China's internal affairs. The Democratic Party members under Martin Lee, Cheung Bing-leung, and Yeung Sum have been condemned since 1994 as foreign subversives. If the Democratic Party stays clear from international complicity, China will have less excuse to appeal to and rely upon nationalism to defend sovereignty and independence against legitimate demands or pleas from pro-Hong Kong residents and elite for faithful implementation of the Basic Law. In that case, China would also be under its own domestic pressure to experiment more honestly with 'one country, two systems' in Hong Kong, to impress the Chinese citizens in Taiwan and thus to minimize the US–Japan concern on Beijing's military confrontation in the Taiwan Straits. In conclusion, it is our belief that the pro-Hong Kong elite groups and individuals and the pro-China groups and individuals have more to share implicitly in common than they have explicitly in difference. This is only 'the difference in degree' in their sentiment and in degree of Chinese patriotism. The real policy difference is in choosing priority – which is to be fulfilled first, greater unification with 'greater China' or greater democracy in Hong Kong isolated from instability or chaos in China. This is the difference as often expressed to us by residents in Hong Kong: 'Love Hong Kong, Love China but hate communists.' If the Beijing leadership understands this and performs wisely, it can change its bad image faster and easily. Thus Hong Kong's future political development may not be as bleak as often described in foreign newspapers. The dividing line between pro-Hong Kong and pro-China cannot be accurately drawn. Chinese politics and Chinese people are less scrutable to most foreign observers. Furthermore, the well-chosen and specially trained unit of Chinese troops will soon be stationed in Hong Kong to ensure continuity of law and order against any occurrence resembling the 'turmoil' of the Tiananmen Incident of 1989. Image, sentiment and 'hearts and minds' are at the core to shape the new attitudes of the residents in Hong Kong toward China.

SINO-HONG KONG ECONOMIC INTEGRATION AND POLITICAL DEVELOPMENT IN HONG KONG

Hong Kong is the tenth largest trader in the world. Since China's opening to the outside world in trade and investment, and in the enormous increase of indirect trade between Taiwan and China through Hong Kong, the latter's role in international economic transactions has become indispensable or irreplaceable. It had a per capita GNP of US $21 000 or more and a surplus reserve in international balance of payments of more than US $50 billion in early 1995. Its economy is totally free from government control. Much of this positive achievement has been the result of its geographic advantage as China's outpost for import and export trades. On China's side, several Special Economic Zones (SEZ) were built near Hong Kong in the 1980s to absorb foreign investments in China. Hong Kong was and still is China's economic transition belt in technology and in management science from abroad. Because of the cheap labor in China and the low cost in production management, Hong Kong itself has become the largest economic investor in China. This capital outflow has also changed the infrastructure of manufacturing in Hong Kong. The colony has transformed from labor-intensive manufacturing to tertiary services management. Its import and re-export capacity has been growing fast. New facilities in travel, service, transportation, harbor and new airport expansion have been much in demand. Foreign countries, especially Japan, the United States, Taiwan and China have also been new investors in Hong Kong. As of 31 March 1993, China had invested, for example, in at least 15 major areas of 'listed companies'.[50] These include Merchant-Holding Group, the metal industry, construction engineering, aerospace industry and petroleum. The cash value in 1993 was US $56 966 839 915. As one author estimated the outlook in Hong Kong–China economic relations:

With the economic reform in China going full speed, Hong Kong's economy is becoming more and more closely knit with that of its northern neighbor, which will become its master on 1 July 1997. In fact, Hong Kong and South China have already become economically so closely integrated that many people refer to these two places as having a borderless economy. Hong Kong operates thousands of manufacturing concerns in China, mostly in Guangdong, and it invests in a wide range of projects, including property development, hotels and tourism and infrastructure such as roads, energy and communications. China's investment in Hong Kong is believed to be of the same magnitude as that of Hong Kong's in China, if not greater. With the recent pace of acquisition of listed companies in Hong Kong, China's cumulative direct investment in Hong Kong, including property, may have reached hundreds of billions in U.S. dollars. . . . The positive side of China's investment in Hong Kong is that it helps to build up the investor's confidence in the future of the territory. The more China invests in Hong Kong, the more interdependent the two economies will become.[51]

Since labor, land and services are cheap in China, Hong Kong manufacturing industries will continue to shift to Southeastern China, while tertiary services of importing and re-exporting will steadily increase because of the demands from the vast hinterland in China and the markets for China's goods aboard. Hong Kong, in turn, must continue to update its service facilities. The United States extension to China of the 'most-favored-nation' status is indeed critical in Hong Kong's re-exporting to America.[52] After 1997, it will be largely China's responsibility to promote economic prosperity in Hong Kong. Whatever happens in the future in the Southeastern section of China will directly influence the economic life in Hong Kong. However, Hong Kong itself will continue to retain much of her liberty in economic relations with all her trading partners and in furthering China's trade expansion.[53] At the same time Hong Kong may remain China's largest foreign investor and port of exports. This close economic relationship, on the other hand, creates problems for both China and Hong Kong. For example, Hong Kong's industrial structure is undergoing a sort of 'de-industrialization'. Between 1984 and 1994, only half of the 898 947 manufacturing employees were retained. This was a 50 per cent dismissal of the workforce in ten years. Workers must switch rapidly from job to job to adapt to the flexibility of the economy. The government in the future may have to set up job training centers to help in the relocation of workers. Such rapid change in Hong Kong's economic restructuring is taking place in many sectors including wholesale, retail, tourism, real estate, and so on. It is said:

> Any one here may be a textile worker in one month, a salesman in another, and a property agent in yet another. This does not augur well for the long-run prospect of productivity enhancement, which requires specialization, professionalization, and accumulation of expertise in specific areas. It adds force to the skeptical view that the Hong Kong economy is still ravelling in the bonanza of the China factor for cost reduction and 're-rating' by international investors and speculators.[54]

These are examples illustrating how interdependent and how far integrated economically are China and Hong Kong. Political change cannot be too far behind economics.

Another increasing phenomenon is the rapid development of trade and investment between Taiwan, Hong Kong and China. The three economies, separate a decade ago, are now moving together. Taiwan is doing exactly what Hong Kong started ten years ago in investment on mainland China. Trade with and investment in China are mutually beneficial to both. For Taiwan, cheap labor and resources are abundant on the mainland. For mainland China, investment and technology from Taiwan are most useful and welcome in the coastal region for rapid economic development. Next to Hong Kong, Taiwan has been the second largest investor on mainland China. In trade, for example, Taiwan's export to mainland China in 1979 was US $21.3 million which jumped to US $16 066 million by 1994. Her imports from mainland China in 1979 totalled US $55.8 million and reached US $1858.7 million in 1994.[55] All these economic activities took place through Hong Kong because there has been no direct trade across the Taiwan Straits. These two 'small dragons',

Taiwan and Hong Kong, are moving toward greater inter-dependence with China in marketing, production and trade.

The linkage we are making is that political development may have to follow the track of economic development among Hong Kong, Taiwan and China. In the case of Hong Kong, it is already 'fully integrated' into the Southeastern region of China. As one publication recently indicated: 'If the future development in this regard is moving in the most ideal direction, the solid foundation of the Southeast China Growth Triangle, will not be too far away. Integration of economic capacity will place the three Chinese economies as one of the major economic powers in the world – being top in net foreign exchange reserves and the top three in volume of international trade.'[56] China's paramount leader Deng Xiaoping in 1992 'electrified the southeast coast region' on his tour by irreversibly committing China to 'socialist' market economy. In this perspective, a stable and prosperous Hong Kong is indispensable to Beijing's plan for rapid catch-up growth for the 1990s and beyond. In the three Chinese economies context Hong Kong's multifaceted roles are all the more important. The problem is how to convince the territory's people that there will be correspondence between Beijing's (good) intentions and the actions of its appointed officials.[57] The same author further observes that 'the notion of the three Chinese economies as a formal grouping would further solidify Hong Kong's status as a truly autonomous Special Administrative Region'. If the three Chinese economies become a 'free trade grouping', many economists believe that an agreed procedure of gradual political reunification can be found between Taiwan and mainland China. It really does not matter whether such a peaceful step-by-step political process for eventual integration is called federal or confederate or 'one country, two systems'.[58]

Political development between Hong Kong and Beijing aside, the economic impact of Hong Kong on both Taiwan and China has been the focus of many economists. In 1994 China replaced the emphasis on rapid economic growth with new focus on 'the macroeconomic control policy aiming primarily to suppress inflation, to reform state enterprises, and to improve agricultural inputs and agricultural structural adjustment'.[59] The new policy puts stability and control ahead of rapid growth and inflation. This emphasis will give Hong Kong and Taiwan more confidence in the safety of coordinating their trade and investment on mainland China. The businessmen and corporations in Hong Kong, on the other hand, have taken into account the impact of sovereignty transfer in 1997 concerning their investment strategies under a 'changing economic environment'. They expect government bureaucracy and political climate to become major factors to influence their investment adjustment. Hong Kong's economy will continue, after 1997, to be subject to restructuring from 'manufacturing base to service-dominated metropolitan economy. Hong Kong's trading comparative advantage will enhance the economy's evolution towards an entrepot and regional financial center. Such an environment will also make Hong Kong one of the most internationalized economies in the Asian Pacific region'.[60]

In conclusion, real but unsubstantiated anxiety and fear, or even anger, over the sovereignty transfer in 1997, reflects politically an emotional maladjustment on the part of those less informed and, thus, less prepared residents for the coming historical change. Psychological preparedness by others, ready to celebrate the big occasion, should be in the majority among the residents in Hong Kong. The new political climate, the British celebration for its noble departure, and individual reflections and excitement will make the transfer a happy occasion after all. Change and adjustment, as a common experience, should be nothing new to the people of Hong Kong. A bright economic future for Hong Kong is what most of the people have always wanted. Economic positivism will seem to be able to overcome the anxiety and fear of political negativism. What one often reads and hears as bad messages from foreign journalists and newspapers are not always as impartial as expected. In-depth interviews with average people and with members of the Hong Kong elite can help in gaining wisdom and insight into the complex political history of British colonialism and Chinese nationalism and their interactions in twentieth-century Hong Kong. For the six million residents of Hong Kong to witness a major change from British colonialism to Chinese sovereignty is a major step affecting their personal life. Political change, economic opportunities and psychological adjustment are now taking place. However, for generations since at least the dawn of the twentieth century, the people of Hong Kong have seen revolutions, warlordism, civil wars and Japanese aggression in China. Many of them were victims of destruction and chaos before their final escape to Hong Kong in 1949 or even later. They must know by now how to make the political transition in a non-violent environment.

8 The Court of Final Appeal and Human Rights

INTRODUCTION

Political development and legal development are closely related. It is obvious, however, that in the case of Hong Kong politics will prevail over law in the future. In spite of the fact that the Joint Declaration guarantees the continuity of the current British legal system for 50 years beyond 1997, the coexistence of a common law system with an independent judiciary and socialist China for 50 years is, indeed, like 'walking on a rocky bottom of rapid currents', to quote from Mao's writing. The people in Hong Kong are, however, by and large, realistic and adaptable. They have a very good sense of what will be tolerated and accepted by China and what will not. They are willing and able to make the necessary changes to accommodate China's wishes. The Western nations, however, do not seem to appreciate the necessity for such adaptations. Many of them are concerned, often unpractically and mistakenly, about the survival of the British legal system, the free style of life, and other legacies of some 150 years of British rule.

The Chinese government and its Hong Kong patriots openly consider 'outside meddling' a gross lack of respect for China's internal sovereignty in managing its national affairs. We have, as researchers, often encountered such complaints and resentment while traveling in China and Hong Kong for interviews. Today China itself is changing rapidly. The countryside is undergoing a facelift in economic and social relations. Transportation and communication are improving slowly but steadily and linking the vast rural country together economically and socially. As the socialist market economy and the capitalist free economy move closer and closer, eventually to lose their sharp separate identities, Hong Kong may peacefully lose all its current uniqueness and its concern over 'short-term' uncertainties. Currently, Hong Kong's return to China seems to disturb many Western nations, especially the United States and the British parliament, which repeatedly schedules major debates on the survival of her Common Law, the legal tradition of her independent judicial system, the result of Governor Patten's election reform and, especially, human rights beyond 1997. Amnesty International is monitoring human rights violations in China and expects annual human rights reports from Hong Kong and China after 1997. Such international attention is seen in China as 'hypocritical' interference.[1] We will return to this discussion later in this chapter. Indeed, the interest in Hong Kong's future shown by the United States Congress and the International Commission of Jurists in Geneva, has not gone unnoticed in Beijing. The regrettable reality has been that Britain did not introduce democratic reform until too late: after the Joint Declaration had been signed in 1984. The United States did not pay as much attention to Hong Kong (or Taiwan either) until after the end of the Cold War with the Soviet Union. Ineffective political meddling may only make matters worse for the people of Hong Kong. Critical comments or premature accusations may harden Beijing's greater consciousness of unfriendly meddling by the outside world.[2] Optimistically speaking, we have found also positive determination on the part of many Asian nations not to do anything drastically to 'rock the boat' of peaceful transition. In addition, the Chinese government in Beijing seems aware it cannot afford to fail in Hong Kong's experiment of 'one country, two systems'.

This chapter will be divided into several units discussing the politics of legal transition agreed upon through the Joint Declaration. Certain legal problems, such as the future interpretation of the Basic Law and the jurisdiction of the Court of Final Appeal are being debated between interest groups and political parties in Hong Kong. Britain and China both argue politically but justify their legal stands either through the Joint Declaration or the Basic Law. The people of Hong Kong, as victims of betrayal by prior agreement, only seriously began their own battle for democratic participation since the arrival of Governor Patten in 1992.

However, the people of Hong Kong are handicapped by those limits set in the Sino-British Agreement of 1984 and the Basic Law of 1990. The truth is that all three parties have no real trust or confidence in each other over future developments after British withdrawal. However, future political and legal developments, in all probability, may in fact be much more satisfactory than currently anticipated.

From the point of view of those educated through the British legal system and nurtured by Western democracy, the people of Hong Kong have long been ready for representative government and protection of human rights through independent judiciary. They were denied both under long-term British colonialism.[3] They had guarded optimism in the early 1980s under the future Basic Law, which by 1990 was considered of dubious dependability in protecting their free way of life through a high degree of autonomy. The bloody Tiananmen Incident sadly destroyed their final confidence and trust in China. Thus, they hope to achieve a strong legal shield through the adoption of the United Nations Covenant of Civil and Political Rights (UNCCPR) and the United Nations Covenant of Economic, Social and Cultural Rights (UNCESCR). The LEGCO formally passed a statute in 1991 to incorporate them into a future legal foundation while Britain was still in charge. This accomplished fact has been under challenge from Beijing as a violation of the Basic Law. The people have hoped for a stronger Court of Final Appeal to replace the British Judicial Committee of the House of Lords after 1997. This, too, was not settled satisfactorily in the 1995 Sino-British Agreement. The people's hands were tied each time while their future was betrayed. Whom should they complain to?

From the British colonial point of view, the debate of betrayal has been raised many times in the media,[4] in the House of Commons, and among British diplomats as well. The simple truth is that the British lacked bargaining power, having no choice but to surrender the leased New Territories in 1997. Without the New Territories the colony cannot survive. Had Britain been faithful to representative governments decades earlier in Hong Kong, political self-government would have evolved the colony a long way into the democratic processes – a development which would have given the British diplomats much greater bargaining power in negotiation with China. Today Britain cannot do much to redeem itself. In fact, Britain has done its best to achieve an honorable retreat through Governor Patten's reform.

From China's point of view, she must recover Hong Kong and the leased territories. In such effort, China does have many local patriots in Hong Kong to support the return to China. In diplomacy Beijing blames London for 'dragging its feet'. In Beijing's own perception, Hong Kong should be returned just as it actually is without any 'last moment' reform or change. Any such reform or change constitutes an interference in China's internal sovereign affairs after British withdrawal in 1997. Furthermore China resents 'subversive' activities of certain political groups in Hong Kong. Governor Patten's arrival in 1992 finally destroyed any hope for Sino-British cooperation. The 'victimized' Hong Kong Chinese moved finally to the forefront to try to improve their own lot. What the Beijing leadership will do to repair the wound and to win back the people is something we will soon observe after 1997. In the following pages we will focus on legal discussion of the controversies over the creation of the Court of Final Appeal. We will simply emphasize the policy positions of the Patten government, of the LEGCO, and of Beijing, as well as the public reaction and the external concern in Hong Kong's future human rights practice after 1997. We shall discuss these topics more as political conflicts and less in legal terms for human rights, although the Joint Declaration and the Basic Law are being cited as legal justification for debate.[5]

THE SINO-BRITISH AGREEMENT ON THE COURT OF FINAL APPEAL

Before discussing the Court of Final Appeal (CFA) it is appropriate to summarize the judicial establishment in Hong Kong at the present. The rule of law and judicial independence have been firmly observed under the British and are to be maintained until the year 2047. The Court of Final Appeal to be created will be the only institutional replacement within the present legal structure.[6] Since 1991 the Hong

Kong government had expected the LEGCO's early approval of its draft bill to allow sufficient time for the establishment of the CFA in July 1996. At the same time, local jurisprudence on implementation of the Hong Kong Bill of Rights Ordinance has continued to expand. In 1994 greater attention was given to human rights protection and to efforts for the creation of an Equal Opportunities Commission for all persons, including women's rights.

As long practiced in Hong Kong, the attorney general's division, under the governor, has been responsible for drafting all new legislation in both English and Chinese since 1989. The common law of England and the law of equity are applicable in Hong Kong as a matter of well-established Common Law practice among British colonies everywhere. The transition in 1997, therefore, imposes a critical need for Hong Kong to have a comprehensive body of law through its own legislative process to repeal or to amend the huge body of existing British laws. Such localization and adaptation has begun taking place since 1985. For example, bilingual practice began in the legislature and the court room in 1989.

Judicial independence from executive and legislative interference has, of course, long been the hallmark of British practice in Hong Kong. The Basic Law promises to maintain this independence. As in Britain, the Chief Justice of Hong Kong is the administrative head of the Judiciary. The current Supreme Court consists of nine Appeal Justices and twenty-three High Court Judges, who are aided by the Registrars, as Masters of the Supreme Court. Below the Supreme Court is the High Court, in charge of both civil and criminal cases, which are tried with a small or a large number of jurors as specified by law. Next to the High Court is the District Court, headed by the Chief District Court Judge – one of a group of some thirty judges who handle all cases without a jury. The largest volume of cases are handled in the Courts of the Magistrates, which together manage annually to hear approximately 90 per cent of all cases in Hong Kong. Most of the courts at all levels, together with the solicitors and barristers, have long relied on the English language. Only at the lowest level is Cantonese dialect or mandarin Chinese or another foreign language used with consent from the court.

The transition of sovereignty in 1997 has pressured the government to localize laws and to translate some 600 ordinances from English to Chinese. This task is being guided through the Attorney General's division, which also provides legal advice to all units of the government and the people and is responsible also for drafting all pieces of legislation for introduction in the LEGCO. The legal profession in Hong Kong, as in Britain, consists of some 3000 solicitors who are members of the Law Society, and 550 barristers who are members of the Bar Committee.[7] Both organizations have well-established standards or codes of conduct to govern their members. Thus, in Hong Kong the rule of law governs from the highest levels of government itself to the free legal practice of lawyers. Citizens and corporations depend heavily on contractual legal conduct, which is protected and regulated by the laws of precedent, of equity and of statutes. The public may receive legal services or advice from government agencies and other sources. The rule of law is a cultural tradition from which no one can deviate or escape. As such, Hong Kong is governed free of political and ideological interference. Citizen's rights and privacy are protected from other citizens and, especially, from the abuse of power by the government. What the transition of sovereignty may bring is, therefore, a matter of grave concern to all. Britain, China and the Hong Kong people may each interpret both the Joint Declaration and the Basic Law as they see fit. China has promised to keep the legal system for 50 years after 1997. Few believe it will keep this promise.[8]

There is need to replace the Judicial Committee of the House of Lords with a new Court of Final Appeal, which will exercise the jurisdiction of last resort. The task of negotiating on this replacement occurred within the Sino-British Joint Liaison Group which, after many rounds of talks, finally agreed in 1991 on the following: the CFA's jurisdiction will not include matters of national defense, foreign affairs and those of 'national conduct' in Hong Kong by officials of the Chinese government. The number of judges would be five, and no more than one would be a non-Chinese foreigner. The presiding judge must be a Chinese citizen from Hong Kong who has no foreign abode. The other three Chinese judges must be local Chinese but may have foreign residences.[9] The 1991 agreement was unacceptable to the LEGCO, which joined with the legal profession in opposing the 4:1 ratio between Chinese and foreign judges. Thus the CFA could not be created before 1997. The Executive Council of the Hong Kong government was caught between the LEGCO and the Beijing government, which would not renegotiate for changes. Because their disagreement persisted into 1993–4, the draft bill could not be introduced by the administration. A judicial 'vacuum of authority' will, thus, exist by July 1997. The LEGCO's rejection of the 1991 agreement disturbed both Governor Patten and Lu Ping of Beijing. China threatened to unilaterally create the CFA after 1997 in accordance with the Basic Law if Hong Kong should fail before 1997 to participate in it. Members of the LEGCO hoped to keep the CFA's total number of judgeships flexible so that more foreign judges could be allowed when necessary. Legislator Allen Lee, also head of the Liberal Party, wrote to plead with Lu Ping for such flexibility in judgeships in order to secure LEGCO approval and the support of the legal profession. His effort was rejected by Lu Ping.

By June 1995, the British administration in Hong Kong was again eager to push for a new agreement in order to have the CFA as soon as possible. This would, if successful, allow the court to function and acquire experience long before July 1997. The new agreement, after five long years of bargaining, consists of five major items, as announced in the government gazette in June 1995. The five items: (1) there is an improvement over the 1991 agreement on the basis of the eight recommendations of the Preparatory Working Committee (PWC); (2) included in the next draft bill for the CFA is the 'National Conduct' clause as described by Article 19 of the Basic Law; (3) the CFA cannot come into operation before 30 June 1997; (4) Britain's draft bill for the CFA must deny the future CFA the right to interpret the Basic Law because such right is reserved for the Standing Committee of the National People's Congress (NPC); and finally (5) China agrees that the legislative process to create the CFA must be completed before the end of July 1995. The Hong Kong government, in the new agreement, seemed to have made more concessions and to have reduced the role of the LEGCO to a mere rubber stamp.[10]

The new agreement touched off a major debate in Hong Kong. Some were happy while others were saddened. The Democratic Party claimed that the new agreement would 'serve the British interest at Hong Kong's expense'. Martin Lee warned that the imposition of 'national conduct' as defined by the central government in Beijing would drastically reduce the power or jurisdiction of the future CFA. He registered astonishment over Governor Patten's reversal of his previous firm position and accused him of hastening into agreement 'on his knees' within one week. The Liberal Party also complained, through Chairman Allen Lee, about the 'absence of flexibility' over foreign judges and against the postponement of the CFA's operational date until after 30 June 1997. The pro-China Democratic Alliance for the Betterment of Hong Kong accepted the new agreement with acclamation and considered the agreement very helpful toward 'peaceful transition'. Chairman Fung Kin-kee (Frederick Fung) of the Alliance for Democracy and the People's Livelihood was bitter over the inflexible restriction setting the number of judgeships at five and the allowance for only a single judge from a foreign country.[11] Needless to say, the 1995 agreement greatly lowered Patten's popularity.

Governor Patten denied any concessions made on his part. The postponement of the CFA's date for operation was necessary, he argued, to secure China's consent to the new agreement, which allowed for British participation in the court's creation. He complained angrily against the LEGCO's rejection of the 1991 agreement. It had frozen any effort in the past three years to make progress on the CFA. He warned the LEGCO, in turn, that should it reject the agreement again, there would be a 'judicial vacuum' after 1 July 1997. However, he failed to convince and to silence the members of the legal profession in Hong Kong. Back in Britain, many papers, including *The Times,* accused the governor of 'having lost all the accomplishments he had worked for' and said his new concessions went so far that they 'had ended already the British rule in Hong Kong'.[12] The day after the agreement, the governor sternly declared that he and China would stand by the new agreement. He reaffirmed that if the agreement was rejected, he would hold the LEGCO fully responsible for 'judicial vacuum' after the transition. And finally, he succeeded in outlasting severe criticism. The long dispute over the CFA was finally over.

GOVERNOR PATTEN'S STRUGGLE IN THE HUMAN RIGHTS DEBATE

The Preparatory Working Committee raised many critical issues concerning human rights and other new ordinances which declare that the protection of human rights supersedes six other British laws in conflict with the 1991 Human Rights Ordinance. China has been greatly worried politically about the implementation of human rights after 1997 in violation of the Basic Law, which will be Hong Kong's new constitution. In addition, China argues that the Basic Law itself provides sufficient protection for all rights.[13] China objected to Britain's incorporation of the two United Nations human rights covenants, which had been adopted by the United Nations in 1966, into the Human Rights Ordinance. The British government itself has made no effort to implement these two international rights documents since her assent in 1977. Beijing saw this British inaction as an deliberate plot to supersede the Basic Law and a deliberate show of 'hypocritical arrogance'.

The governor was reported to have always been resentful of the PWC, which had no legal standing in either the Joint Declaration or the Basic Law. Many members of the PWC had been former high-level British appointees who were lately invited to become Beijing's advisers on Hong Kong affairs. They recommended that Beijing abolish portions of the Human Rights Ordinance of 1991 and return to six previous police regulations. The governor's failure to cooperate with members of the PWC further antagonized them, so it was natural for the PWC to confront the governor on his other 'sneaking steps' in violation of the Basic Law. On a broader perspective, it must be remembered that China does not, in principle, want to be interfered or meddled with in any way that restricts its post-1997 sovereignty to voluntarily implement the Basic Law to protect human rights. Beijing cannot be expected to accept any laws which China considers to supersede the Basic Law. In short, any PWC recommendations to abolish or to revise after 1997 will be new sources of conflict, especially in regard to the protection of human rights.[14]

Governor Patten was deeply disturbed over the possibility of abolishing the 1991 Ordinance on Human Rights and restoring the six previous ordinances on liberty over autocracy. On his October 1995 trip to London, he took this concern to Cabinet level, reporting it directly to Prime Minister Major. He also raised British public attention and media discussion on human rights practice in Hong Kong after 1997. The entire concern was soon discussed at the highest diplomatic level.[15] On 20 October 1995 Chinese Deputy Foreign Minister (current Ambassador to Britain) Jiang Enchu and British chief delegate Mr Davis of the Sino-British Joint Liaison Group met to discuss formally the recommended changes on human rights legislation in Hong Kong and the future implementation of the Basic Law on civil and political rights. Again, Jiang was concerned about the supersessory nature of the recent LEGCO laws. There was no meeting of minds. Each side simply restated its own position. China declared it reserved the right to re-examine all British 'newly-revised laws' after the 1997 takeover to prevent the superseding imposition on the Basic Law.[16]

The human rights dispute does not seem to discourage China's confident claim that it will retain the Hong Kong people's support through its long-term success in preserving 'stability and prosperity' in Hong Kong. The deputy foreign minister again reassured the people publicly that 'all their existing rights will be fully protected'. He urged Britain to 'cooperate and to avoid new troubles'.[17] Mr Davis, on his part, reaffirmed that 'the British Hong Kong government's position on human rights has been quite clear. That is that human rights laws do not contradict the Basic Law.' The PWC accusation of violation of the Basic Law and the proposed restoration of the six replaced previous laws remain very serious political problems for the majority of people in Hong Kong. The Hong Kong government itself has never claimed that the Human Rights Ordinance of 1991 have any superseding force above the Basic Law. After 1997, any laws on human rights protection will emerge from Article 39 of the Basic Law. This is the juridical interpretation of the current official position of some in the British government in Hong Kong. Until 1997, the government depends on Order-in-Council as the source of human rights legislation, not on the United Nations covenants as mistakenly construed juridically by China to justify its fear of a superseding illegitimacy. Others in the Hong Kong government are much more critical of the PWC's recommendations on human rights protection. Chief Justice T.L. Yang has taken, so far unsuccessfully, a high road of 'silence over Sino-British controversy' on human rights because, as he claimed, the dispute has been 'politicized and sentimentalized far beyond judicial clarification with equity. Governor Patten and Chan Fang On-Sang, on the other hand, have been the strongest proponents of the incorporation of the two United Nations covenants into Hong Kong's legal protection of human rights. There is, no doubt, overwhelming public support, in addition to widespread support among members of the legal profession, in favor of a strong entrenchment in human rights protection before the transition in July 1997.

Legally and politically, defending Hong Kong's free way of life is foremost on the agenda of the Democratic Party, which wants new laws before 1997, especially in the establishment of independent agencies to protect human rights. Late in 1995 when China, for the second time, sentenced human rights fighter Wei Jingsheng to another 14 years of imprisonment, the leaders of this largest party in the LEGCO sought an urgent meeting with the governor for a series of new legislation to protect human rights in Hong Kong. Martin Lee and his party were most concerned in late 1995 over the formation of the Preparatory Committee in early 1996. As China's 'shadow government', the PC might soon interfere in the British process of governing. According to the Basic Law stipulation, the Hong Kong government must cooperate with the PC immediately after its formation. Thus, the Democratic Party leaders on 18 December 1995, requested the governor to undertake the following three measures:

(1) Establishment of an Independent Human Rights Commission;
(2) Establishment of an Independent Legal Service Organization;

(3) Abolition of all colonial ordinances against rebellion and the overthrow of government, which have provided penalties of various kinds and degrees.[18]

These requests carry with them serious political implications. For example, Governor Patten in 1994 had decided not to create a Human Rights Commission for fear of Beijing's strong opposition. However, Martin Lee and his LEGCO colleagues were certain that, under the new popular feeling in Hong Kong, they could deliver the passage of a draft bill on human rights. Such a new law would strengthen the administration of complaints on human rights violations after 1997. In addition, the Foreign Affairs Committee of the House of Commons in London and the International Commission of Jurists have all urged the establishment of such a Human Rights Commission.

On its own initiative, the Hong Kong government long ago started to gather together the scattered edicts and ordinances on rebellion to overthrow the regime for consideration and discussion at Sino-British Joint Liaison Group. However, leaders of the Democratic Party urged the governor not to wait for the JLG's decision and asked him to introduce a draft bill through the LEGCO within two months. If no such bill was introduced within two months, members of the LEGCO might take the initiative to introduce their own 'private member's bill'.[19] In short, the governor remains in charge. However, Beijing's PC is already in operation, and the governor must cooperate with it as required under the Joint Declaration.

THE LEGCO AND THE PWC STRUGGLE OVER HUMAN RIGHTS AND LOCALIZATION OF LAWS

As just described, the unusually bitter disagreement between the governor and the LEGCO took place over the 1995 Sino-British Agreement on the Court of Final Appeal. To the overwhelming criticism of Governor Patten in the LEGCO and the legal profession in Hong Kong, we must add the media attack on Patten in Britain. *The Times* of London, in its editorial, suggested that the new CFA agreement reflected

'Britain's return to the pre-1992 policy toward China', a policy no longer willing to protect the people's interest in Hong Kong. The pro-labor *Observer* of London attacked the governor on his retreat from his support of the CFA's early start before July 1997. The paper also admitted Britain's early defeat on the 'through train' and now said that Britain had 'reneged on the protection of the CFA's jurisdiction' and judgeship flexibility. The new CFA agreement put the court totally under Beijing's control from the very first day after 1 July 1997. London officials, however, firmly held the LEGCO responsible if it would choose to reject the agreement.[20]

Within the LEGCO, the Democratic Party members moved to oppose the PWC recommendations to Beijing to abolish part of the 1991 Human Rights Ordinance and to restore part of the old anti-liberty ordinances concerning human rights in Hong Kong. One of the LEGCO motions urged the government to continue its revision of still other regulations in support of human rights practice. At the same time in 1995, five LEGCO members attended the United Nations Human Rights Conference of 1995 in Geneva. LEGCO members Emily Lau and Christine Loh reported from the Geneva Conference that (1) the United Nations expected Britain to continue to submit an annual report on the human rights record in Hong Kong; (2) whether China would make such a report on behalf of Hong Kong or would authorize the Hong Kong government to do so remains in doubt until after 1997; (3) the UN Conference was seriously concerned about the PWC's recommendations to revise other Hong Kong ordinances after 1997. Since China has not been a member of the United Nations Human Rights Conference, whether the Beijing government will make such a report, as required through the Joint Declaration, remains to be seen. Other delegates to the Geneva Conference criticized the disingenuity of the British delegate's responses to questions at the conference and criticized those delegates representing the British Hong Kong government at the conference for following principles that violated the United Nations Covenants on Human Rights.[21] Within the LEGCO, on 27 October 1995, a motion was approved to send LEGCO delegations to Beijing and London to request information about how Hong Kong will make the human rights report to the United Nations after 1997. The motion further urged London and Beijing to reach agreement on this quickly.[22]

The PWC subgroup on law, on the other hand, remained firm in its recommendations to the Chinese government to oppose the 1991 ordinance that human rights be incorporated into Hong Kong's legal system. This subgroup on law had worked carefully for nearly two years. It had reviewed some 600 British ordinances, approximately 20 of which were recommended for abolition. For example, the 1994–5 election laws calling for three-tier government were included for abolition. Despite bitter popular opposition, the subgroup voted in Beijing on 7 November 1995 to firmly maintain its original recommendations.[23]

As indicated in previous chapters, the PWC was a major instrument set up to conduct serious research and policy studies unilaterally, leading to recommendations which were to be made to the yet-to-be-organized Preparatory Committee, which itself could only be created in early 1996 according to the Basic Law. Indeed, the 150-member PC later voted to accept the entire PWC recommendations by all five subgroups, each of which had worked for nearly two years. The tasks of these subgroups were broad and covered all aspects of policy-making relevant to the transition in July 1997.

Seven current LEGCO members are simultaneously members of the PWC who are also Beijing's advisers on Hong Kong affairs. They actively participated in the LEGCO's debates on human rights and on all statutes passed since 1990, when human rights covenants were incorporated. All seven took a unanimous stand in defense of the PWC recommendations. Some of them insisted that the decision to oppose the PWC recommendations and to strengthen human rights practice should be left for the future SAR government to decide after 1997. The motion to oppose the PWC recommendations was introduced in the LEGCO by joint effort of both the Democratic Party and the Liberal Party, with strong support from the Alliance for Democracy and the People's Livelihood. Members of the pro-China Democratic Alliance for the Betterment of Hong Kong opposed the motion, of course. Meanwhile, the governor's Executive Council declared that Hong Kong's human rights statutes did not contradict the Joint Declaration and the Basic Law.

Officials in charge came to attend the LEGCO debate on 13 November 1995. They reaffirmed that 'all human rights statutes in Hong Kong are in accord with the Basic Law'. They cited the Joint Declaration and the Basic law as supporting, after 1997, the continuity of both the United Nations Covenant of Civil and Political Rights and the United Nations Covenant of Economic, Social and Cultural Rights. Thus, there were 'no reasons to meddle with Human Rights Statutes'.[24]

On 15 November 1995 the LEGCO passed the 'motion to oppose the PWC recommendations on human rights legislation' by 40 to 15. What the SAR government in Hong Kong or the National People's Congress in Beijing will do after July 1997 on human rights practice will be of great concern to the six million residents in Hong Kong. During the LEGCO debate, officials of the government pledged to 'take all opportunities' to explain to China the PWC's misinterpretation of human rights statutes and also to explain that Basic Law Article 39 clearly supports what the Hong Kong government has achieved in the human rights field for now and for the future after 1997. On the other hand, pro-China LEGCO members insisted (1) that the PWC recommendations did not oppose human rights in Hong Kong, but opposed only the portions of the statutes that superseded and contradicted the Joint Declaration and the Basic Law; (2) that the superseding aspects tended to reduce the executive power of the government; (3) that Britain never promoted human rights before 1990 and that the United States, a super champion for rights, did not even sign up the UNCCPR and the UNCESCR, and that, furthermore, human rights practice and the superseding statutes in Hong Kong had no direct relations; and (4) that Article 3 of the draft bill stated that it supersedes other laws and, therefore, this is a clear contradiction; (5) that the 1984 Joint Declaration pledged to retain, without change, the legal foundation of law in Hong Kong. But, in spite of this, the British unilaterally began promoting human rights legislation during the transition stage and drastically revising other laws. Britain 'has violated the principle of the Joint Declaration'. From the perspective of international law or practice, China has certainly the right not to accept all such drastic revisions.[25]

We believe both China and Britain failed to use the JLG, which was designed to bridge communications, to keep each other well informed and to reach agreement, for example on the new airport and the Court of Final Appeal. They avoided constructively using the JLG on political serious issues including incorporating human rights legislation into Hong Kong's legal system. Britain, perhaps, should bear more responsibility for the failure of prior discussion and agreement with China on human rights. Since Governor Patten came to Hong Kong, confrontation and unilateral implementation of both the Joint Declaration and the Basic Law have led to mutual animosity. The human rights crisis was but one of many such examples.

China since early 1994 relied heavily on the PWC, which had some 57 members (27 from Hong Kong and 30 from China and 13 more added later) who produced policy papers *vis-à-vis* Governor Patten's unilateral election reform. Perhaps too long an intervening period between 1984 and 1997 has been the major reason that unexpected events have destroyed mutual trust: for example, the Tiananmen Incident and Britain's surprise decision to implement Patten's unilateral reform. The Beijing regime did not want to accept the consequences of reform. The PWC was merely acting as Beijing's invisible 'shadow' in this serious undertaking.

BEIJING'S ARGUMENTS ON THE COURT OF FINAL APPEAL AND THE HUMAN RIGHTS DEBATE

Before we describe the Chinese positions on both human rights and the Court of Final Appeal (CFA), we must first note a philosophical difference between the Chinese and Western outlook on future human rights development. The Beijing *People's Daily*, the official mouthpiece of the Communist Party, accused 'Western critics of seeking to impose on China their own lofty standards'.[26] China resented the US Department of State's characterization of her human rights performance as an 'unprovoked accusation and attack on a different society'. To the Chinese government, there is a strong link between traditional cultural concepts and contemporary human rights performance. China should pursue 'its own path' and 'ignore foreign threats'. Beijing dislikes 'Hegemonism and strong arm tactics'. China reacted often sharply to the US State Department's reports of its failure to meet 'accepted norms' on human rights. Beijing often cites as an example of the American failure on human rights, the discrepancy between promised constitutional equality without discrimination and the actual racial struggle from 1789 to the present. Beijing points out that the modern Western colonial conquest in the name of 'survival of the fittest' was a gross violation of rights. It was used to justify colonialism and American slavery. However, the world is changing. The 'developing world' should not blindly accept the doctrines of the West. There are other, non-Western, civilizations. Each nation should follow its own history and development. Anti-Semitism, old and new, in the West, and lynching in America were examples of 'domestic' affairs. Each country should seek improvement internally. On this basis of such sovereign independence in internal affairs, the Beijing government has negotiated with Britain on the CFA after 1997.

According to Basic Law stipulations, the court of Final Appeal was to operate beginning 1 July 1997 when Britain departs. But in February 1988 Britain suggested that the CFA be created and begin operation earlier. China yielded and negotiated for the successful agreement of September 1991. The agreement designated four 'standing judges' and one 'non-standing judge' who was to be chosen by the chief judge from the list of non-standing Chinese judges or from the list of non-standing foreign judges as the trials on hand may so dictate. Additionally, Britain agreed in 1991 to negotiate with China during each stage of the organization of the CFA about the court's jurisdiction, its civil and criminal procedures, and judges' 'appointment and dismissal'. Unfortunately in December 1991 Britain chose to submit the agreement to the LEGCO for approval. The LEGCO rejected it on the grounds that there would not be enough foreign judges in the court. To Beijing, Britain deliberately placed the LEGCO above the Executive Council by allowing the LEGCO to judge and veto an agreement between two sovereign countries. Beijing pointed out that as the LEGCO had never been more than an advisory body to the governor according to well-established practice in colonial Hong Kong, it could not be allowed to supersede the sovereign authority of Beijing and London. This was clearly 'Britain's trap of a three-legged chair', thereby making Hong Kong 'an independent or semi-independent' political entity. Beijing saw this as further proof of Britain's lack of honesty in carrying out the agreement. Again, Britain did nothing for three years on the CFA establishment until late 1994 when she delivered for China's consideration a revised court draft. Britain's lack of honesty, or at least, total honesty, can be indicated by the following:

1. Oppressive pressure was applied to obtain China's quick reaction to the draft. This was an attempt to hold China responsible for any delay after Britain gave the draft to China in early 1995. The governor and his officials publicly and repeatedly called for the early creation of the CFA to avoid a 'judicial vacuum' after July 1997.

2. Britain refused to promise not to proceed unilaterally. Because the CFA rides the 'through train' into post-1997 Hong Kong judiciary and because the CFA must converge with the Basic Law to assure stability in Hong Kong, China requested the British to allow it sufficient time for careful study. This request was rejected by Britain because of its 'legislative timetable'.

3. Britain violated the Joint Declaration by not keeping negotiations in the JLG secret. Britain further deliberately distorted China's negotiating position. In May 1995, the Hong Kong government falsely leaked to the media that China would allow the 'CFA jurisdiction to handle only economic matters'. The Hong Kong government further gave out misinformation that China would set up an organization to repudiate the CFA's decision whenever Beijing disapproved of a court decision. Britain let the Hong Kong residents know that she herself was 'defending Hong Kong's final jurisdiction'.

4. Taking advantage of the large number of pro-British LEGCO members 'to proceed with the debate' in the LEGCO, Britain was both able to know the size of LEGCO support and to put pressure on China.[27] The Beijing regime accused the Hong Kong government

of attempting to create the CFA unilaterally to preserve its colonial legacy. To counter this distortion,
China's PWC issued an eight-point statement of principles. Beijing allowed that the CFA would be created
before 1 July 1997 but would not be operative until
after 1 July 1997. The so-called 'judicial vacuum' simply
was never intended.[28]

On balance and after five years of dispute over the scope
of jurisdiction, over judgeships and over the flexibility of
foreign judges of the CFA, the Beijing government appeared
to have gotten the better of the 1995 negotiation. Perhaps,
Governor Patten tacitly admitted this when he hailed it as
'the best arrangement' without suggesting any positive virtue in Hong Kong's favor. The LEGCO could not amend
the new agreement when Patten threatened with his veto
against any major changes proposed by the LEGCO. One
of Beijing's major victories in the 1995 negotiations was that
the CFA could be set up only after July 1997 and was to be
structured according to the PWC's eight-point principles.
The court was mainly to be the responsibility of Beijing's
Preparatory Committee, with the British Hong Kong government playing only a minor assisting role. Moreover, a new
feature of the Sino-British agreement included the designa-
tion of CFA's jurisdiction as 'National Conduct' according
to Article 19 of the Basic Law. This 'National Conduct' clause
may actually reduce the court's power, because politically
sensitive issues may be referred to the central government
for assistance.[29] According to point 4 of the new agreement,
the LEGCO must complete the legislative process before the
end of July 1995. The new agreement was signed on 9 June
1995. In short, Britain and the LEGCO came to accept what
China had all along insisted regarding the Court of Final
Appeal to replace the Privy Council's Judicial Committee.[30]
   The Chinese government in late 1995 realized, perhaps,
that the PWC's firm position in recommending the abolition of portions of human rights statutes and the restoration of six previous colonial regulations concerning rights
protection was, indeed, very unpopular in Hong Kong. The
Hong Kong and Macao Affairs Office (HKMAO) in October
1995 took two major steps to reassure the six million resi-

dents. The first step was to restate in an eight-point announcement by one of Mr Lu Ping's deputy directors:

1. The Hong Kong Special Administrative Region (HKSAR) keeps its capitalist economic system and trade relations;
2. The HKSAR keeps its free port status in trade and capital free flow policies;
3. HKSAR keeps its independent customs practice. In the name of 'China, Hong Kong', it participates in customs union, and trade tariff agreement, and other 'most-favored' trade arrangements;
4. HKSAR keeps its current status as an international financial center, including its present currency system;
5. The HKSAR can freely adopt its currency policy and protect its currency market management;
6. The Hong Kong dollar remains as the SAR's own currency for free flow;
7. HKSAR keeps its own harbor and sea trade management and ship registration system, including those to be authorized by the central government; and
8. HKSAR may propose new expansion, adopting new managements to keep its international and regional current aviation status.[31]

These reassurances to the people in manufacturing and commerce in Hong Kong affect nearly the entire population of the colony. They have been seriously concerned about other emerging seaports and trade centers along the long coast of Chinese provinces. The second step of the HKMAO leadership was to reassure the Hong Kong residents that the current capitalist system of government and trade may never change, not even 50 years beyond 1997.

British concessions making the future new CFA too weak to protect the rule of law was very 'provocative and much resented' by the general population, especially among the legal profession, the civil service and political parties. On the other hand, pro-China leaders felt ignored by the Beijing government; they felt they were isolated by the anti-China sentiment. In response to this situation, Beijing dispatched to Hong Kong three legal experts, who were also members of the PWC subgroup on law, to explain Beijing's position and to answer questions from those leaders who have, for years, represented the Hong Kong people in the National People's Congress, or in the Chinese People's Political Consultative Conference, and those who have recently been appointed as Hong Kong Affairs Advisers and District Affairs Advisers. On 27 October 1995, through local NCNA arrangement, the three PWC members met with many groups to make clear to their pro-China audiences two major points: (1) the PWC recommendations to abolish portions of human rights statutes and to restore six pre-1991 ordinances would not change; and (2) Britain was guilty of spreading false information in an attempt to influence and deceive the public in Hong Kong.

The three legal expert members of the PWC met with some 90 local pro-China representatives. While meetings were held inside, protests took place outside. The protesters were angry students and pro-human rights local organizations. It was reported that nothing of substance was achieved by the legal experts of China. Those at the meetings complained that they did not have time to express their own views and those who did speak disagreed with the guest experts.[32]

The three experts also made their point through the local media. They directly accused the governor of leading the protesters to challenge the PWC recommendations. They defended and justified these recommendations as being necessary, correct and constructive. They accused the governor of trying to influence those who did not understand the 'real situation'. They further accused Britons of using human rights covenants 'to heap up restrictions' against China after 1997. Britain had not allowed such restrictions before 1990 against its colonial government, yet Britain wanted the people to restrict and criticize the future SAR government after 1997. In Beijing's judgment, this was a 'British plot' to stir up anti-China public sentiment. They observed, finally, that 'a legal vacuum' may indeed come into existence after British withdrawal if the six pre-1990 statutes can not be restored after 1997.

Many pro-China leaders commented after the meeting that they had not been convinced by the legal experts. Some said that the Basic Law itself provides commitment to uphold human rights in Hong Kong after 1997. Some repeated that the human rights issue could not be settled until after

1997 when the first SAR government takes over. Others re-iterated that public confidence in the SAR government was much compromised already regardless what might happen after the British withdrawal. Allen Lee, as Chairman of the Liberal Party and a Hong Kong Affairs Adviser, commented that he 'had not learned anything new' and remained 'opposed to the PWC recommendations'. In short, human rights legislation in Hong Kong, at any time and under any regime, will remain more political in nature and substance, and less constitutional and legalistic. Among politicians, between political parties, and within the academic community, the human rights debate will continue after 1997. Average residents in Hong Kong are likely to remain less concerned and less interested. For them, Hong Kong does not have a long tradition of popular human rights culture or consciousness. What the Beijing government has failed, in our judgment, to realize is that it has elevated the debate itself to a high consciousness, a greater seriousness, and a politicized new popular awareness. As such, human rights issues before 1997 will likely bring harm to 'smooth governing'. Besides, the future 'politics by consultation' will be the real victim because many residents will not speak out their true judgment if what they say cannot influence the policy-makers.[33]

PUBLIC REACTIONS TO THE COURT OF FINAL APPEAL AGREEMENT AND THE HUMAN RIGHTS DEBATE

As just described above, even pro-China Hong Kong representatives in the NPC and the CPPCC and those serving as Hong Kong Affairs Advisers were uncomfortable on the issues of both the CFA and human rights.[34] In defense of Beijing's position on human rights, Deputy Director Zhang Junsheng of local NCNA even cited Chief Justice T.L. Yang's private comments publicly, claiming new human rights statutes were a source of conflict with the Basic Law. Chief Justice Yang felt betrayed by Zhang for quoting from his casual and private dinner conversation. He suddenly was criticized for an ethical violation of judicial neutrality over political debate. The media pursued him for a response to Deputy Director

Zhang Junsheng's citation. He regretted being dragged into debate over sensitive issues, complained that he had been misquoted, and revealed that he had learned his lesson and would not make such private conversation in the future.[35]

Many members of the public supported the positions taken by the Democratic Party and the Liberal Party in the LEGCO. The public was apprehensive that future interpretation of the 'national conduct' included in the new CFA agreement might allow the central government to encroach upon future court jurisdiction. The public expected the LEGCO's motion to revise the agreement although they were aware of the governor's power to disallow and to prevent such revision. Many agreed with Allen Lee's argument that the agreement not to organize the CFA long before 1997 would prevent it from acquiring valuable judicial experience while the British remained in charge. Such unnecessary delay till after 1997 was also one of the complaints of the professional organizations of the solicitors and barristers.[36]

Attorney Lau Yao-chu (Dorothy Lau), a member of NPC, in a speech agreed with Tsang Yok-sing, chairman of the pro-China DAB Party, that the PWC's announcement of its recommendations on human rights was untimely and destructive when human rights experts from all parts of the world were at a world conference on human rights. As a well-known legal expert, Dorothy Lau observed that after 1997 the Basic Law itself will be able to supersede any other law. She pointed out that Chapter 3 of the Basic Law (Articles 23–41) pledges to protect human rights. Article 38 reads: 'The provisions of the International Covenant on Civil and Political Rights and the International Covenant on Economic, Social and Cultural Rights as applied to Hong Kong shall be implemented through legislation by the Hong Kong Special Administrative Region.'

Article 38 is more than sufficient to sweep away and to supersede any other obstacles after 1997. Attorney Dorothy Lau directed her criticism against the PWC's 'unnecessary interference' and said that she expected China's explanation after 1997 to eliminate any obstacles to implementing the Basic Law on human rights. Her contention further pointed out the NPC's lack of power to accept the PWC's recommendations to eliminate some of the statutes in

Hong Kong.[37] Rather, the Preparatory Committee, which will institute the new SAR government according to the Basic Law or the future SAR government itself, has power, through simple legislation, to nullify all of the 'unconstitutional laws'.

Tsang Yok-sing agreed with Dorothy Lau that the Standing Committee of the NPC could not have the power expected of it by the PWC without contradicting the Basic Law. He reminded the public that Beijing had long declared that it did not recognize the new laws unilaterally made 'during the twilight of British withdrawal'. Tsang reiterated that human rights legislation came late and suddenly and thus violated the spirit of the Joint Declaration and the Basic Law. However, he did not see serious violations by the new legislation.[38] The conservative *Ming Bao Daily* in Hong Kong declared in its editorial that the PWC recommendations 'should be in accord with the primary interests of Hong Kong' as a basic assumption. If so, the recommendations should be considered absurd because these 'recommendations are not related to post-1997 national defence, foreign policy or relations between central and SAR government'. In addition, the recommendations had been attacked by the two legal societies, by pro-China groups, and even by the middle-of-the-road Liberal Party in the LEGCO. Under such circumstances, if the NPC Standing Committee should accept the 'bad recommendations', it would violate the Basic Law's promise of 'Hong Kong people governing Hong Kong' and would thus go against 'people's interest in Hong Kong'. If the Beijing government would not concede on the human rights dispute, it would be creating a crisis to repeat the recent dispute over the Court of Final Appeal that had produced an enormous conflict and much animosity.

The media people in Hong Kong delivered an 'opinion paper' which declared, in case the NPC's Standing Committee should approve the PWC recommendations, that Hong Kong's 'spirit for freedom and its international reputation' would be seriously damaged. In that case, people in all walks of life would sharply lose their confidence in 'one country, two systems'.[39] The 'opinion paper' of the press people continued, saying that so long as the Basic Law is fully adhered to, and so long as the new statutes are intended to promote human rights and to eliminate or revise the brutal and out-dated colonial ordinances, such new statutes cannot be considered as violating the Basic Law.[40] The opinion paper suggested, in conclusion, that the whole matter should be referred to the future SAR Chief Executive and legislature to settle.

In response to questions in the LEGCO on 16 November 1995, the governor chided the PWC and the Chinese officials for the anti-Basic Law recommendations. On the other hand, he called for an end to the dispute in order to prevent international loss of confidence in Hong Kong's future. He went on to deny the charge that the British and Hong Kong governments instigated the dispute in debate as accused. The governor added, furthermore, that a new possible violation of the Joint Declaration and article 39 of the Basic Law would be committed if China should prohibit the future SAR government from making an annual report to the United Nations Human Rights Commission on progress in Hong Kong.[41]

On 17 November 1995 some 50 students from the University of Hong Kong marched to the front gate of the Chinese NCNA in protest against the PWC recommendations on human rights. The students on their way were several times obstructed by police interference. These students asked the Beijing government to come down and consult the majority of people on human rights issues. They also accumulated a list of more than one thousand names from the teaching faculty and staff of the University of Hong Kong which they intended to present to Hong Kong's delegates to the National People's Congress in Beijing.

By October and November of 1995, the human rights debate over the power and jurisdiction of the Court of Final Appeal became a major controversy dividing the public and the officials in the government in Hong Kong. The promise of 'a high degree of autonomy and free life-style' of the Joint Declaration seemed at stake in such debate. Thus, the application of Basic Law after 1997 depends on public consensus over the controversy and Beijing's willingness not to interfere in the court's exercise of the common law tradition by explaining, applying, interpreting and updating the meaning of the Basic Law. Many lawyers and legal experts are seriously concerned about Beijing's attitude toward the court's power. Human rights enforcement and judiciary independence in Hong Kong are inseparable.[42]

What worries the public and experts in Hong Kong is why the PWC had to recommend, and why Beijing's media in Hong Kong firmly supported, the repeal of new laws and the restoration of six brutal outdated British ordinances. Britain's colonial government should be hailed in the 1990s for its willingness to sponsor pro-human rights legislation and to give up administrative authority to restrict such freedom of speech, the right to assemble, and so on. This liberalization of what in the past had been undemocratic control was certainly welcomed by most of the residents of Hong Kong. Such voluntary relinquishment of oppressive administrative ordinance was in accord with Article 29 of the Basic Law. If Beijing understands the impact of the Tiananmen Incident of 1989, it will certainly agree with the residents of Hong Kong on their peaceful demand for such liberal legislation as 'an insurance to protect their free way of life'. In the spirit of 'one country, two systems', the people of Hong Kong can certainly exercise their right under the Basic Law to make such new laws after transition in 1997.[43]

INTERNATIONAL INTEREST IN HONG KONG AND ITS TRANSITION IN 1997

Hong Kong's return to China did not attract much international attention until after the Tiananmen Incident in 1989. Suddenly after the incident, anti-China sentiment grew and has remained constant from concern over one issue or another. Hong Kong has occupied continuing attention from many quarters of the world, especially the US government and the governments of Western Europe. China has painfully engaged in cultural explanation and political self-defense in response to outside criticism against Beijing's handling of the Hong Kong transition or the Tibetan unrest, the prison labor and the military exercise in the Taiwan Strait in March 1996. Basically, with anger, Beijing has labeled all such outside interests as ranging from pure unfriendly complaints to hostile meddling in China's human rights record in domestic affairs. The external interference that disturbs Beijing most has been the intense concern over human rights violations – not the real violations committed by the British in the past in Hong Kong, but the 'presumed' violations China may commit in its future dealings with Hong Kong.

The *People's Daily* in Beijing and pro-China media in Hong Kong report regularly on external meddling in the human rights controversy in Hong Kong. Several pro-Beijing papers in Hong Kong, such as the *Ta Kung Bao* and *Wen Hui Bao* have deeply engaged in China's defense against the so-called 'British or external' complicity or conspiracy in Hong Kong's future affairs. The truth may, for most casual readers, be difficult to uncover, for it depends on which daily in Hong Kong one reads – for example, the English *South China Morning Post* or the Chinese language *Wen Hui Bao*. The official NCNA had repeatedly repudiated deception by the Hong Kong government in publicly saying that its human rights legislation had no supersessory validity over or above the Basic Law, while privately admitting that it does.[44] The Beijing government claimed that such legislation legally violated the Basic Law and was a political obstruction to 'peaceful and smooth' transition before 1997. The Chinese foreign ministry in Beijing declared that such 'unilateral revision of pre-1991 security or police ordinances' was in violation of the Joint Declaration and the Basic Law. Hence, China will not recognize its validity. Furthermore, the same foreign ministry spokesman, Chen Jiang, declared, according to the United Nations Charter and its Articles 1 and 2, that the United Nations itself 'has no right to interfere in China's internal affairs'.[45] There seems to be a growing crisis over human rights in Hong Kong after 1997.

On the other hand, since the Tiananmen Incident, the people have in truth lost confidence in China's desire to genuinely implement the Joint Declaration on Human Rights. They did not want to rely on Article 29 of the Basic Law to protect global standards on human rights. The International Commission of Jurists (ICJ) in 1992 released its long report, which criticizes both Britain and China. This juristic report can be further discussed in terms of political developments in both Hong Kong and China. The major points of contention of the ICJ report include the following:

1. The people of Hong Kong were not allowed to exercise 'the right of self-determination';
2. Before the Joint Declaration was signed, Britain should have had a 'referendum' on the wishes of the people;
3. The British should have helped to provide the right of 'abode for all' British citizens there; and
4. The Joint Declaration failed 'to ensure' the election of the Chief Executive democratically and to subsequently hold him accountable to the people of Hong Kong.[46]

Such charges by the ICJ are oversimplifications. The political reality in 1992 was far beyond the British legal ability to handle. The British had little power to bargain with China. Our discussion of the ICJ'S major points of contention will follow later.

United States interest in Hong Kong has received many hostile comments from Beijing. The American Congress has often expressed in an unfriendly manner its deep concern about presumed human rights violations after 1997. One recent comment, however, came from the retiring US consul-general in Hong Kong, whose words were far more diplomatic than the expressions from Congress or the American media have been. He avoided commenting on the provisional legislature to replace the popularly elected LEGCO, but stressed American expectations of continuous human rights protection, freedom of the press and hence free information flow. He referred to American support for successful transition: one that would keep the political system open to reflect the public opinion of all Hong Kong residents. He praised Governor Patten's political reform to involve popular participation as a new spirit which the American government continues to support in Hong Kong's development.[47]

Very few Asian countries, however, have expressed hostile or strong policy differences against the British or China. Singapore's former Prime Minister Lee Kuan Yew was, perhaps, the only Asian leader who openly criticized Governor Patten's 1994–5 election reform. Collectively, at the Bangkok Conference of Asian Countries in March 1993, the participants signed a Bangkok Declaration. The Asian countries declared their strong opposition to the 'concept of universality' of human rights derived from 'Western liberal thinking'.[48] Ross Daniels wrote in Hong Kong that he feared the Bangkok Declaration 'could enable China to introduce its own rules in Hong Kong after 1997'. The World Conference on Human Rights put the Bangkok Declaration on its 1993 agenda for discussion to prevent 'a step backwards'. It is clear that the human rights debate is a way to put pressure on China. It seems that the West presumes to set the standard for human rights. However, many African, Asian and the Islamic nations cannot live up to the Western standard. Even the USA still has racial and religious crises and discrimination. Fully realizing all this, China seems determined not to accept external interferences in its domestic sovereignty.

The United Nations Human Rights Commission (UNHRC) is, of course, rightfully concerned about the human rights record in all countries. On 3 November 1995 in the midst of human rights conflicts between Britain and China, the UNHRC in its written statement declared its support of the British revision of colonial outdated ordinances in protection of international human rights incorporation into Hong Kong's political system. The Commission further declared that China 'will be obligated to submit annual reports' as Britain had done in recent years. The UNHRC commented upon and then recommended for improvement six areas of human rights in Hong Kong, such as the election system, the Court of Final Appeal and women's rights. More specifically, the Commission criticized the British discrimination in the election system which allocates seats to groups on the basis of wealth and their social function. Thus, Britain has violated Article 25 of the Civil and Political Covenant. The Commission reiterated that the improvement in human rights should not be affected by the transfer of sovereignty to China. Such comments and recommendations, contrary to the PWC recommendations to the Beijing regime, were very much appreciated by the Hong Kong delegates to the 1995 Geneva Conference of the United Nations on Human Rights.[49] Again, we perceive that China is under great pressure from the outside world to improve its policy and performance on human rights. The Bangkok Declaration signed in 1993 by most Asian countries is squarely in conflict with the United Nation's position. In short, Hong Kong's access to all trading nations after its return to China in 1997 is, indeed, a major concern to her trading partners and investors. Its continuing stability and prosperity will affect many aspects of international economy. China's good faith and ability to maintain Hong Kong's system unchanged still concern other nations, especially in view of the Tiananmen Incident and the Hong Kong people's reaction to the incident.

The 1992 report by the International Commission of Jurists (ICJ) named four jurists – Sir William Goodhart of Britain, Y.M. Raja Aziz Addruse of Malaysia, The Honorable John Dowd of Australia, and Professor Hans-Heiner Kuehne of Germany – who came to Hong Kong in June 1992 'to take evidence and hear the views of the Hong Kong people'. In the Preface to the Report, the ICJ Secretary-General Adam Bieng stated: 'There is relatively little cause for concern about human rights in Hong Kong at present. The problem lies in the future.' And he stated in conclusion: 'The Report which follows is disturbing. The Mission is critical of the Basic Law which represents in many respects an evasion by China of the terms which it had agreed with the United Kingdom to apply to Hong Kong. The Report is also critical of the British government for its failure to allow the people of Hong Kong to exercise a right of self-determination and for its failure to object to the unsatisfactory provisions of the Basic Law.'[50] The Report correctly commented on a paradox for the people in Hong Kong, who are 'rich, well-educated, sophisticated' and capable of democratic self-government and 'yet governed with little dissent by an alien and authoritarian' colonial regime. Such a historical paradox logically, in our judgment, could only be understood because the people, in the last several decades, have resented communist government in the 'home country'. The four Mission members, unfortunately, stayed only ten days in Hong Kong to conduct research. During that time the Mission met only 'representatives of the legal profession, the press, the business community, the human rights organizations and the political parties'.[51] The majority average residents did not seem to have any opportunity to be interviewed in that short ten-day stay.

The Mission Report recognized the change in political atmosphere in Hong Kong before and after the Tiananmen

Incident. The following paragraph from the Report tells us a great deal about what has happened because of the unexpected events in China that subsequently compelled Britain, China and the residents in Hong Kong to respond as they each saw necessary in self-interest.[52]

When the first draft of the Basic Law was published in April 1988 for 'solicitation of opinions', the large majority of the people in Hong Kong showed little or no interest in it. An opinion survey conducted at the end of the five-month consultation period revealed that, of those who were interviewed, only one per cent claimed to have read the draft from cover to cover. But by 4 April 1990 when the final draft was adopted by the NPC, Hong Kong was no longer politically apathetic. A territory frightened by the brutal crackdown in June 1989 – the Beijing massacre – had been shaken out of its complacency. Efforts to obtain a reasonable measure of democracy, an effective Bill of Rights, and a judicial autonomy had all failed. Instead, curbs on 'subversion' and restrictions on those who had obtained foreign passports were included. Within three hours of the adoption of the Basic Law in Beijing, Hong Kong's reconstituted legislature voted to reject it. In a more dramatic gesture, the 170 000 strong Hong Kong Federation of Students dumped hundreds of torn copies of the draft Basic Law on the steps of the New China News Agency and condemned the drafting exercise as a 'shameful sell-out of Hong Kong's interests by Beijing and London'.

On page 193 we listed four ICJ complaints against Britain's failure to allow the residents in Hong Kong to decide whether they wanted 'self-determination' or independence. Britain was accused also of failure to conduct a public referendum to accept or reject the Joint Declaration. The ICJ holds Britain responsible for providing the right of abode for all Hong Kong residents qualified under British legislation. How, politically and economically, can Britain afford to accomplish these tasks if the residents in Hong Kong realistically would not want to go to Britain because it lacks economic opportunities for such a great number of people? On the other hand, China does not traditionally have a 'human rights culture' which meets high standards; and Britain did not allow human rights in Hong Kong for some

150 years and then suddenly favored a human rights ordinance in 1991. How can any ICJ legal expert realistically prevent future violations after 1997? How can effective monitoring of violations be accomplished if the future SAR government in Hong Kong and the Beijing government both refuse to cooperate after 1997? These realistic questions from the political and ideological standpoints cannot be easily evaded. These are questions the ICJ report did not, and perhaps could not, answer. The four-member mission in 1992 simply did not stay long enough to appreciate or even fully understand the political and economic realities. Britain, on the other hand, simply was incapable of accommodating, on demand, the right of abode in England. The simple truth is that Hong Kong itself never did legally have human rights protection and thus does not itself under the British have 'a human rights culture'. The Hong Kong people, by a huge majority expression, showed little interest in self-determination or independence before or after the Tiananmen Incident. Only recently have they wanted to use their 'people power' to demonstrate and to confront the Beijing government with the fact that they want Hong Kong to remain unchanged. This they can do without Britain and the West, and can continue to demonstrate until they are satisfied. We echo the ICJ's legal concern but not its unrealistic expectation in the report. The Mission's recommendations and conclusions are good reference for legal analysis when future human rights conflicts occur.[53] The Report was biased and unrealistic in both conclusions and recommendations.

On the other hand, China, from all indications, will not be able to comprehend all these human rights debates and arguments. This is true because, as the ICJ's mission to Hong Kong has pointed out, China's long history has not included the nurturing of a human rights culture. Confucian humanism was China's closest substitute for Western concepts of a human rights culture, but it was postulated on the premise of highly structured human group relations in a broader social context. With regard to Hong Kong, the Chinese counter argument or defense can be advanced that it is not a treaty-signer obligated to observe external demands on human rights performance under the International Covenants of Civil, Political, Economic, Social and Cultural Rights of

1966 of the United Nations. China was even excluded in 1966 from membership in the United Nations.

The other Chinese defense has been its strong objection to external interference in its sovereign domestic jurisdiction. China claims that it would never want, under international law, to interfere in the internal affairs of any other nation on human rights performance, whether there is a violation in the United States or elsewhere in racial inequality or lack of equal opportunities. Beijing relies, as just indicated, on Articles 1 and 2 of the United Nations Charter to make the cardinal distinction between external and internal affairs for all sovereign states. One of the strongest Chinese counter arguments has been its equal treatment since 1949 of some 55 ethnic minorities in all parts of the country. Its socialist economic system 'guarantees job opportunities for all, promotion of equal educational opportunities for all ethnic minorities in Tibet, Inner Mongolia, Yunnan, Guangxi and in Manchuria for the Korean ethnic minority in China'. Having one-sixth of the global population in China alone, the government claims as its great achievement in human rights its commitment to simply feed and clothe this huge number. This is considered by the Chinese to be a much greater accomplishment in human rights. There has been practically no legal barrier against women in China since the 1950s. The right of each of the 55 minority ethnic groups in China to use its own language in educational textbooks and media communication is another feature of pride. Because of international pressure, the Information Office of the State Council in Beijing published a book in 1991 explaining to the outside world China's efforts and unique culture on human rights. The Preface of the publication says:

> Old China lived under foreign imperialism, feudalism, and bureaucracy. There was no human rights to speak of. Since the overthrow of the old regime (in 1949) the status of human rights has drastically changed ... Those nations, which truly understand this change without preconceived bias, understand Chinese culture and problems and have openly given just praise to our achievement ... Globally human rights is a major concern everywhere. China too

strives to improve our records. However, human rights development in any single nation is conditioned by that nation's history, society, economy and culture . . . There is no single model for all other nations to follow. From China's own history and internal conditions at the present, and based on long time experience in practice, the Chinese people have developed their own concepts on human rights problems . . .[54]

In view of the long history of China and the current ideology of government under Marxism, there are vast differences between what the International Commission of Jurists has concluded and recommended on human rights records in Hong Kong and what the Beijing government is and is not able to do to comply. The ICJ in its 'Conclusions and Recommendations' made some 45 points either blaming Britain and China or trying to guide future human rights development in Hong Kong. While some of these points are worthy of praise, the majority are so impracticable politically as to be labeled 'wishful thinking'.[55] For example, in view of China's 'one country, two systems' experiment, the report says, 'The Chief Executive should report to but should not be made accountable to the government of the PRC. . . . Another recommendation states, 'The power of interpreting the Basic Law in its application to the SAR and the power of deciding whether the existing laws contravene the Basic Law should be transferred from the Standing Committee of the National People's Congress to the courts of Hong Kong.' All such suggestions had been tried by Britain and Hong Kong at the time when the Basic Law was being drafted, but failed.

The British government and the Chinese government, through their Joint Liaison Group, might again have tried to negotiate on the two items mentioned above immediately after the ICJ report in 1992. We found no evidence of this, however. *The Mission Report* itself never suggested how such efforts could be accomplished. The British tried diplomatically and failed in 1993 before taking steps to implement the Patten reform without 'unilateral violation' of the Joint Declaration. The Beijing government, likewise, tried to stop Patten before following its own 'unilateral implementation' of both the Joint Declaration and the Basic Law. Both countries have turned deaf ears to the ICJ or again have failed in legal compliance. From now on, only the people of Hong Kong can help themselves to minimize legal violations through internal political progress. Outside interference may or may not help promote human rights in Hong Kong. The Beijing government will probably continue to suspect American or British interference from hidden motives to cause embarrassment to China. In our judgment, political democratization in China alone will gradually promote a 'human rights culture' and protection with Chinese 'indigenous characteristics'.

9 Prospects for the Unification of China

HONG KONG'S IMPACT ON CHINA'S UNIFICATION

We cannot predict whether 'one country, two systems' will successfully meet the expectations of the majority of the people in Hong Kong, because many variables can affect the outcome. For example, the Sino-British Joint Declaration and its three Annexes remain to be interpreted and applied during and after 1997. The Basic Law, although promulgated in 1990, is not legally in force yet. Political parties and functional groups are struggling to find ways to compete, to integrate, or to realign themselves in the current legislature.[1] The future chief executive's degree of autonomy from Beijing's interference is an open question. How the self-censoring media will behave under direct influence from Beijing and how the Court of Final Appeal of Hong Kong will uphold the British legal tradition are difficult to predict. Up to 1 July 1997, a great many questions will go unanswered.[2] Furthermore, it may take five years, a decade, or even longer, to determine the overall success or failure of the experiment of 'one country, two systems'.

Although we are interested in observing changes in Hong Kong itself as China's first Special Administrative Region, more important to us is the influence Hong Kong may have on the people of both Communist China and Taiwan. The possible impact of 'one country, two systems' in Hong Kong on mainland China was briefly explored in Chapter 1. Hong Kong's impact on Taiwan is examined below.

If, during the first five years after the takeover, prosperity and stability prevail, life-style is not interfered with, and media freedom remains largely unrestricted, then the six million people will be favorably disposed to accept and support their SAR government. If this occurs, then we may consider the Hong Kong experiment a success – one which may have a positive impact on China's unification with Taiwan. On the other hand, if the Hong Kong experiment fails, Beijing will also fail in its attempt to achieve an early reunification with Taiwan.

TAIWAN'S GUIDELINES FOR UNIFICATION

The National Unification Council of Taiwan, a governmental organization established in 1990 and headed by President Lee Teng-hui, sets peaceful unification with China as its goal. In 1991 the Council passed the Guidelines for National Unification, which state that China's unification should be achieved in three phases: a short-term phase of exchanges and reciprocity, a medium-term phase of mutual trust and cooperation, and a long-term phase of consultation and unification. The phased approach was chosen in full realization that the eventual unification of China will be a long and arduous political process and that China's unification will not be achieved quickly because the two sides have divergent social, political and economic systems, not to mention vastly different life-styles. Therefore, the Council has set no timetable for unification. Nor has China. Mao, Zhou Enlai, and Deng have all said that it may take as long as 100 years. Lee Kuan Yew of Singapore predicted that it may take at least 40 years. Taiwan suggested that the right time for unification would be when the distance (political, economic, and so on) between the two sides of the Taiwan Straits is substantially shortened.

COULD THERE BE A TIMETABLE?

Tao Bo-chuan, a former member of the Exam Yuan of the Republic of China and a member of the National Unification Council, suggested that the demarcation line between the short-term and medium-term phrases should be three years after Hong Kong's reversion, that is, in the year 2000. He did not suggest a specific year for the demarcation line between the medium-term and long-term phases.

We basically agree with him regarding the demarcation line between the first two phases, because his rationale is to wait and see how China treats and manages Hong Kong during the first three years after its reversion. We would, however, change the date from the year 2000 to 2002, because Macao will revert to China in 1999. These two additional years will reveal how China treats and manages Macao as well.

Recent developments between China and Taiwan, especially since the establishment of Taiwan's Straits Exchange Foundation and China's Association for Relations Across the Taiwan Straits in 1991, have been generally positive. The only exception was the period from President Lee Teng-hui's visit to the United States in June 1995 to his re-election to the presidency in March 1996. There have, however, been some improvements since May 1996.

The current relationship between the two sides of the Taiwan Straits appears to be somewhere between the short-term phase of exchange and reciprocity and the medium-term phase of mutual trust and cooperation. Should China treat both Hong Kong and Macao well after 1997 and 1999 respectively, can Taiwan and China move completely into the second phase? There is no reason why the answer should not be in the affirmative. If that trend of cooperation and mutual trust continues, then, could they move into the third stage? And, if the answer is again in the affirmative, then when? We suggest that the most opportune time to move into the third stage is 2012. To be more specific, it should be, if possible, 1 January 2012.

WHY 1 JANUARY 2012?[3]

During the past several years, Dr Sun Yat-sen, who overthrew the Manchu Dynasty in 1911 and founded the Republic on 1 January 1912, has been 'rectified' in mainland China and regained prominence in Taiwan. He is very much respected both as an individual and for his political thoughts and writings on both sides of the Taiwan Straits.[4] The first day of January 2012 will mark the 100th anniversary of the overthrow of the Manchu Dynasty. It is worthy of celebration by itself. Should Taiwan and China be able to move into the third stage as designated in the Guidelines for National Unification, there is more reason to celebrate. Both sides should strive for this goal. Since 2012 will be 15 years after Hong Kong's reversion to China and 13 years after Macao's, there is ample time for China to prove her sincerity in implementing the 'one country, two systems' as well as improving her own domestic political and economic systems. Likewise, there is ample time for Taiwan to prove that it is truly interested in a peaceful solution to unification. It is true that Taiwan is much stronger than Hong Kong in terms of military capability, size of population, geographical location, and so on. However, a direct military confrontation with China, even with the support of other powers, would not result in anything positive for Taiwan.[5] A peaceful solution with China is necessary and 2012 might be the first opportunity to move into the long-term phase of conciliation and unification.

Notes

FOREWORD

1. *International Legal Materials*, Vol. 23, No. 6 (November 1984), pp. 1366–87.
2. *Facts on File*, 1985, Vol. 45, No. 2323 (31 May 1985), pp. 412–43.
3. See, for example, Robert Jennings and Arthur Watts, *Oppenheim's International Law* 9th edn (Harlow: Longman, 1992), Vol. 1, Parts 2–4, 1992, pp. 1207, 1208; and Wang Tieya and Wei Min, *Guojifa* [International Law] (Beijing, Fa-lu chupan she [Law Publisher]), 1981, p. 326.
4. The longest PRC treaty is the 1962 boundary treaty with Mongolia. See *Zhonghua Renmin Gonghe Guo Tiaoyue Ji* [Collection of Treaties of the People's Republic of China], Vol. 11 (1962), pp. 19–32.
5. Article 31 provides: 'The state may establish special administrative regions when necessary. The systems to be instituted in special administrative regions shall be prescribed by law enacted by the National People's Congress in the light of the specific conditions'. In line with this, Article 62(13) of the Constitution provides the National People's Congress with the power 'to decide on the establishment of special administrative regions and the systems to be instituted there'. *The Laws of the People's Republic of China 1979–1982* (Beijing: Foreign Languages Press, 1987), pp. 11, 17.
6. According to PRC law, city residents can elect one delegate for every 130 000 persons, while rural residents can elect one delegate for every 1 040 000 persons. See *1983 Zhongguo baike nianjian* [1983 Yearbook of the Encyclopedia of China] (Shanghai: Xinhua Press, 1983), p. 226. Assuming all Hong Kong residents are considered as city residents, its 5 147 900 (1984) population can elect roughly 40 delegates.
7. See *1983 Yearbook of the Encyclopedia of China*, see note 6 above, p. 227.
8. See, for example, 'Accord Welcomed by Shultz', *New York Times*, 27 September 1984, p. A12, and report of reaction of Japan and Singapore in *Foreign Broadcast Information Service, China*, 2 October 1984, pp. G3, G4–G5.
9. *The Laws of the People's Republic of China* 1979–82 (Beijing: Foreign Languages Press, 1997), p. 11.
10. Ibid., p. 7.
11. Ibid.
12. English translation in *International Legal Materials*, Vol. 29, No. 6 (November 1990), pp. 1519–51.
13. Ibid., p. 1524.
14. Ibid., p. 1545.
15. Ibid., p. 1523.

16. Ibid.
17. Ibid.
18. Ibid., p. 1524.
19. Ibid., p. 1546.
20. Ibid., p. 1527.
21. Ibid., p. 1531.
22. Ibid., p. 1548.
23. Jesse Wong, 'Beijing Toughens Line on Basic Law for Hong Kong', *Asian Wall Street Journal Weekly*, 29 January 1990, p. 4. See also Barbara Basler, 'Draft Law for Chinese Rule Stirs Protest in Hong Kong', *New York Times*, 17 February 1990, p. 3.
24. *Asia 1991 Yearbook* (Hong Kong: Far Eastern Economic Review, 1991), p. 110.
25. See Barbara Basler, 'Democracy Backers in Hong Kong Win Election Landslide', *New York Times*, 17 September 1991, pp. A1, A8; and Stacy Mosher, 'Election Result puts China on the Spot, Liberal Landslide', *Far Eastern Economic Review*, 26 September 1991, pp. 19–20.
26. Barbara Basler, 'Hong Kong Reveals Plan to Broaden Government', *New York Times*, 8 October 1992, p. A11.
27. See ibid. Currently, many functional groups with a right to elect a representative to the Legislative Council have tiny constituencies that are easily manipulated. Governor Patten's plan is to give the right to vote in functional constituencies to each working person. In practice, therefore, 19 new seats in the Legislative Council will be selected through open competition rather than through private influence. Moreover, the voter base of the existing 21 functional constituencies will be enlarged substantially. See Frank Ching, 'Hong Kong cleared for action', *Far Eastern Economic Review*, 22 October 1992, p. 22.
28. See Daniela Deane, 'New Democracy Sought in Hong Kong, China Terms Governor's Proposals "Extremely Irresponsible"', *Washington Post*, 8 October 1992, p. A37; and Barbara Busler, 'Outlook in Beijing Cold for Hong Kong Chief', *New York Times*, 18 October 1992, p. 14; Lincoln Kaye, 'Hong Kong Official Reproof, China uses Patten Visit to Convey Displeasure', *Far Eastern Economic Review*, 29 October 1992, p. 18; and Shi Jiao-ao, 'Comment on Mr. Christopher Patten's Constitutional Reform Plan', *Liaowang* (Outlook), No. 42 (1992), overseas edition, 19 October 1992, pp. 22–3.
29. See Patrick E. Tyler, 'Chinese Verdict Points to an Era of Harsh Rule', *New York Times*, 31 October 1996, pp. A1, A12.
30. This massacre is reported in almost all newspapers. *Foreign Broadcast Information Service – China (FBIS–China)* has an extensive collection of media reports on this subject in its 5 June 1989, issue. See also 'Beijing Bloodbath', *Newsweek*, 12 June 1989, pp. 24–9; 'Despair and Death in a Beijing Square', *Time*, 12 June 1989, pp. 24–7; 'Reign of Terror', *Newsweek*, 19 June 1989, pp. 14–22; *People's Republic of China, Preliminary Findings on Killings of Unarmed Civilians, Arbitrary Arrests and Summary Executions since 3 June 1989* (London: Amnesty Inter-

national, 1989). Although it has become commonplace to refer to the events of 4 June 1989, as the 'Tiananmen massacre', it is now widely accepted that most of the killing that took place on the night in question occurred not in Tiananmen Square proper, but along a three-mile stretch of Fuxing, Fuxingmen, and Changan Boulevard, to the west of Tiananmen. See Robin Munro, 'Who Died in Beijing, and Why?', *Nation*, 11 June 1990, pp. 811–22; and Nicholas D. Kristof, 'How the Hardliners Won', *New York Times Magazine*, 12 November 1989, p. 71.

31. PRC's Foreign Minister Qian Qichen already warned the Hong Kong people on 2 November 1996 that press freedoms would be limited when Hong Kong reverts to Chinese rule in 1997. See 'Hong Kong Warned of press freedom limit', *Sun* (Baltimore), 3 November 1996, p. 27A.

32. See, for example, Wang Dan case in note 29 above.

CHAPTER 1 INTRODUCTION

1. *New York Times*, 19 September 1995. In this election for 60 seats: 20 are popularly elected from 20 geographical districts, 30 from voting members of functional constituencies (occupational groups) and 10 by the newly created Election Committee, consisting of all the members of local District Boards.

2. *South China Morning Post* (*SCMP*), 17–19 September 1995. Nearly half the total population were newly enfranchised by the Patten election reform as adopted by the LEGCO. Many have two votes to cast. Roughly 920 567 registered to vote, but only 35.8 per cent of those registered cast their ballots – an indication that the people have not been fully convinced that voting can change their destiny.

3. Ibid. (*SCMP*, Hong Kong), 18 September 1995. The pro-China Party Democratic Alliance for the Betterment of Hong Kong was bitterly defeated: the party president, vice-president and general secretary were all defeated at the polls. After the election they began publicly redefining the party policy to move closer to the voters and began distancing themselves somewhat from China. Tsang Yok-sing and Cheng Kai-nan are well known among the voters. Their immediate reaction to defeat was, 'We have good connections with China. We try to use our channels to communicate with China. The result of these elections is bound to have a big impact on things to come, on how China sees us.' The President of the victorious Democratic Party, Martin Lee, said, on the other hand, 'Democrats have consistently pushed for genuine democracy over Britain's and China's objections . . . because that is what Hong Kong people want'. A neutral observer, Professor Sunny Lo Shui-hing of Hong Kong University, commented on the election embarrassment to China, 'The most important significance of this election is the participation of pro-China forces. . . . The extent of the participation of pro-China forces is unprecedented.' Governor Christopher Patten, the architect of the election reform, while visiting the polling stations on 17 September, said indirectly

to the Chinese government, 'I think they should think again. And I certainly think they should get a little more into tune with what people in Hong Kong can do . . .' In short, the election delivered almost half of the 60-plus seats to the DP and pro-DP independents in the next LEGCO, which will be dissolved, halfway through its full term, in July 1997.

4. Portugal and China have signed their Joint Declaration for Macao to be returned to China in 1999. Beijing has applied the same 'one country, two systems' to Macao, while Taiwan's future is full of uncertainty.

5. Hungdah Chiu, ed., 'Symposium on Hong Kong: 1997', Occasional Papers/Reprints Series in *Contemporary Asian Studies*, no. 3, 1985, School of Law, University of Maryland, pp. 11–14, and pp. 1–70.

6. Mark Roberti, *The Fall of Hong Kong, China's Triumph and Britain's Betrayal* (New York: John Wiley, 1994), pp. xiv–xv. Roberti complains about neglecting the people's interests in Hong Kong and he suspects the existence of secret agreements which cannot be made public for 30 years in 2014.

7. Ibid., pp. 215–22, and 290–1. The failure to introduce partial direct election for the LEGCO in 1988 bitterly disappointed those who urged the universal popular election under the British. The Chinese further frustrated the democratic followers of Martin Lee and Szeto Hua during the drafting of the Basic Law before 1990.

8. The 23 Hong Kong delegates to the Basic Law Drafting Convention were unfortunately divided among themselves. The pro-British were represented by Vincent Lo and S.Y. Chung, who were rich merchants (the Group of 89), while Maria Tan, Szeto Hua and Martin Lee represented the democratic forces but were defeated repeatedly in debate and voting in 1988.

Britain complied in the process while China dictated the content of the Basic Law.

9. *China Daily*, Beijing, 29 October 1992, pp. 1 and 4, vol. 12, no. 3539 (English language). In addition to the Joint Declaration and the Basic Law, China, on 28 October 1992, made public all seven letters from the British Ambassador and Foreign Minister Douglas Hurd to the Chinese Foreign Minister Qian Qichen and also made public China's replies on political changes and the election of 1991.

Ambassador Alan Donald's letter of 2 February 1990 requested the urgent clarification of the Chinese position on three issues: the grand electoral college, voting procedures, and the imposition of a nationality restriction on membership in the legislature. The British government would also like to know what the Chinese government is planning for the post-1997 political structure. See also NCNA release in Hong Kong on 2 October and *People's Daily* in Beijing on 27 October on Chris Patten's violation of the Basic Law.

10. *World Journal*, 6 September 1995, 10–16. This journal carried good coverage on the campaign in Hong Kong among the eight parties and independent candidates. The LEGCO election has changed Hong Kong's political development in many major ways.

11. Communist Party Central Committee United Front Department, the Third Bureau – Research Center – published six volumes on 'One Country, Two Systems'. Volume 1 and Volume 2 concentrate on Taiwan and on Sino-American relations *vis-à-vis* Taiwan. Volume 3 devotes itself to Hong Kong. Together these essays and comments do not always indicate the consistency of China's position.

12. Dr Sun Yat-sen in his will specifically reminded his followers about unequal treaties and unfair treatment of China by the imperial West: 'In my forty years of national revolution for the purpose of liberty and international equality, I understand fully that to succeed we must wake up our people to unite with those who treat us with the same equality... [and] to abolish the unequal treaties imposed on us by foreign imperialists...' (Our own translation.)

13. *World Journal*, 4–5 October 1995. The visit produced agreements that Britain will have no right to interfere in Hong Kong's selection of the first Chief-Minister; Britain will cooperate with China on international affairs and on British economic-commercial interests in China and both will cooperate fully for smooth transition. See also 4 October 1995, *Hong Kong South China Morning Post*, and 5 October 1995, *Central Daily News*, Taiwan.

14. *Central Daily News*, Taiwan, 5 October 1995, p. 4.

15. We intend to base our description and analysis on our knowledge of Chinese history, revolution and nationalism, focusing on the ways in which foreign conspiracy and imperialism in China contributed to the Chinese nationhood image and national rejuvenation. The ten items interpret and clarify the leadership thinking in response to external challenge.

16. Mark Roberti, *The Fall of Hong Kong*, op. cit., pp. 10–19. In 1971, Beijing's chief delegate to the United Nations, Huang Hua, informed the world organization of China's intention to regain Hong Kong and Macao, and the UN removed both from the list of colonies heading toward eventual independence. Again, in 1978 during Governor Murray MacLehose's visit to Beijing, the Chinese government, seeking to recover sovereignty and administrative independence, flatly rejected the idea of allowing Britain to remain after 1997.

17. Ibid., pp. 7–10.

18. Chu-yuan Cheng, 'Hong Kong's Prosperity: Foundation and Prospect', pp. 61–70, In Occasional Papers/Reprints Series in *Contemporary Asian Studies*, no. 3, 1985. School of Law, University of Maryland, Symposium on Hong Kong: 1997.

19. *The People's Daily*, Beijing, 29 October 1992 (Chinese language). China published, for domestic consumption, all the seven letters from the British on mutual understanding before the Patten reform violated this agreed-upon understanding.

20. Donald H. McMillen and Man Si-wai, eds, *The Other Hong Kong Report*, 1994, Chinese University Press, Sha Tin, New Territories. The election victory of 1991 and the Patten election reform since 1992 have literally transformed the nature of politics in Hong Kong. See pp. 2, 78, 82. Many political leaders in Hong Kong including Emily

Lau advocate direct election for all 60 seats of the LEGCO. See also 'Government Administration of the 1991 Direct Election: A Public Opinion Analysis' in *Hong Kong Public Administration*, vol. 3, No. 1 (March 1994) pp. 95–132.

21. Hungdah Chiu, 'The Koo-wang Talks and Intra-Chinese Relations', a paper presented at the annual meeting of the American Association for Chinese Studies, 15–17 October 1993, University of South Carolina pp. 40–1. In 1993, the *China Times* began reporting on public opinion. It identified that only 10 per cent of the respondents favored an independent Taiwan, while 45.7 per cent favored the status quo. Over two-thirds, a good 68.6 per cent, opposed unification under 'one country, two systems'.

22. In 1995, shortly after President Lee Teng-hui and the Dalai Lama visited the United States, the Congress and the Department of State disagreed on many issues concerning Hong Kong, Tibet and Taiwan. All such expressions were angrily treated in Beijing as interference in China's domestic affairs. See *World Journal* issues in June and August and *The Congressional Record* for the Dalai Lama's reception in the White House at the Vice President's office. See also *Time*, 5 August 1995.

CHAPTER 2 JOINT DECLARATIONS ON HONG KONG AND MACAO

1. Joint Declaration of the Government of the United Kingdom of Great Britain and Northern Ireland and the Government of the People's Republic of China on the Question of Hong Kong (hereinafter cited as the Sino-British Joint Declaration, or Declaration). Signed on 19 December 1984 and effective 27 May 1985, this document consists of the Joint Declaration proper, three annexes, and an exchange of memoranda.

2. Joint Declaration of the Government of the People's Republic of China and the Government of the Republic of Portugal on the Question of Macao (hereinafter cited as the Sino-Portuguese Joint Declaration, or Declaration). Signed on 13 April 1987 and effective 15 January 1988, this document consists of the Joint Declaration proper, two annexes and an exchange of memoranda.

3. Article 1 of the Sino-British Joint Declaration.

4. Article 1 of the Sino-Portuguese Joint Declaration.

5. The treaty can be found in *Consolidated Treaty Series*, vol. 93.

6. Ibid., vol. 123.

7. Ibid., vol. 186.

8. Regarding the Sino-British negotiation, see Frank Ching, *Hong Kong and China for Better or for Worse* (New York: China Council of the Asia Society and the Foreign Policy Association, 1985).

9. See Immanuel C.Y. Hsu, *The Rise of Modern China* (New York: Oxford University Press, 1970), p. 124.

10. Hen-tze Tu, 'On the So-called Question of Future of Macao,' *China*

Times, May 1985 (about late May, exact date missing). The Sino-Portuguese Treaty was signed on 1 December 1887. See John K. Fairbank, et al., *East Asia: The Modern Transformation* (Boston: Houghton Mifflin, 1965), p. 343.

11. Tu, op. cit.
12. Ibid.
13. The Hay-Bunau-Varilla Treaty, Article II. See US Senate, Committee on Foreign Relations. *Background Documents Relating to the Panama Canal*, 95th Cong., 1st Session. pp. 279–80. See also Richard Y. Chuang, 'The Panama Canal Issue' *L'Observateur Diplomatique* (Koln, West Germany), February/March 1978, p. 19.
14. Cited in Jerome Alan Cohen and Hungdah Chiu, *People's Republic of China and International Law: A Documentary Study*, vol. 1. (Princeton University Press, 1974), p. 380; and Hungdah Chiu, 'The 1984 Sino-British Settlement on Hong Kong: Problems and Analysis', *Journal of Chinese Studies*, vol. 2, no. 1, April 1985, p. 97.
15. Ibid., emphasis added.
16. 'A Significant Concept', *The Hong Kong Solution* (Beijing: Beijing Review Foreign Affairs Series, 1985), p. 88.
17. Ibid., p. 89.
18. Ibid.
19. Frank Ching, op. cit. at p. 20.
20. Article 8 of the Sino-British Joint Declaration.
21. Article 7 of the Sino-Portuguese Joint Declaration.
22. *Free China Review* (Taipei, Taiwan), May 1988, p. 34.
23. This was the wording by the British Embassy in Washington, DC. See its press release on 'Agreement on the Future of Hong Kong', 26 September 1984, p. 1.
24. Article 3 (2) of the Sino-British Joint Declaration.
25. Article 3 (12) of the Sino-British Joint Declaration.
26. Ibid.
27. Article 1 of the Sino-Portuguese Joint Declaration.
28. Article 4, Section I of Annex II to the Sino-Portuguese Joint Declaration.
29. Article 8 of Annex II to the Sino-British Joint Declaration.
30. Section III of Annex I to the Sino-Portuguese Joint Declaration.
31. Section IV of Annex I to the Sino-British Joint Declaration.
32. Section II of Annex I to the Sino-Portuguese Joint Declaration.
33. Section XII of Annex I to the Sino-British Joint Declaration.
34. Ibid.
35. Section XIII of Annex I to the Sino-British Joint Declaration.
36. Ibid., Section I.
37. Section I of Annex I to the Sino-Portuguese Joint Declaration.
38. See Chapter 5 for detailed discussion.
39. Thus, Britain (Hong Kong) is in the process of issuing a new passport, British National (Overseas) replacing the BDTC. This new passport, according to the Exchange of Memoranda, can be issued only to those who hold the BDTC now or to those who are born in Hong Kong on or before 1 July 1997. This document, in so far as China is

concerned, is recognized only as a travel document for traveling outside of China. The Exchange of Memoranda clearly states: 'No person will acquire BDTC status on or after 1 July 1997 by virtue of a connection with Hong Kong.' Nor will any person born on or after 1 July 1997 acquire the BN(O) mentioned above. Thus this BN(O) document/status will disappear after at most one generation following the transfer. See also Chapter 5.

40. *Centre Daily News* (National Edition, published in New York in the Chinese language), 4 June 1987, p. 5.
41. As to the nature of the Sino-British Joint Declaration (including all annexes and memoranda), Professor Hungdah Chiu of the University of Maryland School of Law concluded that the *Agreement on the Future of Hong Kong'* is a formal international agreement similar to a treaty under international law. See Chiu, op. cit., p. 102. The nature of the Sino-Portuguese Joint Declaration will, by analogy, be the same.
42. Bryon S.J. Weng, 'The Hong Kong Model of "One Country, Two Systems": Promises and Problems', *Asian Affairs* (Washington, DC), vol. 14, no. 4, Winter 1987–8, p. 196.

CHAPTER 3 THE STATIONING OF CHINESE FORCES IN HONG KONG

1. 'The Growing Importance of the Military's Deep Involvement in Politics and the Economy', *Inside China Mainland* (Taipei, Taiwan: Institute of Current China Studies, December 1994), pp. 70–2, at 71. Hereinafter it is cited as *Inside China*.
2. Regarding the 'one country, two systems', the best source is *Beijing Review*'s Foreign Affairs Series: no. 6, *China and the World*, 1985, especially the article by Qian Junrue, 'One Country, Two Systems – Key to Settling Hongkong Issue', pp. 105–12.
3. *Central Daily News*, Air Mail Edition, Taipei. (Hereinafter cited as *Central Daily News*), 14 May 1987, 1.
4. Ibid.
5. The proposed reforms included lowering the voting age from 21 to 18; establishing single-seat, single-vote constituencies; abolishing the appointed members to Municipal Councils and District Boards (that is, they were all to be elected); broadening the franchise of the existing functional constituencies and creating nine new functional constituencies; permitting the members of the legislative Council elected in 1995 to complete their four terms through to 1997, and so on. For original documents see *Our Next Five Years: The Agenda for Hong Kong*, address by Governor Christopher Patten at the opening of the 1992/93 session of the Hong Kong Legislative Council, 7 October 1992, especially 30–41; *Hong Kong: Today's Success, Tomorrow's Challenges*, address by Governor Christopher Patten at the opening of the 1993/94 Session of the Hong Kong Legislative Council, 6 October 1993. For more detail, see Chapter 5.

6. *Chinese Daily News* (A Chinese language daily newspaper), West Coast Edition, Los Angeles. 13 April 1993, A10.
7. *Chinese Daily News*, 5 April 1993, A1.
8. Ibid. 17 September 1993, A1.
9. Ibid., 2 October 1993, A1.
10. Ibid, 10 September 1994, A10.
11. Article 1, Joint Declaration.
12. *Centre Daily News* (Published in the United States. Hereinafter to be cited as *Centre*. The paper has ceased publication), 28 January 1989.
13. *Centre*, 7 July 1989.
14. Ibid., 4 January 1990, 4. The other four concerns were China's takeover of Hong Kong, immigration, greater PRC influence over Hong Kong than at present, and Hong Kong's inability to become independent.
15. Ibid., 15 September 1989.
16. For the purpose of ensuring a smooth transfer and effective implementation of the Joint Declaration, the Joint Liaison Group (JLG) will be established (Article 5 of the JD). The JLG is a coordination body, not an organ of power (Article 6 of Annex II to the JD).
17. *Centre*, 16 November 1987, 5.
18. Ibid., 1 February 1988.
19. *Chinese Daily News*, 29 September 1992, A1.
20. An agreement on how to finance the proposed new airport to be built in Chek Lap Kok was, after years of negotiation, reached on 14 November 1994.
21. *Chinese Daily News*, 3 January 1996, A10.
22. *Centre*, 15 December 1988, 4.
23. *Central Daily News*, 1 July 1989.
24. Ibid., 2 July 1989, p. 1.
25. Ibid., 18 August 1989, p. 4.
26. Ibid., 24 October 1989, p. 1.
27. Ibid., 4 August 1993, A10.
28. *Centre*, 20 July 1987, p. 4. There was also information in *Hong Kong 1988* (A Review of 1987), published by the Hong Kong Government Information Service, pp. 236–40. However, there was only a description of the types of forces stationed; no troop level was indicated.
29. *Ibid.*
30. *Centre*, 21 December 1987, p. 2.
31. *Central Daily News*, 5 January 1988, p. 1; *Centre*, 6 January 1988, p. 4.
32. *Chinese Daily News*, 29 May 1996, A10.
33. *Centre*, 14 April 1988, p. 5.
34. *Chinese Daily News*, 6 February 1995, A10.
35. Ibid., 30 January 1996, A10.
36. The so-called Three Headquarters.
37. *Chinese Daily News*, 19 December 1993, A2.
38. Ibid.
39. So named because at midnight on 30 June 1997, China will take over Hong Kong.
40. *Chinese Daily News*, 6 February 1995, A10.
41. Ibid., 12 and 29 January 1996 A10; and A10.

42. Ibid., 2 May 1994, A10.
43. Ibid., 19 December 1993, A2.
44. Ibid., 2 May 1994, A10.
45. Ibid., 1 May 1994, A9.
46. Ibid.
47. Ibid., 4 September 1994, A9.
48. Ibid., 16 February 1995, A10.
49. Ibid., 15 January 1995, A2.
50. Ibid., 23 April 1993, A10.
51. Ibid., 1 July 1994, A10.
52. Ibid., 12 May 1994, A9.
53. Ibid., 4 November 1994, A1.
54. Para. XII, Annex I to the Joint Declaration.
55. Para. XII, Annex II to the JD.
56. Article 14, Basic Law, 1990.
57. Para. 4, Article 18 of the Basic Law.
58. Ibid.
59. We are greatly indebted to the editor of the article, 'What Role Will the PLA Play in Post-97 Hong Kong?' *Inside China Mainland* (Taipei, Taiwan: Institute of Current China Studies). December 1994, pp. 70–3, especially 71–2 from which materials for the remainder of this section are directly taken. It should also be noted that the editor in turn gathered this material from *Cheng Ming* (Hong Kong), 26–27 October 1994, by Fan Jun.

CHAPTER 4 SAFE HAVEN, VISAS, AND RIGHT OF ABODE

1. Published in *Current Law Statutes Annotated* 1981, vol. 2 London, 1982. See also Robin M. White, 'Nationality Aspects of the Hong Kong Settlement', *Case Western Reserve Journal of International Law*, vol. 20, no. 1 (1988), pp. 225–51, and 'Hong Kong: Nationality, Immigration and the Agreement with China', *International and Comparative Law Quarterly* vol. 36 (1987), pp. 483–503, by the same author.
2. The BN(O) status is provided in the Hong Kong Act of 1985 (London: HMSO).
3. *Guardian Weekly*, 31 July 1983, p. 5.
4. *Centre Daily* (in Chinese) (New York), 29 Aug. 1986, p. 1.
5. Ibid., 11 May 1988, p. 5.
6. Ibid., 8 June 1988, p. 5.
7. Ibid., 6 July 1988, p. 5.
8. Ibid., 6 January 1988, p. 4.
9. Ibid., 3 July 1989, p. 4.
10. Ibid., 14 August 1987, p. 5.
11. Ibid., 30 January 1988, p. 4.
12. White, note 5, p. 227.
13. *Current Law Statutes Annotated 1981*, vol. 2, chap. 61, general note.
14. Ibid.
15. *Centre Daily*, 11 January 1989.

16. *Guardian Weekly*, 30 April 1989, p. 10.
17. *Centre Daily*, 20 May 1989.
18. Ibid., 24 June 1989, p. 4.
19. Ibid., 21 June 1989, p. 4.
20. Ibid.
21. *Centre Daily*, 4 June 1987, p. 5.
22. *Guardian Weekly*, 30 April 1989, p. 10; *Centre Daily*, 22 March 1989, p. 6.
23. A term used in a letter to the editor, *Guardian Weekly*, 18 June 1989, p. 2.
24. Ibid., 30 April 1989, p. 10.
25. *Centre Daily*, 3 July 1989, p. 4.
26. Hong Kong Government, *White paper: The Development of Representative Government: The Way Forward*, February 1988.
27. This was actually down from about 47 000 in 1987. *Commonwealth* (Taiwan), 1 January 1990, p. 58. If the massacre had not occurred, the immigration figure have might been substantially less than 42 000.
28. *The Independent*, 9 October 1989.
29. *Hong Kong Digest*, 25 October 1989. This issue contained a summary of Governor Wilson's address to the LEGCO, 11 October 1989, in which the governor announced the project.
30. *Commonwealth*, 1 January 1990, p. 65.
31. *Far Eastern Economic Review*, 9 November 1989, pp. 13–14.
32. *Hong Kong Digest*, 28 August 1989.
33. Ibid., 19 December 1989, p. 4.
34. Phillip M. Chen, ed., *Hong Kong and 1997: Development and Assessment.* (Taipei: Asia and World Institute, 1989), p. 53.
35. *Commonwealth*, 1 January 1990, p. 65.
36. *Hong Kong 1996* (Hong Kong Government Information Services Department, 1996), chart at p. 49.
37. 'Statement on Hong Kong', a document distributed by the Hong Kong Economic and Trade Office (New York) 20 December 1989, p. 1.
38. Ibid., p. 6.
39. *Hong Kong Roundup* (title was later changed to *Hong Kong Digest*), February/March 1990, p. 1.
40. *Hong Kong Digest*, 31 January 1994, p. 3.
41. *Macroview*, 8 April 1994, p. 2.
42. *Hong Kong Digest*, 2 April 96, p. 1.
43. *Guardian Weekly*, 7 April 1996, p. 1.
44. *Hong Kong Digest*, 2 April 1996, p. 1.
45. *Chinese Daily News*, 16 May 1996, A1.
46. Ibid., 23 March 1996, A12.
47. A discussion of Chinese nationality law is beyond the scope of this chapter. See, however, Tung-pi Chen, *The Nationality Law of the People's Republic of China and the Overseas Chinese in Hong Kong, Macao and South East Asia, New York Law School Journal of International and Comparative Law*, vol. 5, no. 7 (1984), 281–340.
48. *Chinese Daily News*, 9 April 1996, A10.

49. Ibid., 12 May 1996, A12.
50. Ibid., 19 April 1996, A10.

CHAPTER 5 BRITISH IMPLEMENTATION OF THE JD AND THE BASIC LAW

1. The Hong Kong editions of *Ta Kung Bao* and *Wen Hui Bao* were the two major daily papers. Both attacked Patten after his October 1992 reform speech.
2. *South China Morning Post* (SCMP), *Cheng Ming Monthly*, *The Nineties* and the Hong Kong Government Information Service's Publications (especially 'The Week in Hong Kong' as one official release), and so on.
3. See the Basic Law, Article 45.
4. Chan Yu-xiong, *The Blueprint for 97* (Hong Kong: Wide Angle Press, 1998) especially on 'the 1991 LEGCO Election', pp. 25–9.
5. *The Other Hong Kong Report*, 1994, Donald H. McMillen and Man Si-wai, eds, (Hong Kong: Chinese University Press), pp. 125–48.
6. *The Memoir of Xu Jiatun*, and also *World Journal*, 9 September 1993.
7. 'How Much Autonomy?' by Martin C.M. Lee in William McGurn, ed., *Basic Law and Basic Questions* (Hong Kong: Review Publishing Co. Ltd, 1988), pp. 38–52.
8. *Wen Hui Bao*, Hong Kong, 8 October 1992.
9. Zhou Yizi, 'Hong Kong's Return and One Country Two Systems', in *Collection of Essays on One Country Two Systems*, Vol. 5, pp. 1–13; also Xu Jiatun's News Conference in Hong Kong in May 1984, pp. 23, 24 (of the same vol.) published by the United Front Department of the Chinese Communist Party, Beijing, 1988.
10. See articles 16 and 17 of the Basic Law.
11. Mark Roberti, *The Fall of Hong Kong, China's Triumph and Britain's Betrayal* (New York: John Wiley, 1994), pp. 192–3. Deng Xiaoping declared that democracy does not suit Hong Kong and can destroy Hong Kong.
12. Ibid. Chapter 18, 'The Drafting Basic Law and Consultation for Review', pp. 211–22.
13. Roberti, *The Fall of Hong Kong*, op. cit., pp. 146–51.
14. *The Memoir of Xu Jiatun* on selection of the Hong Kong delegates to the Basic Law drafting convention and also see *World Journal* of 15–30 June 1993 on his role in the making of the Basic Law.
15. Roberti, *The Fall of Hong Kong*, op. cit., p. 147.
16. Szeto Hua and Martin C.M. Lee, *A Critical Outlook of the Draft Basic Law*, May 1988. They analyzed all major articles first and made a recommendation for each major article. (Our translation.)
17. *The Other Hong Kong Report*, ed. Choi Po-king (Chinese University Press, Hong Kong: 1993), chapter 22 'China's Investment in Hong Kong', pp. 426–54. It is an excellent factual report.
18. Gerd Balke in *One Country, Two Systems and Taiwan*, ed. Li Dah, (Hong Kong: Wide Angle Press, 1988), pp. 22–5.

19. David Bonavia, in Foreword to *Basic Law, Basic Questions*, ed. William McGurn (Hong Kong: Review Publishing, 1988) p. vii.
20. Louis Ha in chapter 7, 'Human and Civil Rights', McGurn, *Basic Law, Basic Questions*, op. cit., p. 114.
21. See Governor MacLehose's 1978 'Government Work Report'. Also Hung Tze-lian, 'Systemic Development Prospectus in 50 years, 1968–2017', *Hong Kong Toward the 21st Century* (Hong Kong: Chung Hwa Press, 1989), pp. 85–160.
22. Chan Yu-shong, 'Forecasting the 1991 LEGCO Direct Election' in *The Blueprint for 1997* (Hong Kong: Wide Angle Press, 1981), pp. 25–9.
23. Ibid., p. 254. See also *The Memoir of Xu Jiatun*, which was also carried in *World Journal*, 25 and 26 June 1993, on democratic consultation.
24. Roberti, *The Fall of Hong Kong*, op. cit., p. 256–60.
25. *South China Morning Post (SCMP)*, 20 May – 10 June 1989.
26. Action in the House of Commons, London, 30 June 1989. See also *SCMP*, 1 and 2 July 1989.
27. Roberti, *The Fall of Hong Kong*, op. cit., pp. 285–8. Also 'The Week in Hong Kong', Issue No. 433/89, 30 October – 5 November 1989, p. 1, on the end of the Basic Law consultation (Hong Kong Government Public Relations Division).
28. *South China Morning Post*, 8 October 1992.
29. Prior to Governor Patten's 1994–95 election reform: about 30 percent of LEGCO, 38 percent of the Urban Council, 33 percent of Regional Council, 2/3 of all District Board members were elected indirectly. The rest were all appointed by the government.
30. *China Daily*, Beijing, 21, 22 and 23 October 1992 (an English paper).
31. *People's Daily*, Beijing, 8 October 1992.
32. *South China Morning Post*, 8 October 1992, Hong Kong, p. 1.
33. Beijing has all along insisted that Hong Kong is to be transferred back to China, not to local Hong Kong officials. British localization of power is a violation of the Basic Law and the Joint Declaration. Also see *The Memoir of Xu Jiatun* and *World Journal*, 26 June 1993 for Xu's article.
34. *The Other Hong Kong Report, 1994*, eds D.H. McMillen and Man Si-wai (Hong Kong: Chinese University Press), p. 103.
35. Robert T.Y. Chung, Social Science Research Center Analyst, in *The Other Hong Kong, 1993*, pp. 410–11.
36. 'Public Opinion' in ibid., 1994 edition, pp. 103–23.
37. Ibid. see charts on pages 114–18 on Patten's popularity in 1992–4. He remained popular at all times among all who paid attention to politics.
38. His *Asian Time* interview, 9 November 1992, *China Daily* (English language) Beijing, 31 October 1992; also 30 November 1992, *Ta Kung Bao*, Hong Kong.
39. *South China Morning Post*'s International Weekly edition, 26–27 February 1994, pp. 1–2. Patten's first part of the reform bill was passed by 36–23 in the LEGCO, with 15 Liberal Party members and seven pro-China independents led by Councilwoman Elsie Tu in opposition.

40. See *World Journal*, 4 June 1993. Patten brought the LEGCO's support behind him to apply pressure on Beijing while the diplomatic round of talks were just beginnning.
41. *South China Morning Post*, 29 June 1993.
42. *World Journal*, 20 July 1993.
43. Ibid., 2 October 1993.
44. *South China Morning Post*, 7–8 October 1993.
45. Ibid., 20 January 1994; *World Journal*, 21 January 1994.
46. *South China Morning Post*, International Edition, 23–24 April 1994.
47. On 26 March 1994, the 1–2–3 Democratic Alliance was organized to contest the September 1995 election and won one seat. It was pro-Taiwan. See *SCMP* International Weekly of 23–24 April 1994.
48. *SCMP*, 18 September 1995, Hong Kong.
49. Ibid., p. 3; see also *New York Times*, 19 September 1995.
50. *SCMP*, International Weekly, 23 April 1994.
51. *SCMP*, 19 September 1995, Hong Kong.
52. *New York Times*, 18 September 1995.
53. *World Journal*, 22, 26 April 1996.
54. *SCMP*, 9 April 1996. China refused to allow Governor Patten to attend the ceremony of transfer on 1 July 1997. Britain disagreed and expected big media presence. The JLG is still discussing it.
55. On 12 October 1995 Governor Patten announced his full cooperation in the transfer.
56. Secretary Chan Fang On-Sang was formally invited to Beijing as a Hong Kong Government official to discuss the transfer; see *World Journal*, 27 April 1996.
57. *SCMP*, 4 February 1996.
58. Ibid., 4 March 1996.
59. Ibid., 1 March 1996.

CHAPTER 6 CHINESE IMPLEMENTATION OF THE JD AND THE BASIC LAW

1. Deng Xiaoping, *The Selected Works of Deng Xiaoping* (Beijing: The People's Press). Three vols, especially vol. 3. There are seven units about Hong Kong.
2. See the Joint Declaration, Paragraph 3, Section 2 on defence and foreign policy concerning Hong Kong after 1997.
3. Deng told Margaret Thatcher bluntly in 1992 that Hong Kong and Kowloon are Chinese territories. Britain, he said, had imposed treaty stipulation on China by force of war. This constituted a legal violation of international law of the West. China could not, therefore, accept the treaty as valid.
4. See the *Shanghai Communique* of February 1972 and also the *Joint Communique* on formal diplomatic recognition between the USA and China on 16 December 1978.
5. Deng Xiaoping, 'One Country Two Systems', United Front Department, Communist Party, vol. 1 (His speech on 22 June 1984, in Beijing), pp. 278–82.

6. Ranbir Vohra, *China's Path to Modernization* (Englewood Cliffs, NJ: Prentice-Hall), pp. 57–8.
7. Deng Xiaoping, *Selected Works*, op. cit., pp. 144–70.
8. Deng Xiaoping spoke to the visiting delegation from Hong Kong. *World Journal*, 3 October 1984.
9. Deng's speech to the Basic Law drafters. *World Journal*, 16 April 1987.
10. Deng Xiaoping, *Selected Works*, vol. 3 (Beijing: People's Press).
11. Hong Kong Government Information Service, *The Week in Hong Kong*, Issue No. 25, 18–24 June 1990, p. 1.
12. *South China Morning Post (SCMP*, Hong Kong), 27 August 1992.
13. Ibid., 1 September 1992.
14. *World Journal*, 26 September 1992, a Chinese language daily with global circulation. Its North American edition has daily coverage of development in Hong Kong.
15. *SCMP*, 1 October 1992.
16. See Article 68 of the Basic Law and also its Annex II.
17. *SCMP*, 16 October 1992.
18. Ibid.
19. *World Journal*, and *SCMP*, 28 October 1992.
20. Ibid.
21. *The People's Daily* of Beijing, Overseas Edition, 22 November 1992.
22. *World Journal*, 30 November 1992.
23. See *SCMP*, 14 January 1993.
24. *World Journal*, 4 January 1993.
25. NCNA, Hong Kong release, 12 November 1992.
26. Ibid. Also *World Journal*, 13 November 1993; and the *People's Daily*, Overseas Edition, 13 November 1992.
27. *World Journal*, 8 February 1993.
28. Ibid., 6 March 1992.
29. *SCMP*, 14 April 1993.
30. *World Journal*, 18 March 1993.
31. Ibid.; *SCMP*, 17 March 1993.
32. *World Journal*, 18 March 1993.
33. *SCMP*, 26 May 1993.
34. Danny Gittings, *SCMP* International Weekly, 12–13 June 1993.
35. *World Journal*, 15, 18 June 1993.
36. *SCMP*, 14 June 1993.
37. *People's Daily*, Overseas Edition, 15 June 1993.
38. *SCMP*, 9–10 July 1993.
39. Robert T.Y. Chung, Social Science Research Center, University of Hong Kong, who released data to us. See also *World Journal*, 9 July 1993.
40. *World Journal*, 11 July 1993.
41. *People's Daily*, Overseas Edition, 21 July 1993.
42. *World Journal*, 4 October 1993.
43. Donald H. McMillen and Man Si-wai, eds, *The Other Hong Kong Report, 1994* (Hong Kong: Chinese University Press) p. xxxi.
44. Robert T.Y. Chung, op. cit., Director of polling analysis.
45. *SCMP*, 13 October 1993.

46. *SCMP*, International Weekly, 17, 30 October; 6–7, 28–29 November 1993.
47. *Wen Hui Bao* (Hong Kong), 24 November 1993.
48. *People's Daily*, 3 December 1993.
49. *Wen Hui Bao*, 3 December 1993.
50. *World Journal*, 23 June 1993.
51. Ibid., 24 June 1993.
52. *SCMP*, 14 July 1993.
53. Ibid., 27 September 1993.
54. *People's Daily*, Overseas Edition, 10 December 1993.
55. After the September 1995 election, the British could do no more, the Chinese were coming down from Beijing. The people were watchful, uncertain of their destiny and unwilling to demonstrate or protest. Read *SCMP*: 21 October 1995, 8 December 1995, and 19 March 1996.
56. See report of PWC (Preparatory Working Committee), and the *People's Daily*, 25 December 1995.
57. *World Journal*, 8 and 20 March 1996.
58. On permanent residency and HKSAR passports, see Chapter 4 above.
59. *World Journal*, 11 November 1995.
60. *People's Daily*, Overseas Edition, 21 December 1995.
61. Ibid., 28 January 1996.
62. Ibid., 16 February 1996.
63. *World Journal*, 17 February 1996.
64. *SCMP*, 16 February 1996.
65. *World Journal*, 29 February 1996.
66. Report from Beijing, see also *World Journal*, 3 March 1996.
67. *People's Daily*, Overseas Edition, 25 March 1996; *World Journal*, 21 March 1996.
68. *SCMP*, 25 March 1996.
69. Ibid., 30 March 1996.
70. Ibid., 3 April 1996.
71. Author Yan Jiaqi, former director of the Center of Political Science, Social Science Academy, Beijing. See *World Journal*, 7 April 1996.
72. Ibid., 7 April 1996.
73. *SCMP*, 14 April 1996.
74. *World Journal*, 16 April 1996.
75. Ibid., 2 May 1996.
76. *People's Daily*, Overseas Edition, 6 May 1996.
77. *World Journal*, 21 April 1996.
78. *People's Daily*, 19 April 1996
79. Ibid., 13 April 1996.
80. Ibid., 20 April 1996.
81. Ibid., 8 December 1995.
82. For more details on both candidates, see *World Journal*, 22 December 1995.
83. For details, see ibid., 27 January 1996.

CHAPTER 7 POLITICAL DEVELOPMENTS IN HONG KONG

1. Chan Kai-Cheung, chapter 23, 'History', in *The Other Hong Kong Report*, 1993, ed. by Choi Po-king (New Territories, Hong Kong: Chinese University Press), pp. 455–84.
2. Milton D. Yeh, 'The Peking–London Dispute over Hong Kong's Political Reform', *Issues and Studies*, vol. 29, no. 4, Institute of International Relations, Taipei, Taiwan, pp. 131–2.
3. Chan Kai-Cheung, op. cit., footnote no. 1, pp. 462–70.
4. George Shen, 'China–Hong Kong Integration' in *The Other Kong Report*, 1994, edited by Donald H. McMillen and Man Si-wai (Hong Kong: Chinese University Press, 1994), pp. 469–84.
5. Benjamin K.P. Leung, ed., 'Introduction', *Social Issues in Hong Kong* (Hong Kong: Oxford University Press, 1990), pp. 1–12.
6. Malinda Liu, *Beijing Spring* (Tokyo: Toppan Printing Company, 1990). A good introduction by Orville Schell (a picture publication with explanation).
7. Frank Ching, 'Politics, Politicians and Political Parties' in *The Other Hong Kong Report*, 1993, op. cit., pp. 23–38.
8. Chan Yu-xiong, 'Winners and Losers Over the Basic Law' in *The Blue Print for 1997* (Hong Kong: Wide Angle Press, 1981) pp. 21–4.
9. Yeung Sum, *Hong Kong's Systemic Reform* (Hong Kong: Wide Angle Press, 1986). Yeung is opposed to 'one partyism and elitism'. He advocates multi-party pluralism and direct popular election to keep the system open to all. See pp. 78–81. On opposition to functional representation and indirect election, on social mobilization and pluralist direct multi-party system election, see pp. 186–97.
10. Albert H.Y. Chen, *Legal System and the Basic Law* (Hong Kong: Wide Angle Press, 1986), pp. 2–50, 266–71 on legal systems in Hong Kong and in China and the Basic Law.
11. Yeung Sum, op. cit., pp. 63–77, on District Board elections and the LEGCO election and power. The author is eager for reform.
12. John Walden, 'Accountability: Past, Present and Future' in William McGurn, ed., *Basic Law and Basic Questions* (Hong Kong: Review Publishing, 1988), pp. 53–68.
13. Martin C.M. Lee, chapter 2: 'How Much Autonomy?' in William McGurn, op. cit., pp. 37–52. He believes in popular, direct, open and competitive election as the ultimate guarantee for autonomy.
14. *South China Morning Post* (SCMP), 19 February 1994, p. 11.
15. 1995 election for the LEGCO seats distribution: DP 20; LP 10; ADPL 4; four small parties each received one seat; and the independent candidates won 15 in the 60-seat LEGCO.
16. *Chicago Tribune*, 5 November 1995.
17. Yeung Sum, op. cit., pp. 3–18, 206–28.
18. *SCMP* International Weekly, 23–24 April 1994.
19. *World Journal*, 1 February 1993.
20. Ibid., Sunday Weekly Edition, 23 January 1994.
21. UDKH, see *1991 Election Platform*, which was a long publication com-

mitting the party to reform in many areas for equality among classes of unequal incomes.

22. *Central Daily News*, 7 October 1995, 'Democracy Faces Challenge in Hong Kong'.
23. *World Journal*, 6 January 1996.
24. Ibid., 27 March 1996.
25. Ibid., 14, 27–28 April 1996.
26. Ibid., 1 March 1993.
27. Ibid., p. 4. Also see *SCMP*, 28 February 1996.
28. *SCMP*, 18 December 1993.
29. Ibid.
30. See the 'Transition Project Visual Data Surveys', Baptist University Transition Research Centre, Hong Kong.
31. Michael E. DeGolyer, 'Politics, Politicians, and Political parties', in *The Other Hong Kong Report*, 1994, ed. by Donald H. McMillen and Man Si-wai, op. cit., pp. 75–102.
32. Chan Hoi-man, 'Culture and Identity' in *The Other Hong Kong Report*, 1994, op. cit., pp. 443–68, at p. 444.
33. Ibid., pp. 447–8.
34. Ibid., pp. 450–2.
35. Robert Chung Ting-yui, chapter 7, 'Public Opinion' in *The Other Hong Kong Report*, Donald H. McMillen and Man Si-wai, eds, op. cit., pp. 103–24.
36. His survey data were related to one of us during an interview in April 1995 at his office. See also *The Other Hong Kong Report*, 1994.
37. Basic Law, Article 45, and its Annex I.
38. Michael E. DeGolyer, op. cit., pp. 75–102.
39. Joseph S.Y. Cheng, ed., *Hong Kong in Transition* (Hong Kong: Oxford University Press, 1986), p. 11. The truth has always depended on when and how Hong Kong returns to China. Less that 8 per cent on average of Hong Kong residents in three consecutive pollings within 12 months in 1993–4 called themselves 'Hong Kong British'. The rest called themselves 'Chinese', 'Hong Kong Chinese' or 'Hong Kong person'.
40. *The Other Hong Kong Report, 1994*, pp. 87–8.
41. Ibid., pp. 89–92.
42. Ibid., p. 99.
43. Ian Scott, 'Legitimacy and its Discontents: Hong Kong and the Reversion to Chinese Sovereignty', *Asian Journal of Political Science*, vol. 1, no. 1 (June 1993), pp. 55–75. The author doubts Beijing's command in 'moral authority' to instill affective responses from the population.
44. See 'Student Politics in Hong Kong' in *One Culture, Many Systems: Politics in Re-Unification of China*, edited by Donald H. McMillen (Hong Kong: Chinese University of Hong Kong Press, 1993).
45. Sunny Lo Shiu Hing and Donald Hugh McMillen, 'A Profile of the Pro-China Hong Kong Elite: Images and Perceptions', *Issues and Studies* (Taipei, Taiwan: Institute of International Relations), June 1995, pp. 98–127.

46. Ibid., p. 98.
47. Emily Lau, 'The Right to Write', chapter 4 in *Basic Law and Basic Questions*, edited by William McGurn, op. cit., pp. 69–79. She believes 'freedom to disseminate and gather information is the foundation of most other freedoms'. p. 79.
48. See Sunny Lo Shiu Hing and Donald Hugh McMillen, *op. cit.*, p. 103, where the authors divide Beijing leadership into 'hardliners', 'moderates' and 'softliners'. Currently 'hardliners' Lu Ping and Zhou Nan are in daily charge over transition under the 'moderate' foreign minister Qian Qichen.
49. See releases by the office of the Hong Kong Transition Project, Hong Kong Baptist College, for details on Hongkongese identity in March 1994.
50. Georg Shen, 'China's Investment in Hong Kong', in *The Other Hong Kong Report*, 1993, op. cit., p. 45.
51. Ibid.
52. Henry C.Y. Ho, chapter 6, 'The State of the Economy', in *The Other Hong Kong Report*, pp. 75–94.
53. Y.C. Jao, Chapter 7, 'Monetary and Financial Affairs', in *The Other Hong Kong Report*, pp. 94–146.
54. Tang Shu-ki, Chapter 8, 'The Economy' in *The Other Hong Kong Report, 1994*, p. 133.
55. Chu-yuan Cheng, 'The Role of the Republic of China in the World Trade', a paper presented at the annual meeting of the Association of Chinese Social Scientists in North America, 11–13 November 1995, Reno, Nevada, p. 10.
56. Linda Fung-Yee Ng and Chyau Tuan, eds, *The Three Chinese* Economies, China, Hong Kong and Taiwan: Challenges and Opportunities (Hong Kong: Chinese University of Hong Kong Press, 1996), p. xiv.
57. Anthony M. Tang, chapter 1, 'Some Reflections on the Three Chinese Economies', op. cit., p. 2.
58. Ibid., p. 5.
59. Chyau Tuan and Linda Fung-yee Ng, 'The post-1997 Hong Kong and Its Impacts upon the Economic Relations between the Two Sides of the Taiwan Strait', paper presented at the 37th American Association for Chinese Studies annual convention, 11–13 November 1995, Reno, Nevada.
60. Linda Fung-Yee Ng and Chyau Tuan, 'Changing Business Environment and Investment Strategies in the Post-1997 Hong Kong's Responses to Transfer of Sovereignty', a paper presented at the same convention 11–13 November 1995, in Reno, Nevada, p. 13.

CHAPTER 8 COURT OF FINAL APPEAL AND HUMAN RIGHTS

1. *World Journal* 14 June 1996. A Chinese Foreign Ministry spokesman at a news conference, in response to question related to the US concern over Hong Kong's transition and after 1997, said on 13 June 1996 that: 'the American Congress should pay more attention to its

own internal affairs. Hong Kong's affairs do not require the U.S. to be concerned.... I suspect the American Congress knows little about Hong Kong's history.'

2. International Commission of Jurists, *Countdown to 1997: Report of a Mission to Hong Kong*, 1992, Geneva, Switzerland.
3. Martin Lee, on Basic Law revision, *SCMP*, 15 July 1988, p. 6.
4. *The Fall of Hong Kong*, Mark Roberti, 1994, op. cit., pp. 129–41.
5. John D. Ho, 'The Legal System: Are the Changes Too Little, Too Late?' in the *Other Hong Kong Report, 1994*, op. cit., pp. 9–22.
6. Government Information Service, *Hong Kong 1995*, chapter 3, 'The Legal System', pp. 49–58.
7. Ibid. pp. 50–1.
8. International Commission of Jurists, op. cit., 'Preface' to the Report, by Adam Bieng, Secretary-General of ICJ.
9. See *World Journal*, 9, 15 June 1993 and *Hong Kong 1994*, Government Information Service, chapter on legal system.
10. *World Journal*, 10 June 1994, A4.
11. *SCMP*, 11 June 1995.
12. Ibid., 12–13 June. See also the *Central Daily News*, the Republic of China, Taiwan, 12 June 1995.
13. See Chapter III of the Basic Law, Articles 23–42 on fundamental rights and duties of inhabitants in Hong Kong. Among them Article 39 is controversial in subjecting those rights to 'other prescriptions by law'.
14. *World Journal*, 14 November 1995.
15. *SCMP*, 10 October 1995.
16. *SCMP* and *World Journal*, 21 October 1995.
17. Ibid., and *World Journal*, 30 May 1995.
18. *SCMP*, 18 December 1995.
19. Ibid., and also 8–9 July 1995.
20. *World Journal*, 12 June 1995.
21. Ibid., 24 October 1995, *SCMP*, 4 November 1995.
22. *SCMP* and *World Journal*, 28 October 1995.
23. *World Journal*, 8 November 1995.
24. *World Journal*, 14 November 1995.
25. *SCMP*, 15 November and *World Journal*, 16 November 1995.
26. *SCMP*, 19 February 1994.
27. *People's Daily*, Beijing, overseas edition, 27 May 1995.
28. Ibid., 18 May 1995, p. 5.
29. *Central Daily News*, Taiwan, 11 June 1995.
30. *People's Daily*, ibid., 10 June 1995, p. 5.
31. *SCMP*, 27 October 1995; *World Journal*, 28 October and ibid., 28 October. *Ta Kung Bao*, Hong Kong, 27 October 1995.
32. Ibid., *SCMP*, 28 October 1995.
33. *World Journal*, 14 November 1995.
34. Ibid., 27 October and *SCMP*, 4 November 1995.
35. *World Journal*, 13, 18 November 1995.
36. *Central Daily News*, Taiwan, 11 June 1995.
37. *SCMP* and *World Journal*, 22 October 1995, A4.

38. Ibid., *World Journal* above.
39. Ibid., 31 October 1995.
40. Ibid., 17 November 1995.
41. *South China Morning Post*, 18 November 1995.
42. *World Journal*, 7 November 1995.
43. Editorial Essay: 'China's Intent on Hong Kong Debate on Human Rights Practice', 18 November 1995 and also Ma Yu: 'Hong Kong's Human Rights Storming Controversy', ibid., 19 November 1995, *World Journal*.
44. *People's Daily*, overseas edition, 15 November 1995.
45. *World Journal*, 10 October 1995.
46. International Commission of Jurists: *Countdown To 1997*, op. cit., p. 107.
47. *SCMP* and *World Journal*, 15 June 1996.
48. *SCMP*, 5 June 1993.
49. Ibid, and *World Journal*, 4 November 1995.
50. International Commission of Jurists (ICJ), op. cit., 'Preface'.
51. Ibid., p. 3.
52. Ibid., pp. 7–8.
53. Ibid., p. 108.
54. Council of State, Information Office, Beijing, *The Status of Human Rights in China*, 1991, pp. 1–3.
55. International Commission of Jurists, op. cit., chapter XV, 'Conclusions and Recommendation', pp. 116–20.

CHAPTER 9 PROSPECTS FOR THE UNIFICATION OF CHINA

1. Michael E. DeGolyer, 'Politics, Politicians, and Political Parties' in *The Other Hong Kong Report of 1994*, pp. 75–101. In addition to non-party groups, there were in 1994 a total of 12 registered political parties. In 1994 the United Democrats merged with the Alliance for Democracy and the People's Livelihood. Now the largest party in the LEGCO since the 17 September 1995 election, the new party's name is simply Democratic Party. Party politics is just beginning in Hong Kong.
2. See Bruce Bueno de Mesquita et al., *Red Flag Over Hong Kong* (Chatham, NJ: Chatham House Publishers, 1996) pp. 121–40.
3. See Richard Chuang, 'Can There Be a Timetable for Unification?', *Ming Bao Monthly* (Hong Kong), July 1991, pp. 103–4.
4. There are many programs on the study of Sun Yat-sen and his thoughts, established in both universities or research institutions on both sides of the Taiwan Straight. A recent conference on Dr. Sun Yat-sen's Thoughts, held in Chicago 26–28 June 1996 and sponsored by the Sun Yat-sen Institute in America, attended by more than 150 scholars and interested persons from ten different countries in four continents, is an indication of his popularity.
5. See Richard Chuang, 'The Achievements, Image Problems and Future of the Republic of China', *American Journal of Chinese Studies*, October 1996, Section 3.

Chronology

1573	Portugal acquires the de facto rights to govern Macao.
1842	Treaty of Nanking signed, ceding Hong Kong Island to Britain.
1860	Convention of Peking signed, ceding the Southern tip of Kowloon Peninsula and Stonecutters Island to Britain.
1887	Treaty signed by China giving Portugal the right to perpetual jurisdiction over Macao.
1898	Convention of Peking signed, leasing the New Territories to Britain for 99 years.
1941–45	Occupation of Hong Kong by the Japanese.
1949	People's Republic of China founded.
1966	Beginning of the Cultural Revolution.
1976	Death of Mao Zedong; end of the Cultural Revolution.
1979	Sir Murray MacLehose, governor of Hong Kong, raises the question of Hong Kong land leases expiring in 1997.
September 1982	Margaret Thatcher and Deng Xiaoping open diplomatic channels for preliminary negotiations.
Spring 1983	Thatcher's private messages to Premier Zhao Ziyang suggest sovereignty issue be set aside, thereby breaking deadlock in preliminary negotiations.
12 July 1983	Substantive negotiation begins; first of 22 rounds of talks.
October 1983	Beijing sets September 1984 as deadline for reaching agreement; otherwise Beijing will proceed with its own plans for Hong Kong.
Fall 1983	Beijing guarantees that Hong Kong's existing system will remain unchanged for 50 years after 1997.
20 April 1984	Sir Geoffrey Howe, British Foreign Secretary states that British administration in Hong Kong will end after 1997.
25 May 1984	Deng Xiaoping declares that the People's Liberation Army will be stationed in Hong Kong after 1997.
18 July 1984	Hong Kong government publishes a green paper on 'The Further Development of Representative Government in Hong Kong'.

1 August 1984	China and Britain agree to establish a Sino-British Joint Liaison Group to ensure smooth transfer and effective implementation of the Joint Declaration.
26 September 1984	Joint Declaration initialed by British Ambassador Sir Richard Evans and Deputy Foreign Minister Zhou Nan.
19 December 1984	Thatcher and Zhou sign the Sino-British Joint Declaration and three annexes and exchange of memoranda.
10 April 1985	China's National People's Congress (NPC) authorizes the establishment of a Basic Law Drafting Committee (BLDC).
27 May 1985	Joint Declaration comes into effect.
18 June 1985	NPC approves the BLDC membership list.
18 December 1985	Consultative Committee for the Basic Law (CCBL) established.
December 1986	Governor Edward Youde, who came to Hong Kong in 1982, dies in Beijing.
13 April 1987	China and Portugal sign the Joint Declaration on Macao.
April 1987	Governor David Wilson comes to Hong Kong.
June 1987	*Green Paper on Review of Developments in Representative Government* (based on the 1984 White Paper) published.
October 1987	Publication of the Report on Assessment of Public Response to the 1987 Green Paper.
January 1988	Publication of White Paper on 1988 Election.
15 January 1988	Sino-Portuguese Joint Declaration on Macao comes into effect.
April 1988	Publication of the Draft Basic Law of the Hong Kong Special Administrative Region of the People's Republic of China (For Solicitation of Opinions).
February 1989	Basic Law of the Hong Kong Special Administrative Region of the People's Republic of China (Draft) published.
4 June 1989	The Tiananmen Incident.
April 1990	Promulgation of the Basic Law of the Hong Kong Special Administrative Region of the People's Republic of China.
5 April 1990	Britain announces detailed plans to grant the heads of 50 000 households in Hong Kong the right of abode in the United Kingdom.
26 July 1990	British Nationality Act of 1990 (granting right of abode in UK to 50 000 heads of households in Hong Kong) comes into effect.
3 September 1991	Sino-British agreement on a new airport signed after nine months of negotiation.

15 September 1991	Hong Kong directly elects 18 members of the Legislative Council; all pro-China candidates defeated; 16 pro-democracy candidates elected.
1 October 1991	China announces that it does not recognize the Legislative Council (LEGCO) as a legislature, but only as a consultative body.
3 October 1991	New China News Agency announces that China's acceptance of the 'through train' is contingent upon Hong Kong people's support of the People's Republic of China.
23 January 1992	Report states that China will appoint Hong Kong Affairs Advisers.
25 January 1992	China instructs its cadre in Hong Kong to prepare for the 1995 election.
March 1992	China appoints the first group of 44 Hong Kong Affairs Advisers, an act which begins the 'second power center'.
3 July 1992	Governor Wilson retires.
8 July 1992	Governor Christopher Patten arrives in Hong Kong.
7 October 1992	Patten delivers the political reform policy statements to the LEGCO.
29 October 1992	Patten makes his first visit to Beijing, where he receives a cold reception.
3 December 1992	Despite China's strong objection, Patten is determined to go ahead with the reform.
3 December 1992	Hang Shen Index drops 433 points, or 7 per cent.
15 March 1993	Macao Basic Law promulgated.
26 March 1993	The Presidium of the 8th People's Congress announces that it will establish a 'Preparatory Working Committee' when the time is right.
29 March 1993	Publication of the list of the second group of Hong Kong Affairs Advisers.
22 April 1993	The 17 rounds of Sino-British negotiation on political reforms begins.
2 July 1993	Preparatory Working Committee formally established.
6 October 1993	Patten makes his second annual address to the LEGCO, declaring that political reforms would proceed.
26 November 1993	End of the 17 rounds of negotiation; no indication of whether the two sides will meet again in the future.
15 December 1993	Patten formally introduces the first stage of political reform proposals to the LEGCO; China immediately announces that the negotiation is off and it will not recognize the 1994 and 1995 elections.

4 January 1994	Hong Kong governor receives Taiwan's representative for the first time in 40 years.
31 January 1994	China indicates that it will appoint District Affairs Advisers.
23 February 1994	LEGCO passes the first-stage reform proposals.
24 February 1994	Britain publishes a White Paper detailing why the 17 rounds of negotiation failed.
25 February 1994	Patten announces the second stage of political reform.
28 February 1994	China publishes the 'True Picture' on negotiation.
4 March 1994	China publishes list of the first group of District Affairs Advisers.
9 March 1994	Patten formally introduces the second stage of political reform in the LEGCO.
11 April 1994	China publishes list of the third group of Hong Kong Affairs Advisers.
1 May 1994	Lu Ping, Director-General of the Hong Kong and Macao Office of the State Council, visits Hong Hong and refuses to see Patten.
2 May 1994	The Political-Economic Affairs Section of the Preparatory Working Committee meets in Hong Kong for the first time.
2 May 1994	The Bank of China issues Hong Kong currencies.
30 June 1994	China and Britain reach an agreement on military bases, facilities and lands after seven years of negotiation.
31 August 1994	NPC Standing Committee formally resolves to abolish the three-tier legislative set-up in Hong Kong after 1997.
7 September 1994	Reports circulate about setting up a 'provisional legislative council' on 1 July 1997.
18 September 1994	Direct election of District Board members held in accordance with Patten's reform proposals.
5 October 1994	Patten makes his third annual report to the LEGCO.
6 October 1994	Hong Kong's Economic and Trade Association exhibits a 'countdown clock' – only 1000 days to 1 July 1997.
4 November 1994	China and Britain sign an agreement on Hong Kong's new airport after three years of negotiation.
March 1995	Municipal Council elections.
7 June 1995	Taiwan President Lee Teng-hui visits the United States.
9 June 1995	After four years of negotiation China and Britain sign an agreement establishing a Court of Final Appeal for Hong Kong.

5 July 1995	China and Britain sign the financial support agreement for the new airport and airport railway, paving the way for the Airport Authority and the Mass Transit Railway Co. to borrow funds for the project.
17 September 1995	For the first time in Hong Kong's history, all the members of the new LEGCO are selected through direct or indirect elections; no one appointed.
11 October 1995	Patten's 4th annual report to the LEGCO emphasizes Hong Kong's economic achievements.
28 December 1995	China announces the appointment of a 150-member Preparatory Committee to oversee the setting up of the post-1997 political structure for Hong Kong.
9 January 1995	Britain and China agree in principle on financing the Container Terminal No. 9 project.
10 January 1996	Britain and China reach agreement on the future HKSAR passports.
26 January 1996	Preparatory Committee formally established, replacing Preparatory Working Committee established 2 July 1993. PC's first plenary session held in Beijing, marking the last phase of Hong Kong's transition.
17 February 1996	A committee of the Preparatory Committee announces that the method by which the Selection Committee (for selecting the first Chief Executive of the HKSAR after 1 July 1997) will be determined in April 1996.
17 February 1996	'Countdown clock' counts only 500 days to 1 July 1997.
4 March 1996	Britain announces that holders of the future HKSAR passports will be permitted to enter UK without visas.
13 March 1996	A survey indicates that 80 per cent of Hong Kong people are against the use of force by China to solve the Taiwan question.
20 March 1996	A committee of the Preparatory Committee meeting in Beijing recommends that the Hong Kong LEGCO cease functioning on 1 July 1997 and be replaced by a 'provisional legislative council'.
23 March 1996	First direct election held of the president of the Republic of China. Lee Teng-hui and Lien Chan elected as president and vice president respectively.
31 March 1996	Last day for applying for a British passport: more than 50 000 apply before midnight, the highest one-day record in Hong Kong's history.

15 May 1996	NPC passes a resolution that holders of foreign passports will be required to make a choice between permanent residency and foreign consular protection after 1997.
20 May 1996	Lee Teng-hui inaugurated for another four-year term of presidency.
16 June 1996	Hong Kong government's position on opposing the establishment of 'Provisional Legislative Council' after 1997 unchanged.
1 July 1996	'Countdown clock' counts only one year to Hong Kong's reversion to China.
December 1996	Report states that the Chief Executive for the future HKSAR will be Tung Chee-hwa.
1 July 1997	Hong Kong reverts to China.

Appendix

Agreement between the Government of the United Kingdom of Great Britain and Northern Ireland and the Government of the People's Republic of China on the Future of Hong Kong

26 September 1984

INTRODUCTION

1. On 26 September 1984 representatives of the Governments of the United Kingdom and of the People's Republic of China initialled the draft text of an agreement on the future of Hong Kong. The agreement, contained in the second part of this White Paper, consists of a Joint Declaration and three Annexes. There is an associated Exchange of Memoranda. These documents are the outcome of two years of negotiations between the two Governments, undertaken with the common aim of maintaining the stability and prosperity of Hong Kong.

2. The purpose of this White Paper is to explain the background to the last two years' negotiations and their course, and to present the documents in their proper context. The text of this White Paper is also being published in Hong Kong by the Hong Kong Government, and the people of Hong Kong are being invited to comment on the overall acceptability of the arrangements which it describes. Thereafter the matter will be debated in Parliament.

History

3. During the nineteenth century Britain concluded three treaties with the then Chinese Government relating to Hong Kong: the Treaty of Nanking,[1] signed in 1842 and ratified in 1843 under which Hong Kong Island was ceded in perpetuity;

---

[1] British State Papers Vol. 30, p. 389

the Convention of Peking[2] in 1860 under which the southern part of the Kowloon peninsula and Stonecutters Island were ceded in perpetuity; the Convention of 1898[3] under which the New Territories (comprising 92 per cent of the total land area of the territory) were leased to Britain for 99 years from 1 July 1898. It was the fact that the New Territories are subject to a lease with a fixed expiry date which lay behind the decision by Her Majesty's Government to seek to enter negotiations with the Government of the People's Republic of China (referred to hereafter as 'the Chinese Government') on Hong Kong's future.

4. The Chinese Government has consistently taken the view that the whole of Hong Kong is Chinese territory. Its position for many years was that the question of Hong Kong came into the category of unequal treaties left over from history; that it should be settled peacefully through negotiations when conditions were ripe; and that pending a settlement the status quo should be maintained. The Chinese Government made its views of Hong Kong's status clear in a letter to the Chairman of the United Nations Special Committee on the Situation with regard to the Implementation of the Declaration on the Granting of Independence to Colonial Countries and Peoples in March 1972. This maintained that the settlement of the question of Hong Kong was a matter of China's sovereign right and that consequently Hong Kong should not be included in the list of colonial territories covered by the Declaration on the Granting of Independence to Colonial Countries and Peoples.

The Background to the Negotiations

5. In the late 1970's, as the period the termination of the New Territories lease continued to shorten, concern about the future of Hong Kong began to be expressed both in the territory itself and among foreign investors. In particular there was increasing realization of the problem posed by individual land leases granted in the New Territories, all of which are set to expire three days before the expiry of the New Territories lease in 1997. It was clear that the steadily shortening span of these leases and the inability of the Hong Kong Government to grant new ones extending beyond 1997 would be likely to deter investment and damage confidence.

6. Her Majesty's Government had by this time, following a detailed examination of the problem conducted in consultation with the then Governor, concluded that confidence would begin to erode quickly in the early to mid-1980's if nothing was done to alleviate the uncertainty caused by the 1997 deadline. Accordingly, when the Governor of Hong Kong visited Peking in March 1979 at the invitation of the Chinese Minister of Foreign Trade, an attempt was made, on the initiative of Her Majesty's Government, to solve the specific question of land leases expiring in 1997. These discussions did not result in measures to solve the problem.

7. In the course of the next two years there was increasing awareness of the need to remove the uncertainty which the 1997 deadline generated. The importance of the issue was publicly stressed by the senior Unofficial Member of the Executive Council in May 1982. In January 1982 Sir (then Mr) Humphrey Atkins, Lord Privy Seal, visited Peking and was given significant indications of Chinese policy towards Hong Kong by Chinese leaders, which confirmed the view of Her Majesty's Government that negotiations should be opened with the Chinese Government.

[2] British State Papers Vol. 50, p. 10
[3] British State Papers Vol. 90, p. 17

The Prime Minister's Visit to China

8. Against this background Her Majesty's Government decided that the Prime Minister's visit to China in September 1982 would provide an opportunity to open discussions with the Chinese Government on the future of Hong Kong. It was evident that the Chinese Government had reached the same conclusion, and substantive discussions took place during the visit. Following a meeting between the Prime Minister and Chairman Deng Xiaoping on 24 September 1982 the following joint statement was issued:

'Today the leaders of both countries held far-reaching talks in a friendly atmosphere on the future of Hong Kong. Both leaders made clear their respective positions on this subject.

They agreed to enter talks through diplomatic channels following the visit with the common aim of maintaining the stability and prosperity of Hong Kong.'

The Course of the Negotiations

9. The Prime Minister's visit was followed by the first phase of negotiations conducted by her Majesty's Ambassador in Peking and the Chinese Foreign Ministry. These consisted of exchanges between the two sides on the basis on which the negotiations would be conducted, and on the agenda. On 1 July 1983 it was announced that the second phase of the talks would begin in Peking on 12 July. The pattern of negotiation in the second phase, which was continued until the end of the negotiations, was for formal rounds of talks to be held between delegations led by Her Majesty's Ambassador in Peking and a Vice or Assistant Minister of the Chinese Foreign Ministry, supplemented as necessary by informal contacts between the two delegations. The Governor of Hong Kong took part in every round of formal talks as a member of the British delegation.

10. In the course of the negotiations Her Majesty's Government explained in detail the systems which prevail in Hong Kong and the importance for these systems of the British administrative role and link. Following extensive discussion, however, it became clear that the continuation of British administration after 1997 would not be acceptable to China in any form. After full consultation with the Governor and the Executive Council of Hong Kong, Her Majesty's Government therefore proposed that the two sides discuss on a conditional basis what effective measures other than continued British administration might be devised to maintain the stability and prosperity of Hong Kong and explore further the Chinese ideas about the future which had at that stage been explained to them, in order to see whether on this basis arrangements which would ensure lasting stability and prosperity for Hong Kong could be constructed. The Chinese Government was told that, if this process was successful, Her Majesty's Government would consider recommending to Parliament a bilateral agreement enshrining the arrangements. Her Majesty's Government also undertook in this event to assist in the implementation of such arrangements. Following this, Her Majesty's Government sought to explore with the Chinese Government the implications of the Chinese Government's concept of Hong Kong as a Special Administrative Region of the People's Republic of China. In response, the Chinese side further elaborated its policies and ideas.

11. In April 1984 the two sides completed initial discussion of these matters. There were a number of outstanding points, but it was by then clear that an acceptable basis for an agreement might be possible. At the invitation of the Chinese Government the Secretary of State for Foreign and Commonwealth Affairs visited Peking from 15 to 18 April. During his meetings with Chinese leaders the two sides reviewed the course of the talks on the future of Hong Kong, and

further progress was made. In Hong Kong on 20 April Sir Geoffrey Howe made a statement on the approach of Her Majesty's Government to the negotiations. He said that it would not be realistic to think of an agreement that provided for continued British administration in Hong Kong after 1997: for that reason Her Majesty's Government had been examining with the Chinese Government how it might be possible to arrive at arrangements that would secure for Hong Kong, after 1997, a high degree of autonomy under Chinese sovereignty, and that would preserve the way of life in Hong Kong, together with the essentials of the present systems. He made it clear that Her Majesty's Government were working for a framework of arrangements that would provide for the maintenance of Hong Kong's flourishing and dynamic society, and an agreement in which such arrangements would be formally set out.

12. After Sir Geoffrey Howe's visit in April 1984 negotiations continued. A working group was established on 21 June 1984 to meet full-time in Peking and consider documents tabled by both sides. From 27 to 31 July 1984 the Secretary of State for Foreign and Commonwealth Affairs again visited Peking. The visit was devoted almost entirely to the future of Hong Kong. Sir Geoffrey Howe announced in Hong Kong on 1 August that very substantial progress had been made towards agreement on the form and content of documents which would set out arrangements for Hong Kong's future with clarity and precision in legally binding form.

13. Sir Geoffrey also announced on the same occasion that the two sides had agreed to establish a Sino-British Joint Liaison Group which would come into being when the agreement came into force and continue until the year 2000. It would meet in Peking, London and Hong Kong. It was agreed that the Group would not be an organ of power. Its functions would be: liaison, consultation on the implementation of the agreement, and exchange of information. It was agreed that it would play no part in the administration of Hong Kong. Her Majesty's Government would continue to be responsible for the administration of Hong Kong up to 30 June 1997.

14. Following Sir Geoffrey Howe's visit the negotiations continued on the remaining unresolved issues and three further rounds of plenary talks took place. A further ad hoc working group was established in Peking on 24 August. By 18 September negotiators on both sides had approved the English and Chinese texts of the documents that make up the agreement and the associated Exchange of Memoranda. These were submitted to British Ministers and Chinese leaders for final approval. The texts were initiated by the two delegation leaders on 26 September.

Consultation with the People of Hong Kong

15. From the beginning of the negotiations Her Majesty's Government have been conscious that the negotiations concerned the interests and future of the five and a half million people of Hong Kong. It has been the consistent position of Her Majesty's Government that any agreement with the Chinese Government on the future of the territory should be acceptable to the people of Hong Kong as well as to the British Parliament and the Chinese Government.

16. The negotiations had to be conducted on a basis of confidentiality. This was crucial to their success, but the maintenance of confidentiality also caused much concern and anxiety among the people of Hong Kong who were understandably anxious to know what was being negotiated for their future. All members of the Executive Council, as the Governor's closest advisers, were kept fully informed on the negotiations and consulted on a continuing basis throughout the period. The Unofficial Members of the Executive and Legislative Councils (UMELCO) provided invaluable advice to the Governor and to Ministers on the course of the negotiations and on the attitude of the people of Hong Kong.

17. At a number of crucial points in the negotiations the Governor and Unofficial Members of the Executive Council visited London for consultations with the Prime Minister and other Ministers. British Ministers also paid a series of visits to Hong Kong, to consult the Governor, the Executive Council and the Unofficial Members of the Executive and Legislative Councils and to keep in touch with option in the territory. The Secretary of State for Foreign and Commonwealth Affairs was able to describe the approach of Her Majesty's Government to the negotiations in his statement in Hong Kong on 20 April 1984, and to fill in more details of what might eventually be included in an agreement in a further statement in the territory on 1 August 1984. In the course of the negotiations, and in particular since the statement of 20 April, numerous individuals and groups in Hong Kong have made specific proposals on what should be included in an eventual agreement. The Legislative Council of Hong Kong has debated aspects of the future of the territory on a number of occasions. Her Majesty's Government have paid close attention to these expressions of opinion which the Hong Kong Government have relayed to Ministers, and to views about the future expressed through a variety of channels – by and through UMELCO, through the press, through individual communications addressed to Her Majesty's Government or the Hong Kong Government. In this way Her Majesty's Government have sought to take into account the views of the people of Hong Kong to the maximum extent possible during the negotiations.

18. In the same way the maintenance of confidentiality has made the task of consulting Parliament on the negotiations more difficult. Despite this there were debates on Hong Kong in October and November 1983 and in May 1984, and part of the Foreign Affairs Debate in March 1984 was also devoted to Hong Kong. Members of Parliament have kept in close touch with the people of Hong Kong, both through visits to the territory and through meetings with Hong Kong delegations visiting the United Kingdom.

Introduction to the Agreement

19. The full text of the draft agreement is included in the second part of this White Paper. It consists of a Joint Declaration and three Annexes. Each part of the agreement has the same status. The whole makes up a formal international agreement, legally binding in all parts. An international agreement of this kind is the highest form of commitment between two sovereign states.

20. The Joint Declaration consists in part of linked declarations by Her Majesty's Government and the Chinese Government. In paragraph 1 the Chinese Government declares that it will resume the exercise of sovereignty over Hong Kong on 1 July 1997. In paragraph 2 Her Majesty's Government declare that they will restore Hong Kong to the Chinese Government from that date. In paragraph 3 the Chinese Government sets out its policies towards Hong Kong after 30 June 1997. In paragraph 4 the two Governments jointly declare that Her Majesty's Government will remain responsible for the administration of Hong Kong up to 30 June 1997. Paragraphs 5 and 6 deal with the Joint Liaison Group and land. Paragraph 7 constitutes the important link between the declarations by the two parties; it has the effect of making the Joint Declaration and the Annexes to it legally binding in their entirety on the two Governments. Paragraph 8 provides for the agreement to enter into force on ratification. Ratification will take place before 30 June 1985.

21. The agreement sets out clearly the relationship between the provisions which it contains and the future Basic Law of the Hong Kong Special Administrative Region, to be promulgated by the National People's Congress of the People's Republic of China. Paragraph 3(12) of the Joint Declaration provides that the basic policies in the Joint Declaration and the elaboration of them in Annex I will be stipulated in the Basic Law. They will remain unchanged for 50 years.

22. Annex I contains an elaboration of Chinese policies for the Hong Kong Special Administrative Region. The Annex deals in detail with the way Hong Kong will work after 1 July 1997, and describes the extent of the autonomy and continuity which will prevail then. The subjects dealt with in the various sections of this Annex are:

(I) constitutional arrangements and government structure;
(II) the laws;
(III) the judicial system;
(IV) the public service;
(V) the financial system;
(VI) the economic system and external economic relations;
(VII) the monetary system;
(VIII) shipping;
(IX) civil aviation;
(X) culture and education;
(XI) external relations;
(XII) defence, security and public order;
(XIII) rights and freedoms;
(XIV) right of abode, travel documents and immigration.

23. Annex II sets out the provisions concerning the establishment of a Sino-British Joint Liaison Group. The Joint Liaison Group will be established on the entry into force of the agreement and will meet in Peking, London and Hong Kong. From 1 July 1988 it will be based in Hong Kong, although it will also continue to meet in Peking and London. It will continue its work until 1 January 2000. The Annex includes terms of reference which clearly indicate that the Group will be a forum of liaison only and not an organ of power. It will neither play a part in the administration of Hong Kong nor have any supervisory role.

24. Annex III deals with land leases. It covers leases that have already been issued by the Hong Kong Government, leases to be issued between the entry into force of the agreement and 1977, certain financial arrangements, and arrangements for the establishment of a joint Land Commission.

25. Associated with the agreement is a separate Exchange of Memoranda on the status of persons after 30 June 1997 who at present are British Dependent Territories citizens, and related issues. The Memoranda will be formally exchanged in Peking on the same day as the signature of the Joint Declaration.

26. The last part of this White Paper contains further explanatory notes on the text of the Annexes to the Joint Declaration and the Exchange of Memoranda.

Views of Her Majesty's Government on the Agreement

27. As recorded in paragraph 10 above, Her Majesty's Government have sought to see whether on the basis of proposals put forward by the Chinese Government arrangements could be constructed which would ensure lasting stability and prosperity for Hong Kong. They have negotiated energetically and they believe successfully to secure an agreement which meets the needs and wishes of the people of Hong Kong. The negotiations have been hard and long. Taking the agreement as a whole Her Majesty's Government are confident that it does provide a framework in which the stability and prosperity of Hong Kong can be maintained after 1997 as a Special Administrative Region of the People's Republic of China.

28. The text of the agreement has been initialled by both sides. This represents a certification by the negotiators that it represents accurately the outcome of the negotiations. However, as is normal with international agreements negotiated between nations there is no realistic possibility of amending the text. The agreement must be taken as a whole.

29. Her Majesty's Government have a duty to make clear beyond any possibility of misunderstanding the alternative to acceptance of the agreement set out in this White Paper. In their view, there is no possibility of an amended agreement. The alternative to acceptance of the present agreement is to have no agreement. In this case the Chinese Government has made it plain that negotiations could not be reopened and that it would publish its own plan for Hong Kong. There is no guarantee that such a unilateral plan would include all the elements included in the draft agreement, nor would it have the same status as a legally binding agreement between the two countries. Whether or not there is an agreement between Her Majesty's Government and the Chinese Government the New Territories will revert to China on 1 July 1997 under the terms of the 1898 Convention. The remainder of Hong Kong (Hong Kong Island, Kowloon and Stonecutters Island) would not be viable alone. Hong Kong, including the New Territories, has since 1898 become an integral whole and Her Majesty's Government are satisfied that there is no possibility of dividing the New Territories which revert to China on 1 July 1997 from the remainder. The choice is therefore between reversion of Hong Kong to China under agreed, legally binding international arrangements or reversion to China without such arrangements. This is not a choice which Her Majesty's Government have sought to impose on the people of Hong Kong. It is a choice imposed by the facts of Hong Kong's history.

30. Her Majesty's Government believe that the agreement is a good one. They strongly commend it to the people of Hong Kong and to Parliament. It provides a framework in which Hong Kong as a Special Administrative Region of the People's Republic of China will be able to preserve its unique economic system and way of life after 1 July 1997. The agreement preserves Hong Kong's familiar legal system and the body of laws in force in Hong Kong, including the common law. The agreement gives Hong Kong a high degree of autonomy in which it will be able to administer itself and pass its own legislation. It will enable Hong Kong to continue to decide on its own economic, financial and trade policies, and to participate in international organisations and trade agreements such as the General Agreement on Tariffs and Trade (GATT). **Her Majesty's Government are confident that the agreement provides the necessary assurances about Hong Kong's future to allow the territory to continue to flourish, and to maintain its unique role in the world as a major trading and financial centre.**

The Agreement and the People of Hong Kong

31. Her Majesty's Government have consistently stated that an agreement on the future of Hong Kong must be acceptable to the people of Hong Kong as well as to Parliament. In his statement on 20 April 1984 in Hong Kong the Secretary of State for Foreign and Commonwealth Affairs stated that the people of Hong Kong would need to have time to express their views on the agreement, before it was debated by Parliament. The people of Hong Kong will now have this opportunity.

32. The text of this White Paper is also being published in Hong Kong by the Hong Kong Government and will be circulated through a wide variety of channels in the territory. An Assessment Office has been set up in Hong Kong under the charge of a senior official of Hong Kong Government, directly responsible to the Governor. This office will provide Her Majesty's Government and Parliament with an analysis and assessment of opinion in Hong Kong on the draft agreement. Two monitors, Sir Patrick Nairne and Mr Justice Simon Li, have been appointed by Her Majesty's Government to observe the work of the Assessment Office and to report independently to the Secretary of State for Foreign and Commonwealth Affairs on whether they are satisfied that the Assessment Office has properly, accurately and impartially discharged its duties. In the light of these two reports Her Majesty's Government will decide what recommendation to make to Parliament.

33. The people of Hong Kong are now invited to comment on the overall acceptability of the draft agreement on Hong Kong negotiated between Her Majesty's Government and the Chinese Government, against the background set out in this White Paper.

JOINT DECLARATION
OF THE GOVERNMENT OF THE UNITED KINGDOM OF
GREAT BRITAIN AND NORTHERN IRELAND
AND
THE GOVERNMENT OF THE PEOPLE'S REPUBLIC OF CHINA
ON THE QUESTION OF HONG KONG

The Government of the United Kingdom of Great Britain and Northern Ireland and the Government of the People's Republic of China have reviewed with satisfaction the friendly relations existing between the two Governments and peoples in recent years and agreed that a proper negotiated settlement of the question of Hong Kong, which is left over from the past, is conducive to the maintenance of the prosperity and stability of Hong Kong and to the further strengthening and development of the relations between the two countries on a new basis. To this end, they have, after talks between the delegations of the two Governments, agreed to declare as follows:

1. The Government of the People's Republic of China declares that to recover the Hong Kong area (including Hong Kong Island, Kowloon and the New Territories, hereinafter referred to as Hong Kong) is the common aspiration of the entire Chinese people, and that it has decided to resume the exercise of sovereignty over Hong Kong with effect from 1 July 1997.

2. The Government of the United Kingdom declares that it will restore Hong Kong to the People's Republic of China with effect from 1 July 1997.

3. The Government of the People's Republic of China declares that the basic policies of the People's Republic of China regarding Hong Kong are as follows:

(1) Upholding national unity and territorial integrity and taking account of the history of Hong Kong and its realities, the People's Republic of China has decided to establish, in accordance with the provisions of Article 31 of the Constitution of the People's Republic of China, a Hong Kong Special Administrative Region upon resuming the exercise of sovereignty over Hong Kong.

(2) The Hong Kong Special Administrative Region will be directly under the authority of the Central People's Government of the People's Republic of China. The Hong Kong Special Administrative Region will enjoy a high degree of autonomy, except in foreign and defence affairs which are the responsibilities of the Central People's Government.

(3) The Hong Kong Special Administrative Region will be vested with executive, legislative and independent judicial power, including that of final adjudication. The laws currently in force in Hong Kong will remain basically unchanged.

(4) The Government of the Hong Kong Special Administrative Region will be composed of local inhabitants. The chief executive will be appointed by the Central People's Government on the basis of the results of elections or consultations to be held locally. Principal officials will be nominated by the chief executive of the Hong Kong Special Administrative Region for appointment by the Central People's Government. Chinese and foreign nationals previously working in the public and police services in the government departments of Hong Kong may remain in employment. British and other foreign nationals may also be employed to serve as advisers or hold certain public posts in government departments of the Hong Kong Special Administrative Region.

(5) The current social and economic systems in Hong Kong will remain unchanged, and so will the life-style. Rights and freedoms, including those of the person, of speech, of the press, of assembly, of association, of travel, of movement, of correspondence, of strike, of choice of occupation, of academic research and of religious belief will be ensured by law in the Hong Kong Special Administrative Region. Private property, ownership of enterprises, legitimate right of inheritance and foreign investment will be protected by law.

(6) The Hong Kong Special Administrative Region will retain the status of a free port and a separate customs territory.

(7) The Hong Kong Special Administrative Region will retain the status of an international financial centre, and its markets for foreign exchange, gold, securities and future will continue. There will be free flow of capital. The Hong Kong dollar will continue to circulate and remain freely convertible.

(8) The Hong Kong Special Administrative Region will have independent finances. The Central People's Government will not levy taxes on the Hong Kong Special Administrative Region.

(9) The Hong Kong Special Administrative Region may establish mutually beneficial economic relations with the United Kingdom and other countries, whose economic interests in Hong Kong will be given due regard.

(10) Using the name of 'Hong Kong, China', the Hong Kong Special Administrative Region may on its own maintain and develop economic and cultural relations and conclude relevant agreements with states, regions and relevant international organisations.

The Government of the Hong Kong Special Administrative Region may on its own issue travel documents for entry into and exit from Hong Kong.

(11) The maintenance of public order in the Hong Kong Special Administrative Region will be the responsibility of the Government of the Hong Kong Special Administrative Region.

(12) The above-stated basic policies of the People's Republic of China regarding Hong Kong and the elaboration of them in Annex I to this Joint Declaration will be stipulated, in a Basic Law of the Hong Kong Special Administrative Region of the People's Republic of China, by the National People's Congress of the People's Republic of China, and they will remain unchanged for 50 years.

4. The Government of the United Kingdom and the Government of the People's Republic of China declare that, during the transitional period between the date of the entry into force of this Joint Declaration and 30 June 1997, the Government of the United Kingdom will be responsible for the administration of Hong Kong with the object of maintaining and preserving its economic prosperity and social stability; and that the Government of the People's Republic of China will give its cooperation in this connection.

5. The Government of the United Kingdom and the Government of the People's Republic of China declare that, in order to ensure a smooth transfer of government in 1997, and with a view to the effective implementation of this Joint Declaration, a Sino-British Joint Liaison Group will be set up when this Joint Declaration enters into force; and that it will be established and will function in accordance with the provisions of Annex II to this Joint Declaration.

6. The Government of the United Kingdom and the Government of the People's Republic of China declare that land leases in Hong Kong and other related matters will be dealt with in accordance with the provisions of Annex III to this Joint Declaration.

7. The Government of the United Kingdom and the Government of the People's Republic of China agree to implement the preceding declarations and the Annexes to this Joint Declaration.

8. This Joint Declaration is subject to ratification and shall enter into force on the date of the exchange of instruments of ratification, which shall take place in Beijing before 30 June 1985. This Joint Declaration and its Annexes shall be equally binding.

Done in duplicate at Beijing on 1984 in the English and Chinese languages, both texts being equally authentic.

For the
Government of the United Kingdom
of Great Britain and Northern Ireland

For the
Government of the
People's Republic of China

ANNEX I

ELABORATION BY THE GOVERNMENT OF
THE PEOPLE'S REPUBLIC OF CHINA
OF ITS BASIC POLICIES REGARDING HONG KONG

The Government of the People's Republic of China elaborates the basic policies of the People's Republic of China regarding Hong Kong as set out in paragraph 3 of the Joint Declaration of the Government of the United Kingdom of Great Britain and Northern Ireland and the Government of the People's Republic of China on the Question of Hong Kong as follows:

I

The Constitution of the People's Republic of China stipulates in Article 31 that 'the state may establish special administrative regions when necessary. The systems to be instituted in special administrative regions shall be prescribed by laws enacted by the National People's Congress in the light of the specific conditions.' In accordance with this Article, the People's Republic of China shall, upon the resumption of the exercise of sovereignty over Hong Kong on 1 July 1997, establish the Hong Kong Special Administrative Region of the People's Republic of China. The National People's Congress of the People's Republic of China shall enact and promulgate a Basic Law of the Hong Kong Special Administrative Region of the People's Republic of China (hereinafter referred to as the Basic Law) in accordance with the Constitution of the People's Republic of China, stipulating that after the establishment of the Hong Kong Special Administrative Region the socialist system and socialist policies shall not be practised in the Hong Kong Special Administrative Region and that Hong Kong's previous capitalist system and life-style shall remain unchanged for 50 years.

The Hong Kong Special Administrative Region shall be directly under the authority of the Central People's Government of the People's Republic of China and shall enjoy a high degree of autonomy. Except for foreign and defence affairs which are the responsibilities of the Central People's Government, the Hong Kong Special Administrative Region shall be vested with executive, legislative and independent judicial power, including that of final adjudication. The Central People's Government shall authorise the Hong Kong Special Administrative Region to conduct on its own those external affairs specified in Section XI of this Annex.

The government and legislature of the Hong Kong Special Administrative Region shall be composed of local inhabitants. The chief executive of the Hong Kong Special Administrative Region shall be selected by election or through consultations held locally and be appointed by the Central People's Government. Principal officials (equivalent to Secretaries) shall be nominated by the chief executive of the Hong Kong Special Administrative Region and appointed by the Central People's Government. The legislature of the Hong Kong Special Administrative Region shall be constituted by elections. The executive authorities shall abide by the law and shall be accountable to the legislature.

In addition to Chinese, English may also be used in organs of government and in the courts in the Hong Kong Special Administrative Region.

Apart from displaying the national flag and national emblem of the People's Republic of China, the Hong Kong Special Administrative Region may use a regional flag and emblem of its own.

II

After the establishment of the Hong Kong Special Administrative Region, the laws previously in force in Hong Kong (i.e. the common law, rules of equity, ordinances, subordinate legislation and customary law) shall be maintained, save for any that contravene the Basic Law and subject to any amendment by the Hong Kong Special Administrative Region legislature.

The legislative power of the Hong Kong Special Administrative Region shall be vested in the legislature of the Hong Kong Special Administrative Region. The legislature may on its own authority enact laws in accordance with the provisions of the Basic Law and legal procedures, and report them to the Standing Committee of the National People's Congress for the record. Laws enacted by the legislature which are in accordance with the Basic Law and legal procedures shall be regarded as valid.

The laws of the Hong Kong Special Administrative Region shall be the Basic Law, and the laws previously in force in Hong Kong and laws enacted by the Hong Kong Special Administrative Region legislature as above.

III

After the establishment of the Hong Kong Special Administrative Region, the judicial system previously practised in Hong Kong shall be maintained except for those changes consequent upon the vesting in the courts of the Hong Kong Special Administrative Region of the power of final adjudication.

Judicial power in the Hong Kong Special Administrative Region shall be vested in the courts of the Hong Kong Special Administrative Region. The courts shall exercise judicial power independently and free from any interference. Members of the judiciary shall be immune from legal action in respect of their judicial functions. The courts shall decide cases in accordance with the laws of the Hong Kong Special Administrative Region and may refer to precedents in other common law jurisdictions.

Judges of the Hong Kong Special Administrative Region courts shall be appointed by the chief executive of the Hong Kong Special Administrative Region acting in accordance with the recommendation of an independent commission composed of local judges, persons from the legal profession and other eminent persons. Judges shall be chosen by reference to their judicial qualities and may be recruited from other common law jurisdictions. A judge may only be removed for inability to discharge the functions of his office, or for misbehaviour, by the chief executive of the Hong Kong Special Administrative Region acting in accordance with the recommendation of a tribunal appointed by the chief judge of the court of final appeal, consisting of not fewer than three local judges. Additionally, the appointment or removal of principal judges (i.e. those of the highest rank) shall be made by the chief executive with the endorsement of the Hong Kong Special Administrative Region legislature and reported to the Standing Committee of the National People's Congress for the record. The system of appointment and removal of judicial officers other than judges shall be maintained.

The power of final judgment of the Hong Kong Special Administrative Region shall be vested in the court of final appeal in the Hong Kong Special Administrative Region, which may as required invite judges from other common law jurisdictions to sit on the court of final appeal.

A prosecuting authority of the Hong Kong Special Administrative Region shall control criminal prosecutions free from any interference.

On the basis of the system previously operating in Hong Kong, the Hong Kong Special Administrative Region Government shall on its own make provision for local lawyers and lawyers from outside the Hong Kong Special Administrative Region to work and practise in the Hong Kong Special Administrative Region.

The Central People's Government shall assist or authorise the Hong Kong Special Administrative Region Government to make appropriate arrangements for reciprocal judicial assistance with foreign states.

IV

After the establishment of the Hong Kong Special Administrative Region, public servants previously serving in Hong Kong in all government departments, including the police department, and members of the judiciary may all remain in employment and continue their service with pay, allowances, benefits and conditions of service no less favourable than before. The Hong Kong Special Administrative Region Government shall pay to such persons who retire or complete their contracts, as well as to those who have retired before 1 July 1997, or to their dependants, all pensions, gratuities, allowances and benefits due to them on terms no less favourable than before, and irrespective of their nationality or place of residence.

The Hong Kong Special Administrative Region Government may employ British and other foreign nationals previously serving in the public service in Hong Kong, and may recruit British and other foreign nationals holding permanent identity cards of the Hong Kong Special Administrative Region to serve as public servants at all levels, except as heads of major government departments (corresponding to branches or departments at Secretary level) including the police department, and as deputy heads of some of those departments. The Hong Kong Special Administrative Region Government may also employ British and other foreign nationals as advisers to government departments and, when there is a need, may recruit qualified candidates from outside the Hong Kong Special Administrative Region to professional and technical posts in government departments. The above shall be employed only in their individual capacities and, like other public servants, shall be responsible to the Hong Kong Special Administrative Region Government.

The appointment and promotion of public servants shall be on the basis of qualifications, experience and ability. Hong Kong's previous system of recruitment, employment, assessment, discipline, training and management for the public service (including special bodies for appointment, pay and conditions of service) shall, save for any provisions providing privileged treatment for foreign nationals, be maintained.

V

The Hong Kong Special Administrative Region shall deal on its own with financial matters, including disposing of its financial resources and drawing up its budgets and its final accounts. The Hong Kong Special Administrative Region shall report its budgets and final accounts to the Central People's Government for the record.

The Central People's Government shall not levy taxes on the Hong Kong Special Administrative Region. The Hong Kong Special Administrative Region shall use its financial revenues exclusively for its own purposes and they shall not be handed over to the Central People's Government. The systems by which taxation and public expenditure must be approved by the legislature, and by which there is accountability to the legislature for all public expenditure, and the system for auditing public accounts shall be maintained.

VI

The Hong Kong Special Administrative Region shall maintain the capitalist economic and trade systems previously practised in Hong Kong. The Hong Kong Special Administrative Region Government shall decide its economic and trade policies on its own. Rights concerning the ownership of property, including those relating to acquisition, use, disposal, inheritance and compensation for lawful deprivation (corresponding to the real value of the property concerned, freely convertible and paid without undue delay) shall continue to be protected by law.

The Hong Kong Special Administrative Region shall retain the status of a free port and continue a free trade policy, including the free movement of goods and capital. The Hong Kong Special Administrative Region may on its own maintain and develop economic and trade relations with all states and regions.

The Hong Kong Special Administrative Region shall be a separate customs territory. It may participate in relevant international organisations and international trade agreements (including preferential trade arrangements), such as the General Agreement on Tariffs and Trade and arrangements regarding international trade in textiles. Export quotas, tariff preferences and other similar arrangements obtained by the Hong Kong Special Administrative Region shall be enjoyed exclusively by the Hong Kong Special Administrative Region. The Hong Kong Special Administrative Region shall have authority to issue its own certificates of origin for products manufactured locally, in accordance with prevailing rules of origin.

The Hong Kong Special Administrative Region may, as necessary, establish official and semi-official economic and trade missions in foreign countries, reporting the establishment of such missions to the Central People's Government for the record.

VII

The Hong Kong Special Administrative Region shall retain the status of an international financial centre. The monetary and financial systems previously practised in Hong Kong, including the systems of regulation and supervision of deposit taking institutions and financial markets, shall be maintained.

The Hong Kong Special Administrative Region Government may decide its monetary and financial policies on its own. It shall safeguard the free operation of financial business and the free flow of the capital within, into and out of the Hong Kong Special Administrative Region. No exchange control policy shall be applied in the Hong Kong Special Administrative Region. Markets for foreign exchange, gold, securities, and futures shall continue.

The Hong Kong dollar, as the local legal tender, shall continue to circulate and remain freely convertible. The authority to issue Hong Kong currency shall be vested in the Hong Kong Special Administrative Region Government. The Hong Kong Special Administrative Region Government may authorise designated banks to issue or continue to issue Hong Kong currency under statutory authority, after satisfying itself that any issue of currency will be soundly based and that the arrangements for such issue are consistent with the object of maintaining the stability of the currency. Hong Kong currency bearing references inappropriate to the status of Hong Kong as a Special Administrative Region of the People's republic of China shall be progressively replaced and withdrawn from circulation.

The Exchange Fund shall be managed and controlled by the Hong Kong Special Administrative Region Government, primarily for regulating the exchange value of the Hong Kong dollar.

VIII

The Hong Kong Special Administrative Region shall maintain Hong Kong's previous systems of shipping management and shipping regulation, including the system for regulating conditions of seamen. The specific functions and responsibilities of the Hong Kong Special Administrative Region Government in the field of shipping shall be defined by the Hong Kong Special Administrative Region Government on its own. Private shipping businesses and shipping-related businesses and private container terminals in Hong Kong may continue to operate freely.

The Hong Kong Special Administrative Region shall be authorised by the Central People's Government to continue to maintain a shipping register and issue related certificates under its own legislation in the name of 'Hong Kong, China'.

With the exception of foreign warships, access for which requires the permission of the Central People's Government, ships shall enjoy access to the ports of the Hong Kong Special Administrative Region in accordance with the laws of the Hong Kong Special Administrative Region.

IX

The Hong Kong Special Administrative Region shall maintain the status of Hong Kong as a centre of international and regional aviation. Airlines incorporated and having their principal place of business in Hong Kong and civil aviation related businesses may continue to operate. The Hong Kong Special Administrative Region shall continue the previous system of civil aviation management in Hong Kong, and keep its own aircraft register in accordance with provisions laid down by the Central People's Government concerning nationality marks and registration marks of aircraft. The Hong Kong Special Administrative Region shall be responsible on its own for matters of routine business and technical management of civil aviation, including the management of airports, the provision of air traffic services within the flight information region of the Hong Kong Special Administrative Region, and the discharge of other responsibilities allocated under the regional air navigation procedures of the International Civil Aviation Organisation.

The Central People's Government shall, in consultation with the Hong Kong Special Administrative Region Government, make arrangements providing for air services between the Hong Kong Special Administrative Region and other parts of the People's Republic of China for airlines incorporated and having their principal place of business in the Hong Kong Special Administrative Region and other airlines of the People's Republic of China. All Air Service Agreements providing for air services between other parts of the People's Republic of China and other states and regions with stops at the Hong Kong Special Administrative Region and air services between the Hong Kong Special Administrative Region and other states and regions with stops at other parts of the People's Republic of China shall be concluded by the Central People's Government. For this purpose, the Central People's Government shall take account of the special conditions and economic interests of the Hong Kong Special Administrative Region and consult the Hong Kong Special Administrative Region Government. Representatives of the Hong Kong Special Administrative Region Government may participate as members of delegations of the Government of the People's Republic of China in air service consultations with foreign governments concerning arrangements for such services.

Acting under specific authorisations from the Central People's Government, the Hong Kong Special Administrative Region Government may:

- renew or amend Air Service Agreements and arrangements previously in force; in principle, all such Agreements and arrangements may be renewed or amended with the rights contained in such previous Agreements and arrangements being as far as possible maintained;

- negotiate and conclude new Air Service Agreements providing routes for airlines incorporated and having their principal place of business in the Hong Kong Special Administrative Region and rights for overflights and technical stops; and

- negotiate and conclude provisional arrangements where no Air Service Agreement with a foreign state or other region is in force.

All scheduled air services to, from or through the Hong Kong Special Administrative Region which do not operate to, from or through the mainland of China shall be regulated by Air Service Agreements or provisional arrangements referred to in this paragraph.

The Central People's Government shall give the Hong Kong Special Administrative Region Government the authority to:

- negotiate and conclude with other authorities all arrangements concerning the implementation of the above Air Service Agreements and provisional arrangements;
- issue licences to airlines incorporated and having their principal place of business in the Hong Kong Special Administrative Region;
- designate such airlines under the above Air Service Agreements and provisional arrangements; and
- issue permits to foreign airlines for services other than those to, from or through the mainland of China.

X

The Hong Kong Special Administrative Region shall maintain the educational system previously practised in Hong Kong. The Hong Kong Special Administrative Region Government shall on its own decide policies in the fields of culture, education, science and technology, including policies regarding the educational system and its administration, the language of instruction, the allocation of funds, the examination system, the system of academic awards and the recognition of educational and technological qualifications. Institutions of all kinds, including those run by religious and community organisations, may retain their autonomy. They may continue to recruit staff and use teaching materials from outside the Hong Kong Special Administrative Region. Students shall enjoy freedom of choice of education and freedom to pursue their education outside the Hong Kong Special Administrative Region.

XI

Subject to the principle that foreign affairs are the responsibility of the Central People's Government, representatives of the Hong Kong Special Administrative Region Government may participate, as members of delegations of the Government of the People's Republic of China, in negotiations at the diplomatic level directly affecting the Hong Kong Special Administrative Region conducted by the Central People's Government. The Hong Kong Special Administrative Region may on its own, using the name 'Hong Kong, China', maintain and develop relations and conclude and implement agreements with states, regions and relevant international organisations in the appropriate fields, including the economic, trade, financial and monetary, shipping, communications, touristic, cultural and sporting fields. Representatives of the Hong Kong Special Administrative Region Government may participate, as members of delegations of the Government of the People's Republic of China, in international organisations or conferences in appropriate fields limited to states and affecting the Hong Kong Special Administrative Region, or may attend in such other capacity as may be permitted by the Central People's Government and the organisation or conference concerned, and may express their views in the name of 'Hong Kong, China'.

The Hong Kong Special Administrative Region may, using the name 'Hong Kong, China', participate in international organisations and conferences not limited to states.

The application to the Hong Kong Special Administrative Region of international agreements to which the People's Republic of China is or becomes a party shall be decided by the Central People's Government, in accordance with the circumstances and needs of the Hong Kong Special Administrative Region, and after seeking the views of the Hong Kong Special Administrative Region Government. International agreements to which the People's Republic of China is not a party but which are implemented in Hong Kong may remain implemented in the Hong Kong Special Administrative Region. The Central People's Government shall, as necessary, authorise or assist the Hong Kong Special Administrative Region Government to make appropriate arrangements for the application to the Hong Kong Special Administrative Region of other relevant international agreements. The Central People's Government shall take the necessary steps to ensure that the Hong Kong Special Administrative Region shall continue to retain its status in an appropriate capacity in those international organisations of which the People's Republic of China is a member and in which Hong Kong participates in one capacity or another. The Central People's Government shall, where necessary, facilitate the continued participation of the Hong Kong Special Administrative Region in an appropriate capacity in those international organisations in which Hong Kong is a participant in one capacity or another, but of which the People's Republic of China is not a member.

Foreign consular and other official or semi-official missions may be established in the Hong Kong Special Administrative Region with the approval of the Central People's Government. Consular and other official missions established in Hong Kong by states which have established formal diplomatic relations with the People's Republic of China may be maintained. According to the circumstances of each case, consular and other official missions of states having no formal diplomatic relations with the People's Republic of China may either be maintained or changed to semi-official missions. States not recognised by the People's Republic of China can only establish non-governmental institutions.

The United Kingdom may establish a Consulate-General in the Hong Kong Special Administrative Region.

XII

The maintenance of public order in the Hong Kong Special Administrative Region shall be the responsibility of the Hong Kong Special Administrative Region Government. Military forces sent by the Central People's Government to be stationed in the Hong Kong Special Administrative Region for the purpose of defence shall not interfere in the internal affairs of the Hong Kong Special Administrative Region. Expenditure for these military forces shall be borne by the Central People's Government.

XIII

The Hong Kong Special Administrative Region Government shall protect the rights and freedoms of inhabitants and other persons in the Hong Kong Special Administrative Region according to law. The Hong Kong Special Administrative Region Government shall maintain the rights and freedoms as provided for by the laws previously in force in Hong Kong, including freedom of the person, of speech, of the press, of assembly, of association, to form and join trade unions, of correspondence, of travel, of movement, of strike, of demonstration, of choice of occupation, of academic research, of belief, inviolability of the home, the freedom to marry and the right to raise a family freely.

Every person shall have the right to confidential legal advice, access to the courts, representation in the courts by lawyers of his choice, and to obtain judicial remedies. Every person shall have the right to challenge the actions of the executive in the courts.

Religious organisations and believers may maintain their relations with religious organisations and believers elsewhere, and schools, hospitals and welfare institutions run by religious organisations may be continued. The relationship between religious organisations in the Hong Kong Special Administrative Region and those in other parts of the People's Republic of China shall be based on the principles of non-subordination, non-interference and mutual respect.

The provisions of the International Covenant on Civil and Political Rights and the International Covenant on Economic, Social and Cultural Rights as applied to Hong Kong shall remain in force.

XIV

The following categories of persons shall have the right of abode in the Hong Kong Special Administrative Region, and, in accordance with the law of the Hong Kong Special Administrative Region, be qualified to obtain permanent identity cards issued by the Hong Kong Special Administrative Region Government, which state their right of abode:

- all Chinese nationals who were born or who have ordinarily resided in Hong Kong before or after the establishment of the Hong Kong Special Administrative Region for a continuous period of 7 years or more, and persons of Chinese nationality born outside Hong Kong of such Chinese nationals;

- all other persons who have ordinarily resided in Hong Kong before or after the establishment of the Hong Kong Special Administrative Region for a continuous period of 7 years or more and who have taken Hong Kong as their place of permanent residence before or after the establishment of the Hong Kong Special Administrative Region, and persons under 21 years of age who were born of such persons in Hong Kong before or after the establishment of the Hong Kong Special Administrative Region;

- any other persons who had the right of abode only in Hong Kong before the establishment of the Hong Kong Special Administrative Region.

The Central People's Government shall authorise the Hong Kong Special Administrative Region Government to issue, in accordance with the law, passports of the Hong Kong Special Administrative Region of the People's Republic of

China to all Chinese nationals who hold permanent identity cards of the Hong Kong Special Administrative Region, and travel documents of the Hong Kong Special Administrative Region of the People's Republic of China to all other persons lawfully residing in the Hong Kong Special Administrative Region. The above passports and documents shall be valid for all states and regions and shall record the holder's right to return to the Hong Kong Special Administrative Region.

For the purpose of travelling to and from the Hong Kong Special Administrative Region, residents of the Hong Kong Special Administrative Region may use travel documents issued by the Hong Kong Special Administrative Region Government, or by other competent authorities of the People's Republic of China, or of other states. Holders of permanent identity cards of the Hong Kong Special Administrative Region may have this fact stated in their travel documents as evidence that the holders have the right of abode in the Hong Kong Special Administrative Region.

Entry into the Hong Kong Special Administrative Region of persons from other parts of China shall continue to be regulated in accordance with the present practice.

The Hong Kong Special Administrative Region Government may apply immigration controls on entry, stay in and departure from the Hong Kong Special Administrative Region by persons from foreign states and regions.

Unless restrained by law, holders of valid travel documents shall be free to leave Hong Kong Special Administrative Region without special authorisation.

The Central People's Government shall assist or authorise the Hong Kong Special Administrative Region Government to conclude visa abolition agreements with states or regions.

ANNEX II

SINO-BRITISH JOINT LIAISON GROUP

1. In furtherance of their common aim and in order to ensure a smooth transfer of government in 1997, the Government of the United Kingdom and the Government of the People's Republic of China have agreed to continue their discussions in a friendly spirit and to develop the cooperative relationship which already exists between the two Governments over Hong Kong with a view to the effective implementation of the Joint Declaration.

2. In order to meet the requirements for liaison, consultation and the exchange of information, the two Governments have agreed to set up a Joint Liaison Group.

3. The functions of the Joint Liaison Group shall be:

    (*a*) to conduct consultations on the implementation of the Joint Declaration;
    (*b*) to discuss matters relating to the smooth transfer of government in 1977;
    (*c*) to exchange information and conduct consultations on such subjects as may be agreed by the two sides.

Matters on which there is disagreement in the Joint Liaison Group shall be referred to the two Governments for solution through consultations.

4. Matters for consideration during the first half of the period between the establishment of the Joint Liaison Group and 1 July 1997 shall include:

- (*a*) action to be taken by the two Governments to enable Hong Kong Special Administrative Region to maintain its economic relations as a separate customs territory, and in particular to ensure the maintenance of Hong Kong's participation in the General Agreement on Tariffs and Trade, the Multifibre Arrangement and other international arrangements; and
- (*b*) action to be taken by the two Governments to ensure the continued application of international rights and obligations affecting Hong Kong.

5. The two Governments have agreed that in the second half of the period between the establishment of the Joint Liaison Group and 1 July 1997 there will be need for closer cooperation, which will therefore be intensified during that period. Matters for consideration during this second period shall include:

- (*a*) procedures to be adopted for the smooth transition in 1997;
- (*b*) action to assist the Hong Kong Special Administrative Region to maintain and develop economic and cultural relations and conclude agreements on these matters with states, regions and relevant international organizations.

6. The Joint Liaison Group shall be an organ for liaison and not an organ of power. It shall play no part in the administration of Hong Kong or the Hong Kong Special Administrative Region. Nor shall it have any supervisory role over that administration. The members and supporting staff of the Joint Liaison Group shall only conduct activities within the scope of the functions of the Joint Liaison Group.

7. Each side shall designate a senior representative, who shall be of Ambassadorial rank, and four other members of the group. Each side may send up to 20 supporting staff.

8. The Joint Liaison Group shall be established on the entry into force of the Joint Declaration. From 1 July 1988 the Joint Liaison Group shall have its principal base in Hong Kong. The Joint Liaison Group shall continue its work until January 2000.

9. The Joint Liaison Group shall meet in Beijing, London and Hong Kong. It shall meet at least once in each of the three locations in each year. The venue for each meeting shall be agreed between the two sides.

10. Members of the Joint Liaison Group shall enjoy diplomatic privileges and immunities as appropriate when in the three locations. Proceedings of the Joint Liaison Group shall remain confidential unless otherwise agreed between the two sides.

11. The Joint Liaison Group may by agreement between the two sides decide to set up specialist sub-groups to deal with particular subjects requiring expert assistance.

12. Meetings of the Joint Liaison Group and sub-groups may be attended by experts other than the members of the Joint Liaison Group. Each side shall determine the composition of its delegation to particular meetings of the Joint Liaison Group or sub-group in accordance with the subjects to be discussed and the venue chosen.

13. The working procedures of the Joint Liaison Group shall be discussed and decided upon by the two sides within the guidelines laid down in this Annex.

ANNEX III

LAND LEASES

The Government of the United Kingdom and the Government of the People's Republic of China have agreed that, with effect from the entry into force of the Joint Declaration, land leases in Hong Kong and other related matters shall be dealt with in accordance with the following provisions:

1. All leases of land granted or decided upon before the entry into force of the Joint Declaration and those granted thereafter in accordance with paragraph 2 or 3 of this Annex, and which extend beyond 30 June 1997, and all rights in relation to such leases shall continue to be recognised and protected under the law of the Hong Kong Special Administrative Region.

2. All leases of land granted by the British Hong Kong Government not containing a right of renewal that expire before 30 June 1997, except short term tenancies and leases for special purposes, may be extended if the lessee so wishes for a period expiring not later than 30 June 2047 without payment of an additional premium. An annual rent shall be charged from the date of extension equivalent to 3 per cent of the rateable value of the property at that date, adjusted in step with any changes in the rateable value thereafter. In the case of old schedule lots, village lots, small houses and similar rural holdings, where the property was on 30 June 1984 held by, or, in the case of small houses granted after date, the property is granted to, a person descended through the male life from a person who was in 1898 a resident of an established village in Hong Kong, the rent shall remain unchanged so long as the property is held by that person or by one of his lawful successors in the male line. Where leases of land not having a right of renewal expire after 30 June 1997, they shall be dealt with in accordance with the relevant land laws and policies of the Hong Kong Special Administrative Region.

3. From the entry into force of the Joint Declaration until 30 June 1997, new leases of land may be granted by the British Hong Kong Government for terms expiring not later than 30 June 2047. Such leases shall be granted at a premium and nominal rental until 30 June 1997, after which date they shall not require payment of an additional premium but an annual rent equivalent to 3 per cent of the rateable value of the property at that date, adjusted in step with changes in the rateable value thereafter, shall be charged.

4. The total amount of new land to be granted under paragraph 3 of this Annex shall be limited to 50 hectares a year (excluding land to be granted to the Hong Kong Housing Authority for public rental housing) from the entry into force of the Joint Declaration until 30 June 1997.

5. Modifications of the conditions specified in leases granted by the British Hong Kong Government may continue to be granted before 1 July 1997 at a premium equivalent to the difference between the value of the land under the previous conditions and its value under the modified conditions.

6. From the entry into force of the Joint Declaration until 30 June 1997, premium income obtained by the British Hong Kong Government from land transactions shall, after deduction of the average cost of land production, be shared equally between the British Hong Kong Government and the future Hong Kong Special Administrative Region Government. All the income obtained by the British Hong Kong Government, including the amount of the above mentioned deduction,

shall be put into the Capital Works Reserve Fund for the financing of land development and public works in Hong Kong. The Hong Kong Special Administrative Region Government's share of the premium income shall be deposited in banks incorporated in Hong Kong and shall not be drawn on except for the financing of land development and public works in Hong Kong in accordance with the provisions of paragraph 7(*d*) of this Annex.

7. A Land Commission shall be established in Hong Kong immediately upon the entry into force of the Joint Declaration. The Land Commission shall be composed of an equal number of officials designated respectively by the Government of the United Kingdom and the Government of the People's Republic of China together with necessary supporting staff. The officials of the two sides shall be responsible to their respective governments. The Land Commission shall be dissolved on 30 June 1997.

The terms of reference of the Land Commission shall be:

(*a*) to conduct consultations on the implementation of this Annex;
(*b*) to monitor observance of the limit specified in paragraph 4 of this Annex, the amount of land granted to the Hong Kong Housing Authority for public rental housing, and the division and use of premium income referred to in paragraph 6 of this Annex;
(*c*) to consider and decide on proposals from the British Hong Kong Government for increasing the limit referred to in paragraph 4 of this Annex;
(*d*) to examine proposals for drawing on the Hong Kong Special Administrative Region Government's share of premium income referred to in paragraph 6 of this Annex and to make recommendations to the Chinese side for decision.

Matters on which there is disagreement in the Land Commission shall be referred to the Government of the United Kingdom and the Government of the People's Republic of China for decision.

8. Specific details regarding the establishment of the Land Commission shall be finalised separately by the two sides through consultations.

EXCHANGE OF MEMORANDA

(A) UNITED KINGDOM MEMORANDUM

MEMORANDUM

In connection with the Joint Declaration of the Government of the United Kingdom of Great Britain and Northern Ireland and the Government of the People's Republic of China on the question of Hong Kong to be signed this day, the Government of the United Kingdom declares that, subject to the completion of the necessary amendments to the relevant United Kingdom legislation:

(*a*) All persons who on 30 June 1997 are, by virtue of a connection with Hong Kong, British Dependent Territories citizens (BDTCs) under the law in force in the United Kingdom will cease to be BDTCs with effect from 1 July 1997, but will be eligible to retain an appropriate status which, without conferring the right of abode in the United Kingdom, will entitle them to continue to use passports issued by the Government of the United Kingdom. This status will be acquired by such persons only if they hold or are included in such a British passport issued before 1 July 1997, except that eligible persons born on or after 1 January 1997 but before 1 July 1997 may obtain or be included in such a passport up to 31 December 1997.

(*b*) No person will acquire BDTC status on or after 1 July 1997 by virtue of a connection with Hong Kong. No person born on or after 1 July 1997 will acquire the status referred to as being appropriate in sub-paragraph (*a*).

(*c*) United Kingdom consular officials in the Hong Kong Special Administrative Region and elsewhere may renew and replace passports of persons mentioned in sub-paragraph (*a*) and may also issue them to persons, born before 1 July 1997 of such persons, who had previously been included in the passport of their parent.

(*d*) Those who have obtained or been included in passports issued by the Government of the United Kingdom under sub-paragraphs (*a*) and (*c*) will be entitled to receive, upon request, British consular services and protection when in third countries.

Beijing,   1984

(B) CHINESE MEMORANDUM

Translation

MEMORANDUM

The Government of the People's Republic of China has received the memorandum from the Government of the United Kingdom of Great Britain and Northern Ireland dated . . .   1984.

Under the Nationality Law of the People's Republic of China, all Hong Kong Chinese compatriots, whether they are holders of the 'British Dependent Territories citizens' Passport' or not, are Chinese nationals.

Taking account of the historical background of Hong Kong and its realities, the competent authorities of the Government of the People's Republic of China will, with effect from 1 July 1997, permit Chinese nationals in Hong Kong who were previously called "British Dependent Territories citizens" to use travel documents issued by the Government of the United Kingdom for the purpose of travelling to other states and regions.

The above Chinese nationals will not be entitled to British consular protection in the Hong Kong Special Administrative Region and other parts of the People's Republic of China on account of their holding the above-mentioned British travel documents.

Beijing,   1984

EXPLANATORY NOTES

Introduction

1. The following notes are intended to explain the material in the Annexes to the Joint Declaration and in the associated Exchange of Memoranda. They do not seek to be a comprehensive guide and do not include every point in the texts. They are designed to explain in simple terms, and to illustrate where appropriate, how the Annexes provide for the continuation of the essentials of Hong Kong's systems. Hong Kong is a highly developed industrial, commercial and financial centre and as such is a complex place. The Hong Kong Government, in consultation with Her Majesty's Government, are taking steps to ensure that further guidance and answers to detailed questions will be provided as may be necessary and appropriate.

Annex I: Elaboration by the Government of the People's Republic of China of its Basic Policies regarding Hong Kong

Section 1: Constitutional Arrangements and Government Structure

2. When the People's Republic of China resumes the exercise of sovereignty over Hong Kong on 1 July 1997, Hong Kong will become a Special Administrative Region (SAR) of the People's Republic of China with a high degree of autonomy. A Basic Law to be enacted by the National People's Congress of the People's Republic of China will become the constitutional instrument for the Hong Kong SAR. The Letters Patent and the Royal Instructions, which have hitherto performed this function, will be revoked. As paragraph 3(12) of the Joint Declaration makes clear, the basic policies of the People's Republic of China as set out in the Joint Declaration and elaborated in this Annex will all be stipulated in the Basic Law.

3. This section of the Annex makes clear the important point that the Basic Law will stipulate that the socialist system and socialist policies practised in the rest of the People's Republic of China will not be extended to the Hong Kong SAR and that Hong Kong's capitalist system and lifestyle will remain unchanged for 50 years after the establishment of the SAR.

4. The Annex also states that, except in relation to foreign and defence affairs, which are now the overall responsibility of Her Majesty's Government, and will with effect from 1 July 1997 become the overall responsibility of the Central People's Government of the People's Republic of China, the Hong Kong SAR will enjoy a high degree of autonomy, including executive, legislative and independent judicial power. The SAR will also have authority to conduct its own external affairs in appropriate areas (including those relating to economic, trade, financial and monetary, shipping, communications, touristic, cultural and sporting matters) as amplified in section XI of this Annex, which deals with external relations. The SAR will enjoy a significant degree of autonomy in the maintenance and development of its air transport system as set out in section IX of this Annex, which deals with civil aviation.

5. The section of the Annex which deals with constitutional arrangements and government structure provides that the Hong Kong SAR will be under the direct authority of the Central People's Government. The SAR will therefore not be under the authority of any provincial Government.

6. This section of the Annex lays down the main elements of the structure of government in the Hong Kong SAR. It also states that the Government and legislature of the SAR will be composed of local inhabitants. The chief executive will be selected by election or through consultations held locally and be appointed by the Central People's Government. Officials of the rank equivalent to Secretaries will be nominated by the chief executive and appointed by the Central People's Government. The legislature will be elected.

7. Furthermore the Annex indicates that the executive authorities will be required to act in accordance with the law and will be accountable to the legislature; that both Chinese and English languages may be used in government and in the courts; and that, apart from the national flag and national emblem of the People's Republic of China, the SAR may use a regional flag and emblem of its own.

Section II: The Laws

8. This section of the Annex, which describes how the Hong Kong SAR will have its own system of laws, provides continuity of Hong Kong law beyond 1997. The law of the SAR will include the common law and laws passed by the legislature of the SAR. It will remain, as now, capable of adapting to changing conditions and will be free to take account of developments in the common law elsewhere. That this is so reinforced by specific provisions in section III of this Annex providing that the courts of the SAR will be able to refer to precedents in other common law jurisdictions, that judges of the SAR may be recruited from other common law jurisdictions and that the SAR's court of final appeal may invite judges from other common law jurisdictions to sit on it.

9. Hong Kong laws and those enacted after 1 July 1997 by the legislature of the Hong Kong SAR will be valid unless they contravene the Basic Law. The policies stated in the Joint Declaration and in this Annex will be stipulated in the Basic Law.

10. Laws enacted in the Hong Kong SAR will, as now, have to be passed by the legislature, or under its authority in the form of delegated legislation. Such laws may amend the laws of Hong Kong carried over in 1997 so long as the provisions of the Basic Law are not transgressed. After enactment, laws will have to be reported to the Standing Committee of the National People's Congress of the People's Republic of China for the record.

Section III: The Judicial System

11. The courts of Hong Kong consist of the Supreme Court, the District Courts, the Magistrates' Courts, and various statutory tribunals. The courts are at the heart of Hong Kong's legal system, which plays an important role in maintaining the stability and prosperity of Hong Kong. The Annex contains the very important provision for continuity of the judicial system.

12. The Annex indicates that the main change in the judicial system which will take place is the abolition of the system of appeal to the Privy Council and the substitution of arrangements for the final adjudication of disputes by a court of the Hong Kong SAR.

13. The independent exercise of judicial power and the obligation of the courts to decide cases in accordance with the law are both provided for in this section of the Annex. It also provides that the appointment of judges in the Hong Kong SAR will be subject to the recommendation of an independent commission similar to the existing Judicial Service Commission. The independence of the judiciary is protected by the provisions that judges of the SAR may only be removed from office on the grounds of inability or misbehaviour, and then only on the recommendation of a tribunal of judges of the SAR.

14. The Annex provides that the essentials of the system of appointment and removal of judges will remain unchanged, but the appointment and removal of judges of the highest rank will require the endorsement of the legislature of the Hong Kong SAR and have to be reported for the record to the Standing Committee of the National People's Congress.

15. At present the decision whether or not to prosecute in any particular case is the responsibility of the Attorney General. That responsibility is exercised independently free from government interference. The Annex provides that the responsibility will continue to be exercised in the SAR in the same independent way.

16. The Annex provides that local lawyers and also lawyers from outside Hong Kong, who contribute greatly both to the strength of the present legal system and to the success of Hong Kong as a commercial and financial centre, will continue to be able to practise law in Hong Kong. Provision is also made to enable arrangements to be continued whereby, for example, judgments obtained in Hong Kong may be enforced in foreign states, and evidence may be obtained overseas for use in proceedings in Hong Kong.

Section IV: The Public Service

17. This section of the Annex provides for the continuation in Hong Kong of an impartial, stable and effective public service. This is an essential factor in ensuring Hong Kong's future stability and prosperity.

18. Under the provisions of this section of the Annex serving officers will be able to continue in employment with the Hong Kong SAR Government on terms and conditions, including pay and pensions, no less favourable than before 1 July 1997. Special commissions dealing with pay and conditions of service will be retained. In addition, appointments and promotions will be made on the recommendations of a public service commission and on the basis of qualifications, experience and ability.

19. The Annex states that the Hong Kong SAR may employ foreign nationals in a number of capacities, namely as public officers (except at the highest levels), as advisers and in professional and technical posts.

20. It is explicitly provided that all pensions and other benefits due to those officers leaving the public service before or after 1 July 1997 or to their dependants will be paid by the Hong Kong SAR Government.

Section V: The Financial System

21. This section of the Annex provides for continuity in that the Government of the Hong Kong SAR will determine its own fiscal policy and manage and dispose of its financial resources, in accordance with Hong Kong's own needs. There will be no requirement to remit revenue to the Central People's Government. The Annex also makes clear that the predominant authority of the legislature in financial matters, and the system for independent and impartial audit of public accounts, will continue unchanged.

Section VI: The Economic System and External Economic Relations

22. The Annex deals together with these two subjects, which are both important

for Hong Kong's export-oriented economy. Hong Kong's prosperity is heavily dependent on securing continued access to its principal export markets in the developed world. This section of the Annex provides reassurance both to the community at large in Hong Kong and to its trading partners that the basis for Hong Kong's flourishing free market economy will continue. It also ensures that Hong Kong's distinct position within the international trading community, on the basis of which Hong Kong enjoys its present rights of access, will continue.

23. The Annex provides for:

(*a*) Hong Kong's right to continue to determine its economic policies, including trade policy, in accordance with its own needs;

(*b*) the continuation of the free enterprise system, the free trade policies and the free port, which are the essentials of Hong Kong's consistent and successful economic policies;

(*c*) the continuation of individual rights and freedoms in economic matters, notably the freedoms of choice of occupation, of travel and of movement of capital, and the rights of individuals and companies to own and dispose of property.

All these essential requirements are met in this section of the Annex, read in conjunction with the appropriate paragraphs of section XIII, which deals with rights and freedoms. The right of the future Hong Kong SAR to decide its own economic policies is an essential part of the 'one country, two systems' concept.

24. Hong Kong's participation in the General Agreement on Tariffs and Trade (GATT), through which it enjoys most favoured nation treatment in its major markets, has been an important element in its success as an exporter. Even in textiles and clothing, where the free trade principles of the GATT have been modified by the Multi-Fibre Arrangement (MFA) which is negotiated derogation from the normal GATT rules, Hong Kong is able to develop its trade within the MFA and the bilateral agreements negotiated under its provisions. What is even more important, Hong Kong plays an active role in the GATT and the MFA. The continuation of Hong Kong's participation in the GATT and the MFA (if the latter is extended beyond 1986, in which year it expires) is, therefore, of prime importance: and that too is provided in this section of the Annex.

Section VII: The Monetary System

25. A freely convertible currency and the right to manage the Exchange Fund, which provides the backing for the note issue and is used to regulate the exchange value of the currency, are the essential elements of Hong Kong's monetary system. This section of the Annex clearly stipulates that these essential elements shall be maintained.

26. This section of the Annex also provides for the continuation of the arrangements by which currency is issued locally by designated banks under statutory authority.

27. The changes to the designs of bank notes and coins provided for in this section are a logical consequence of the fact that Hong Kong will become a Special Administrative Region of the People's Republic of China on 1 July 1997.

Section VIII: Shipping

28. A major factor in Hong Kong's trading success is its well-developed deep water port and the capacity to handle cargoes by up to date methods. Hong Kong's position as a major shipping centre will be preserved by this section of the Annex, which provides that systems of shipping management and shipping regulation will continue. Private shipping businesses and shipping-related businesses, including container terminals, may continue to operate freely.

29. The Annex states that the Hong Kong SAR will have its own shipping register and will issue certificates in the name of 'Hong Kong, China'.

30. The Annex also provides that merchant shipping will have free access to the ports of Hong Kong under the laws of the SAR.

Section IX: Civil Aviation

31. This section of the Annex makes clear that Hong Kong will continue as a major centre of regional and international air services, and that airlines and civil aviation related businesses will be able to continue operating.

32. Under the provisions of the Annex the Central People's Government of the People's Republic of China will negotiate agreements concerning air services from and to other points in China through the Hong Kong SAR. However there is also a provision that in dealing with such arrangements the Central People's Government will consult the SAR Government, take its interests into account and include its representatives in delegations to air service consultations with foreign governments. By virtue of section XI of the Annex, which deals with external relations, such representatives may also be included in delegations to appropriate international organisations. The Central People's Government will also consult the Hong Kong SAR Government about arrangements for air services between the SAR and other parts of China.

33. It is clearly provided that all scheduled air services touching the Hong Kong SAR which do not touch the mainland of China will be regulated by separate arrangements concluded by the SAR Government. For this purpose the SAR Government will be given specific authorisations from the Central People's Government to negotiate with foreign states and regions its own bilateral arrangements regulating air services. These will as far as possible maintain the rights previously enjoyed by Hong Kong. The SAR Government will also act under a general authority from the Central People's Government in negotiating all matters concerning the implementation of such bilateral arrangements and will issue its own operating permits for air services provided under these arrangements. The Annex also states that the SAR will have the authority to license local airlines, to keep its own aircraft register, to conduct the technical supervision of civil aviation and to manage airports in the SAR. In addition the general provisions in section II of the Annex, which deals with the laws of the SAR, provide for continuity of previously existing civil aviation laws beyond 1997.

34. Hong Kong's civil aviation industry will thus be able to continue to make an important contribution to the effective functioning of Hong Kong's economy in terms of servicing the needs of both business and tourism.

Section X: Culture and Education

35. This section of the Annex makes clear that Hong Kong's own system of education will be continued and that it will operate separately and differently from that in other parts of China. Although most of the funds for education in Hong Kong are provided by the Government, many educational institutes were founded and are run by community and religious organisations. Explicit provision is made for this system to be maintained.

36. This section also provides for continuity in the application of present educational standards, in the use of teaching materials from overseas and in the freedom to pursue education outside Hong Kong. It therefore provides a second basis for Hong Kong to continue to develop an educational system which will ensure that the population will have the skills and expertise required to enable Hong Kong to maintain and improve its position in the fiercely competitive economic and trading environment within which Hong Kong operates.

37. Hong Kong has come to enjoy a varied cultural and intellectual life. This and other sections of the Annex provide for the present unique mix of cultural and intellectual influences to continue. Provision is made in section XI of the Annex, which deals with external relations, for Hong Kong to continue to participate in international sporting events.

Section XI: External Relations

38. This section of the Annex provides that, subject to the principle that foreign affairs are the responsibility of the Central People's Government, the Hong Kong SAR will manage on its own certain aspects of its external relations, in particular those in the economic field. This is particularly important, since Hong Kong's access to its principal overseas markets in the industrialised world, which is crucial to Hong Kong's industry, depends upon recognition of the separate nature of these interests.

39. In keeping with the general provisions for Hong Kong to be a Special Administrative under Chinese sovereignty, overall responsibility for foreign affairs will lie with the Central People's Government, just as overall responsibility for these matters at present lies with Her Majesty's Government in the United Kingdom. At the same time the Hong Kong SAR will be able, under the provisions of this section of the Annex, to look after its own particular interests in certain areas by virtue of the power to be given to it to conclude agreements in appropriate fields and to be represented in the delegation of the People's Republic of China at negotiations of direct concern to Hong Kong.

40. The detailed method by which the provisions of the second paragraph of this section of the Annex, which deals with the application to the Hong Kong SAR of international agreements, will be implemented will have to be worked out during the transitional period and will be one of the matters to be considered by the Joint Liaison Group. There is a very large number of international agreements which apply to Hong Kong and whose continued application following the establishment of the Hong Kong SAR will need to be secured. This will require consultation with third countries.

41. The Annex provides for continuity of representation by all foreign states and organisations currently represented in Hong Kong, subject to the approval of the Central People's Government. Changes to the status of such missions may be required in order to take account of the existence or otherwise of formal relations between the People's Republic of China and a particular state. The United Kingdom will be represented in Hong Kong by a Consul-General after 1 July 1997.

Section XII: Defence, Security and Public Order

42. With the establishment of the Hong Kong SAR, the British garrison will be withdrawn and the Central People's Government of the People's Republic of China will be responsible for the SAR's defence. This section of the Annex makes clear that the maintenance of public order in the SAR will be the SAR Government's responsibility. It is also stated that military forces sent by the Central People's Government to be stationed in the SAR for the purpose of defence will not interfere in its internal affairs, and that expenditure for these military forces will be borne by the Central People's Government.

Section XIII: Rights and Freedoms

43. This section of the Annex explains that basic rights and freedoms will be protected in the Hong Kong SAR. It covers this important subject without an extended description of the rights and freedoms concerned by providing:

- (*a*) that the rights and freedom previously enjoyed under the laws of Hong Kong will be maintained by the SAR Government; and
- (*b*) that the provisions of the International Covenants on Civil and Political Rights and on Economic, Social and Cultural Rights, as they apply to Hong Kong, will continue to apply to the Hong Kong SAR.

44. It is thus made clear that persons in the Hong Kong SAR will enjoy the same protection of the law against infringements of their basic rights as they did before the establishment of the SAR.

45. While not restricting the range of rights and freedoms the text mentions specifically some of the more important rights and freedoms presently enjoyed under the law.

46. The Covenants are too lengthy to reproduce here but they are public documents.[1] They apply to Hong Kong, with certain reservations, and, in accordance with this section of the Annex, will continue to do so after 30 June 1997. The Covenants were drafted by the United Nations Human Rights Commission and adopted by the United Nations General Assembly, and entered into force in 1976. They state a general consensus of nations on basic rights and identify in detail specific human rights and freedoms: including the right to work, to an adequate standard of living, to life and liberty, and freedom of expression, conscience, religion and association.

47. The reservations entered by the United Kingdom in respect of the application of the Covenants to Hong Kong, which are also public, took account of the realities of the social and economic conditions in Hong Kong: for example, in relation to Hong Kong the United Kingdom made reservations relating to immigration and to the deportation of aliens.

Section XIV: Right of Abode, Travel Documents and Immigration

48. This section concerns the right of abode in the Hong Kong SAR, the travel documents to be used by residents of the SAR, and immigration matters. It provides for a high degree of continuity in these areas consistent with the change in Hong Kong's status on 1 July 1997.

49. The first paragraph defines the categories of people who will have the right of abode (including the right to enter, re-enter, live and work) in the Hong Kong SAR. These include:

- (*a*) Chinese nationals who were born in Hong Kong or have lived there continuously for at least 7 years;
- (*b*) Chinese nationals born outside Hong Kong to Chinese nationals who have the right of abode in Hong Kong;

[1] Command 6702 Treaty Series No. 6 (1977)

(*c*) all non-Chinese nationals who have lived in Hong Kong continuously for at least 7 years and who have taken it as their place of permanent residence; and

(*d*) any others who had the right of abode only in Hong Kong before 1 July 1997.

Non-Chinese nationals born in Hong Kong to parents who have the right of abode there also have the right of abode but will retain it after the age of 21 only if they have met the requirements of seven years' residence and of taking Hong Kong as their place of permanent residence. The SAR Government will issue permanent identity cards to all those with the right of abode in the SAR. These cards will state the holder's right of abode.

50. This section of the Annex states that Chinese nationals who have the right of abode in the Hong Kong SAR will be eligible for passports issued by the SAR Government. Other persons who have the right of abode, or are otherwise lawfully resident, in the SAR will be eligible for other travel documents issued by the SAR Government. Both these categories of persons may also use travel documents issued by the competent authorities of the People's Republic China or by other governments to travel to and from the SAR: these include passports issued by the United Kingdom (see paragraphs 63 to 64 below).

51. The Annex makes clear that the right to leave the Hong Kong SAR for any purpose, e.g. business, study or emigration, will be maintained subject to the normal exceptions under the law. To facilitate entry by SAR residents into third countries, all travel documents issued to them will either include a reference to their right to return to the SAR or refer to the fact that they hold a permanent identity card as evidence of their right of abode in the SAR. The SAR Government will be assisted or authorised by the Central People's Government to conclude agreements with the states or regions which provide for the mutual abolition of visa requirements.

Annex II: Terms of Reference of the Sino-British Joint Liaison Group

52. As the Secretary of State for Foreign and Commonwealth Affairs emphasized in his press conference in Hong Kong on 1 August 1984, it is fully agreed between Her Majesty's Government and the Chinese Government that Her Majesty's Government will remain responsible for the administration of Hong Kong until 30 June 1997. Nonetheless there will, of course, be a number of areas relating to the implementation of the Joint Declaration where further consultation between the two Governments will be required after the Joint Declaration has entered into force. One obvious example in the future is the arrangements for Hong Kong's continued participation in international agreements and organizations. Such consultation will be facilitated by the Sino-British Joint Liaison Group, whose role and functions are clearly defined in Annex II.

Annex III: Land Leases

53. This Annex takes account of the important part which land plays in the development and economy of Hong Kong.

54. It considers existing leases under two main categories: those which continue beyond 30 June 1997 and those which expire before that date. In the case of the first category (mainly 75 year leases renewable for 75 years, and 999 year leases) the rights in the leases are recognised by the Annex and will be recognised and protected under the law of the SAR after 1997. These rights include the right of renewal in the case of renewable leases, as well as rights granted by the leaseholder to other persons, e.g. sub-leases, mortgages and rights of way.

55. Leases which expire before 30 June 1997 (mainly New Territories leases and 75 year non-renewable leases in the urban area) may be extended without premium until 2047. A rent of 3 per cent of current rateable value will be charged from the date of extension, except in the case of village land held by indigenous villagers who will continue to pay a nominal rent.

56. New leases running until 2047 may be issued by the Hong Kong Government in the period up to 30 June 1997. These will continue to be issued under the existing system of land disposal (i.e. by public auction, tender or private treaty grant). A premium will be payable and a nominal rent will be charged up to 30 June 1997. After that date, no additional premium will be payable but the rent will increase to 3 per cent of current rateable value.

57. The concept of charging a rent on the basis of rateable values follows that used since 1973 to fix rents on the renewal of leases. It has, however, been agreed that the rent will be based on current rateable values (i.e. a rent which will change as rateable values change) rather than based, as at present, on a fixed reference point (i.e. a rent which is based on the rateable value at the date of renewal and which remains unchanged for the whole term of the lease).

58. The amount of new land which may be granted by the Hong Kong Government will be limited to 50 hectares a year. The limit does not include land granted to the Housing Authority for the construction of public rental housing.

59. Modifications of lease conditions will continue to be dealt with by the Hong Kong Government in accordance with existing practice.

60. In recognition of the fact that leases which extend beyond June 1997 derive part of their value from the post-June 1997 portion of their term, the Annex provides for net premium income to be shared between the Hong Kong Government and the future SAR Government.

61. A Land Commission, consisting of an equal number of officials appointed by Her Majesty's Government and the Chinese Government, will be set up. This Commission will monitor the implementation of the provisions in this Annex and will consider proposals for increasing the limit on the amount of new land which may be granted and for drawing on the SAR Government's share of premium income. It will not, however, consider individual land cases, nor will it be involved in deciding who should be issued with new leases. The Commission will be dissolved on 30 June 1997.

Associated Exchange of Memoranda

62. The status after 30 June 1997 of persons who are now British Dependent Territories citizens, and related issues, are covered in two Memoranda to be formally exchanged between the British and Chinese Governments on the same day as the signature of the Joint Declaration. These Memoranda set out the respective positions of the two Governments.

63. Since Hong Kong will no longer be a British dependent territory after 30 June 1997, it will not be appropriate for those who are British Dependent Territories citizens by virtue of a connection with Hong Kong to be described as such after that date. The United Kingdom Government will seek Parliamentary approval for legislation which will give such British Dependent Territories citizens the right to a new status, with an appropriate title. This status will not give them the right of abode in the United Kingdom, which they do not possess at present, but it will carry benefits similar to those enjoyed by British Dependent Territories citizens at present, including the entitlement to use British passports and to receive British consular services and protection in third countries. The status will not, however, be transmissible by descent. The United Kingdom Government will do all they can to secure for holders of these British passports the same access to other countries as that enjoyed at present by holders of British Dependent Territories citizen passports.

64. This new status will be acquired by former Hong Kong British Dependent Territories citizens only if they obtain a British passport before 1 July 1997. The only exceptions to this are:

(*a*) persons included in the passport of a parent before 1 July 1997 will be able to acquire this new status and will be able to obtain a British passport of their own after that date;

(*b*) persons who were born between 1 January and 30 June 1997 will be able to acquire this new status if they obtain a British passport, or are included in the passport of a parent, on or before 31 December 1997. Those who are included in the passport of a parent will be able to obtain a British passport of their own after that date.

65. The Chinese Memorandum states the Chinese Government's position that Hong Kong Chinese are Chinese nationals. It indicates, however, that those Chinese nationals who hold British travel documents may continue to use them after 1 July 1997. Such persons will not, of course, be entitled to consular protection by the United Kingdom Government in the Hong Kong SAR or in other parts of China.

Index